DAY HIKES AROUND
Santa Barbara

113 GREAT HIKES

Robert Stone
3rd EDITION

Day Hike Books, Inc.

RED LODGE, MONTANA

Published by Day Hike Books, Inc.
P.O. Box 865
Red Lodge, Montana 59068
www.dayhikebooks.com

Distributed by The Globe Pequot Press
246 Goose Lane
P.O. Box 480
Guilford, CT 06437-0480
800-243-0495 (direct order) · 800-820-2329 (fax order)
www.globe-pequot.com

Photographs by Roy Mata
Design by Paula Doherty

The author has made every attempt to provide accurate information in this book. However, trail routes and features may change—please use common sense and forethought, and be mindful of your own capabilities. Let this book guide you, but be aware that each hiker assumes responsibility for their own safety. The author and publisher do not assume any responsibility for loss, damage, or injury caused through the use of this book.

Cover photo:
La Jolla Trail, Hike 95

Back cover photo:
Davy Brown Trail, Hike 97

ALSO BY ROBERT STONE

Day Hikes On the California Central Coast

Day Hikes On the California Southern Coast

Day Hikes Around Sonoma County

Day Hikes Around Napa Valley

Day Hikes Around Big Sur

Day Hikes Around Monterey and Carmel

Day Hikes In San Luis Obispo County, California

Day Hikes Around Santa Barbara

Day Hikes Around Ventura County

Day Hikes Around Los Angeles

Day Hikes Around Orange County

Day Hikes In Sedona, Arizona

Day Hikes In Yosemite National Park

Day Hikes In Sequoia & Kings Canyon Nat'l. Parks

Day Hikes In Yellowstone National Park

Day Hikes In Grand Teton National Park

Day Hikes In the Beartooth Mountains

Day Hikes Around Bozeman, Montana

Day Hikes Around Missoula, Montana

Day Hikes On Oahu

Day Hikes On Maui

Day Hikes On Kauai

Day Hikes In Hawaii

LINDA STONE

Hiking partner, Kofax

Table of Contents

THE HIKES

Ojai area

Montecito · Summerland · Carpinteria
Romero Canyon · San Ysidro Canyon · Hot Springs Canyon · Cold Spring Canyon

Santa Barbara to Goleta

Rattlesnake Canyon • Mission Canyon • San Roque Canyon

Goleta • Gaviota • Los Olivos

Upper Country
East Camino Cielo Road • Santa Ynez River Valley

Figueroa Mountain Recreation Area

North Coast
Santa Barbara to Santa Maria • Carrizo Plain
National Monument

Hiking Santa Barbara

Santa Barbara is a captivating, inviting community that is located in a beautiful, natural setting along California's Pacific coast. The temperate climate and refreshing ocean breezes, very similar to the Mediterranean, have distinguished this area as "the jewel of the American Riviera."

Santa Barbara lies in a unique area. The landscape around the city includes mountainous terrain, preserved forests and wilderness areas, and stretches of undeveloped coast. To the north of the coast, the Santa Ynez Mountains rise 3,000 feet, serving as a backdrop to Santa Barbara and the nearby coastal communities. These mountains separate the coastal plain from the rolling farmlands and mountainous interior of Santa Barbara County. The incredible Big Sur coastline lies farther up the coast between Santa Barbara and Monterey. The cities of San Luis Obispo (100 miles northwest) and Los Angeles (90 miles south) are a comfortable drive away.

Day Hikes Around Santa Barbara includes 113 day hikes within a 65-mile radius of the city. The trails have been chosen for their scenery, variety, and ability to be hiked within a day. The network of hiking trails around Santa Barbara stretches along the coast, up and over the Santa Ynez Mountains, and throughout the Santa Ynez River Valley. These hikes include an excellent cross section of scenery and difficulty levels, ranging from coastal beach walks to steep canyon climbs with far-reaching views. Highlights include oceanside bluffs; beaches; tidepools; wetland preserves; sculpted gorges; rock outcroppings with caves; numerous waterfalls; secluded pools in mossy canyons;

mountain ridge trails; historical sites; stunning overlooks of wide mountain valleys, towns, and the Pacific Ocean; and some of southern California's best scenery.

HIKES 1—19 are found in the area around the city of Ojai in neighboring Ventura County. Nearly all of the hikes travel along river valleys and canyons. The lightly used trails wind through national forest and wilderness land.

Farther west lie the coastal communities of Carpinteria, Summerland, and Montecito, HIKES 20—41. Coastal hikes include tidepools, beaches, and wildlife viewing areas. A short distance inland, trails and abandoned roads crisscross the foothills and canyons that lead down to the ocean.

HIKES 42—63 are found in the immediate vicinity of Santa Barbara, Goleta, and Isla Vista. Natural undeveloped scenery surrounds the majority of the trails. Several hikes lead up through cool river canyons to great coastal and city overlooks. Undeveloped parks and wildlife habitats offer shady retreats just minutes from the urban areas. HIKES 64—72 continue west along the coast to Gaviota State Park.

The Camino Cielo Road travels along the ridge that divides the coastline from the Santa Ynez River Valley. HIKES 73—89 are found in this area, known as the Upper Country. These backcountry hikes are found from along the ridge to the valley below. Some of the hikes follow the Santa Ynez River Valley and its tributaries. Several others are high elevation climbs that offer the reward of 360-degree panoramic views, from the inland mountains to the Pacific Ocean.

The North Country includes HIKES 90—113 in the area that stretches from Lake Cachuma to the northern county line along the Santa Maria River. Here you will find mountainous backcountry, coastal bluffs, secluded beaches, a historic mission, salt flats along the San Andreas faultline, and the highest sand dunes on the west coast.

All of these hikes are found within an hour's drive of Santa Barbara and can be completed within a day. A quick glance at the hikes' summaries will allow you to choose a hike that is appropriate to your ability and intentions. An overall map on the next page identifies the general locations of the hikes and major roads. Several other regional maps (underlined in the table of contents), as well as maps for each hike, provide the essential details. The Thomas Guide, or other comparable street guide, is essential for navigating through the urban areas. Other relevant maps are listed under the hikes' statistics if you wish to explore more of the area.

A few basic necessities will make your hike more pleasurable. Wear supportive, comfortable hiking shoes and layered clothing. Take along hats, sunscreen, sunglasses, drinking water, snacks, and appropriate outerwear. Bring swimwear and outdoor gear if heading to the beaches. Ticks may be prolific and poison oak flourishes in the canyons and shady moist areas. Exercise caution by using insect repellent and staying on the trails.

Use good judgement about your capabilities—reference the hiking statistics for an approximation of difficulty and allow extra time for exploration.

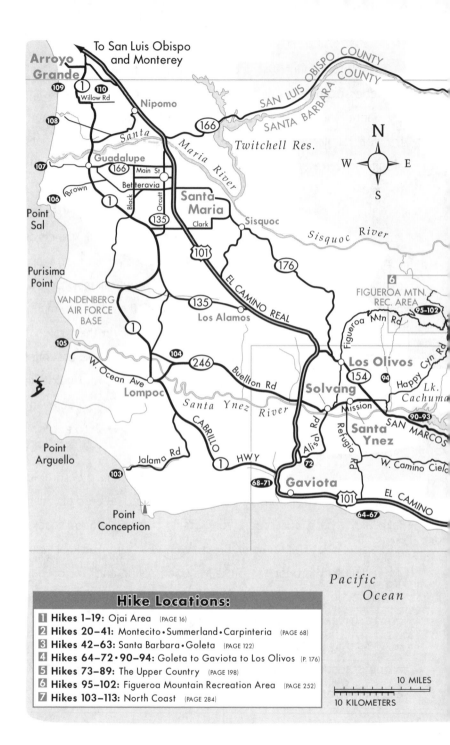

Hike Locations:

1. **Hikes 1–19:** Ojai Area (PAGE 16)
2. **Hikes 20–41:** Montecito • Summerland • Carpinteria (PAGE 68)
3. **Hikes 42–63:** Santa Barbara • Goleta (PAGE 122)
4. **Hikes 64–72 • 90–94:** Goleta to Gaviota to Los Olivos (P. 176)
5. **Hikes 73–89:** The Upper Country (PAGE 198)
6. **Hikes 95–102:** Figueroa Mountain Recreation Area (PAGE 252)
7. **Hikes 103–113:** North Coast (PAGE 284)

10 MILES
10 KILOMETERS

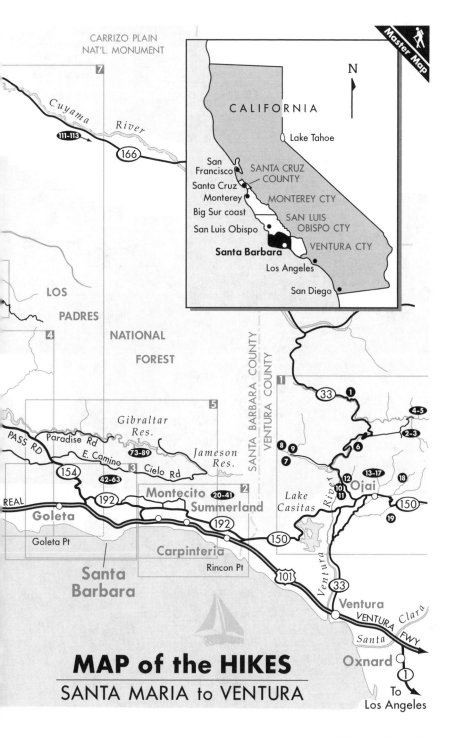

CARRIZO PLAIN
NAT'L. MONUMENT

7

Cuyama *River*

111-113

166

N

CALIFORNIA

Lake Tahoe

San
Francisco
SANTA CRUZ
COUNTY
Santa Cruz
Monterey
MONTEREY CTY
Big Sur coast
SAN LUIS
San Luis Obispo
OBISPO CTY
Santa Barbara
VENTURA CTY
Los Angeles

San Diego

LOS

PADRES

4

NATIONAL

FOREST

5

Gibraltar
Res.

PASS RD
Paradise Rd
E. Camino
73-89
Jameson
Res.

3 Cielo Rd

154

42-63

SANTA BARBARA COUNTY
VENTURA COUNTY

1

33 **1**

4-5

2-3

8 9
7

6

12
13-17
10
11
Ojai
18

REAL

192

Montecito **20-41** **2**

Lake
Casitas

150

19

Goleta

Summerland

192

Goleta Pt

150

Santa

Carpinteria

Rincon Pt

101

33

Ventura

Santa
Barbara

VENTURA FWY

Santa

Clara

MAP of the HIKES

Oxnard

To
Los Angeles

SANTA MARIA to VENTURA

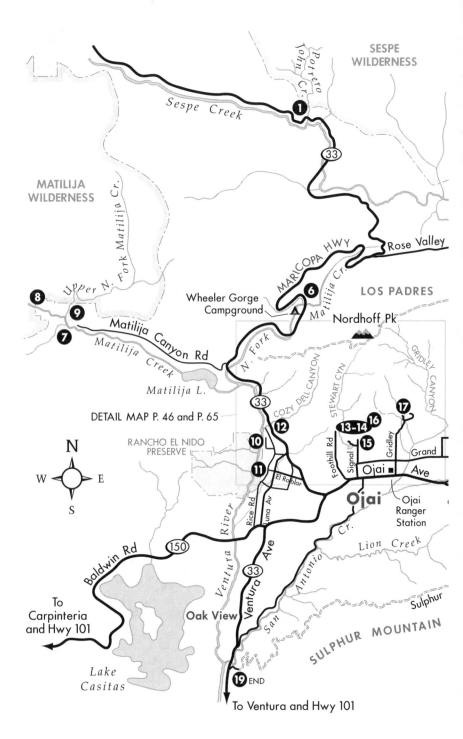

SESPE WILDERNESS

Potrero John Cr.

Sespe Creek

①

33

MATILIJA WILDERNESS

Upper N. Fork Matilija Cr.

MARICOPA HWY

Rose Valley

Wheeler Gorge Campground

⑥

Matilija Cr.

LOS PADRES

Nordhoff Pk

⑧

⑨

⑦

Matilija Canyon Rd

Matilija Creek

Matilija L.

N. Fork

COZY DEL CANYON

STEWART CYN

GRIDLEY CANYON

⑰

DETAIL MAP P. 46 and P. 65

⑬-⑭ ⑯

Foothill Rd

Signal

⑮

Gridley

Grand

RANCHO EL NIDO PRESERVE

⑫

⑩

Ojai ■ Ave

N
W E
S

⑪

El Roblar

Ojai

Ojai Ranger Station

Lion Creek

Rice Rd

Tuna Av

Baldwin Rd

150

Ventura River

33

Ventura Ave

San Antonio Cr.

Sulphur

To Carpinteria and Hwy 101

Oak View

SULPHUR MOUNTAIN

Lake Casitas

⑲ END

To Ventura and Hwy 101

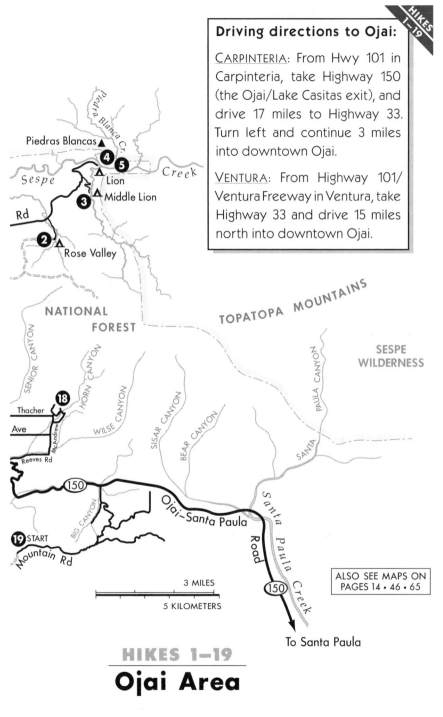

Driving directions to Ojai:

CARPINTERIA: From Hwy 101 in Carpinteria, take Highway 150 (the Ojai/Lake Casitas exit), and drive 17 miles to Highway 33. Turn left and continue 3 miles into downtown Ojai.

VENTURA: From Highway 101/Ventura Freeway in Ventura, take Highway 33 and drive 15 miles north into downtown Ojai.

Piedras Blancas

Piedra Blanca Cr.

Sespe

Creek

Lion

Middle Lion

Rd

Rose Valley

NATIONAL FOREST

TOPATOPA MOUNTAINS

SESPE WILDERNESS

SENIOR CANYON

HORN CANYON

WILSE CANYON

SISAR CANYON

BEAR CANYON

PAULA CANYON

SANTA

Thacher

Ave

McAndrew

Reeves Rd

START

Mountain Rd

BIG CANYON

Ojai-Santa Paula

Santa Paula

Road

Creek

150

150

3 MILES

5 KILOMETERS

ALSO SEE MAPS ON PAGES 14 • 46 • 65

To Santa Paula

HIKES 1–19

Ojai Area

1. Potrero John Trail

Hiking distance: 4 miles round trip
Hiking time: 2 hours
Elevation gain: 600 feet
Maps: U.S.G.S. Wheeler Springs
       Matilija and Dick Smith Wilderness Map Guide
       Sespe Wilderness Trail Map

Summary of hike: Potrero John Canyon is tucked into the southern slopes of Pine Mountain in the 220,000-acre Sespe Wilderness, part of the Los Padres National Forest. The Potrero John Trail is an uncrowded, lightly used trail that begins at an elevation of 3,655 feet, where Potrero John Creek empties into Sespe Creek. The trail follows Potrero John Creek through a narrow gorge and up the canyon. There is also an open meadow dotted with red baked manzanita and views of the surrounding mountains. At the trail's end is Potrero John Camp, a creekside flat shaded with oaks.

Driving directions: OJAI. From Ojai, drive 21 miles north on Highway 33 (Maricopa Highway) to the trailhead parking pullout on the right side of the road. It is located on the north side of Potrero Bridge.

Hiking directions: Hike north past the trailhead sign, immediately entering the narrow, steep-walled canyon on the west side of Potrero John Creek. After three successive creek crossings, the trail enters the Sespe Wilderness. There are eight creek crossings in the first mile while passing various pools and cascades. At one mile, leave the narrow canyon and emerge into a large, open meadow. At the far side of the meadow, the trail ends at Potrero John Camp, a walk-in camp on the banks of the creek. Return to the trailhead along the same route.

To hike farther, a rough, unmaintained trail heads upstream over rocks, downfall, and underbrush. Along the way are continuous pools, cascades, and waterfalls. ■

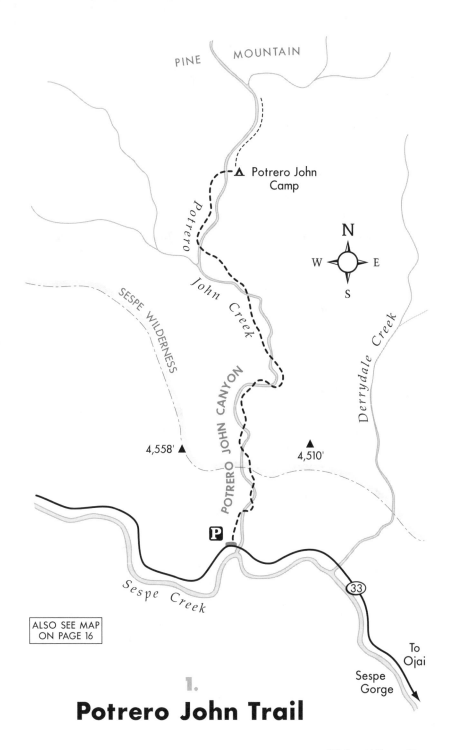

PINE MOUNTAIN

▲ Potrero John
Camp

Potrero

John Creek

SESPE WILDERNESS

POTRERO JOHN CANYON

Derrydale Creek

4,558' ▲

▲ 4,510'

N
W ○ E
S

P

Sespe Creek

(33)

To
Ojai

Sespe
Gorge

ALSO SEE MAP
ON PAGE 16

1.
Potrero John Trail

2. Rose Valley Falls

Hiking distance: 1 mile round trip
Hiking time: 30 minutes
Elevation gain: 300 feet
Maps: U.S.G.S. Lion Canyon
Sespe Wilderness Trail Map

Summary of hike: Rose Valley Falls is a 300-foot, three-tiered waterfall at the northern base of Nordhoff Ridge in the Topatopa Mountains. This hike follows Rose Valley Creek up a shady canyon to the base of the lower falls, a 100-foot, multi-strand waterfall. The tall and narrow waterfall cascades through a notch over the near-vertical cliffs onto the rocks below in a cool, moss-covered grotto. This short, easy trail begins at the Rose Valley Campground at an elevation of 3,450 feet. There are also three lakes near the campground that are stocked with trout.

Driving directions: OJAI. From Ojai, drive 14.6 miles north on Highway 33 (Maricopa Highway) to the Rose Valley Road turnoff and turn right. Continue 3 miles to the Rose Valley Campground turnoff across from the lower lake and turn right. Drive 0.5 miles to the south end of the campground loop road to the signed trailhead by campsite number 4.

Hiking directions: Hike south past the trailhead sign, immediately entering the thick coastal live oak, bay, and sycamore forest on the well-defined trail. Cross a tributary of Rose Valley Creek, and stay on the main path as you make your way up the lush, narrow canyon. The first of several small waterfalls can be spotted on the left at 0.2 miles. Short side paths lead down to the creek by these waterfalls and pools. The trail ends at a half mile at the base of lower Rose Valley Falls with its bridal veil beauty, beneath the colorful mossy rock wall. Return along the same path.

To extend the hike, the Nordhoff Road (a gated road) climbs

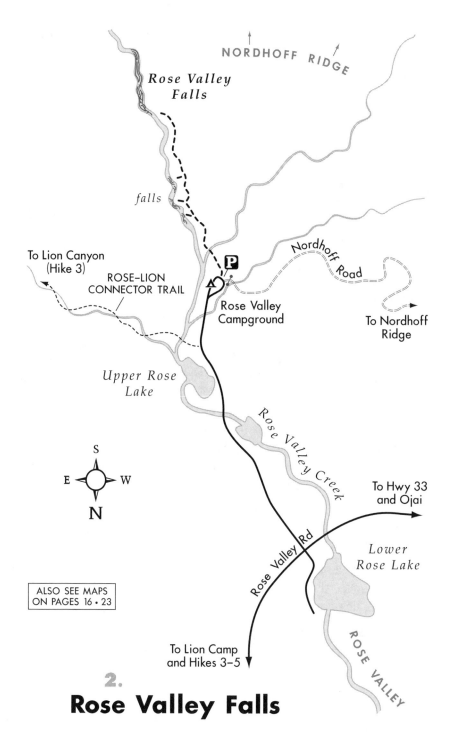

NORDHOFF RIDGE

Rose Valley
Falls

falls

To Lion Canyon
(Hike 3)

ROSE–LION
CONNECTOR TRAIL

Nordhoff Road

P

Rose Valley
Campground

To Nordhoff
Ridge

Upper Rose
Lake

Rose Valley Creek

S

E W

N

To Hwy 33
and Ojai

Rose Valley Rd

Lower
Rose Lake

ALSO SEE MAPS
ON PAGES 16 · 23

ROSE VALLEY

To Lion Camp
and Hikes 3–5

2.
Rose Valley Falls

2.1 miles west to Nordhoff Ridge, with sweeping coastal and mountain vistas. At the entrance gate to the campground, the Rose-Lion Connector Trail heads east to Lion Canyon (Hike 3). ∎

3. Lion Canyon Trail
to West Fork Lion Camp and East Fork Lion Camp

Hiking distance: 5.6 miles round trip
Hiking time: 3 hours
Elevation gain: 350 feet
Maps: U.S.G.S. Lion Canyon
Sespe Wilderness Trail Map

Summary of hike: Lion Canyon Creek flows 6.5 miles from the upper slopes of the Topatopa Mountains through Lion Canyon, emptying into Sespe Creek. The Lion Canyon Trail follows the canyon over five miles, from Middle Lion Campground to 5,160-foot Nordhoff Ridge. The vistas expand across Ojai Valley to the ocean and Channel Islands. This hike follows the lower portion of the trail through the forested canyon along Lion Creek to a three-way trail fork, where the canyon splits at the confluence of the East Fork and West Fork. Footpaths follow each fork to shaded backcountry camps on creekside flats with lush vegetation. Both camps have a beautiful waterfall and pool that are surrounded by rounded boulders.

Driving directions: OJAI. From Ojai, drive 14.6 miles north on Highway 33 (Maricopa Highway) to the Rose Valley Road turnoff and turn right. Continue 4.8 miles to a road split. Take the right fork 0.8 miles down to the Middle Lion Campground and trailhead parking area.

Hiking directions: Walk east along the unpaved campground road, crossing Lion Canyon Creek. Take the signed trail to the right, and head south up Lion Canyon. Continue hiking gradually uphill along the east side of the canyon. At 1.3 miles is a posted

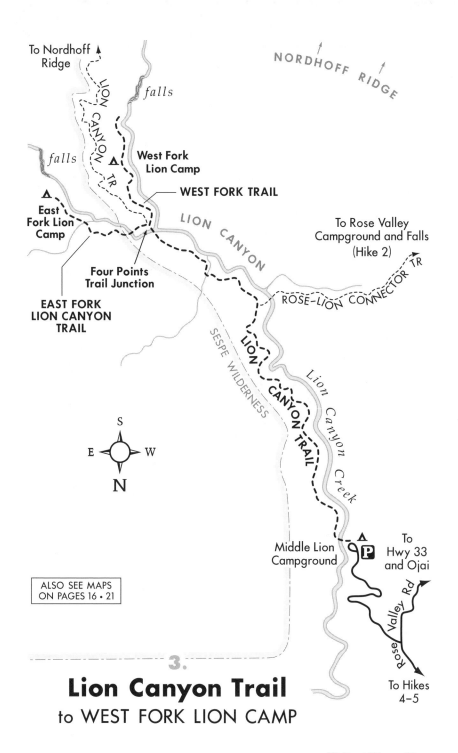

To Nordhoff
Ridge

falls

LION CANYON TR

West Fork
Lion Camp

WEST FORK TRAIL

falls

LION CANYON

East
Fork Lion
Camp

To Rose Valley
Campground and Falls
(Hike 2)

Four Points
Trail Junction

ROSE–LION CONNECTOR TR

EAST FORK
LION CANYON
TRAIL

NORDHOFF RIDGE

SESPE WILDERNESS

LION CANYON TRAIL

Lion Canyon Creek

S
E · W
N

Middle Lion
Campground

P

To
Hwy 33
and Ojai

Rose Valley Rd

ALSO SEE MAPS
ON PAGES 16 · 21

To Hikes
4–5

3.
Lion Canyon Trail
to WEST FORK LION CAMP

junction with the Rose-Lion Connector Trail to the right, which leads to Rose Valley Campground (Hike 2). Proceed straight ahead, staying in Lion Canyon, to another creek crossing at two miles. After crossing is a three-way trail split known as Four Points Trail Junction.

From the Four Point Trail Junction are three options. The left fork (East Fork Lion Canyon Trail) leads a half mile to East Fork Lion Camp and a waterfall and pool within the Sespe Wilderness. The Lion Canyon Trail (middle route) continues straight ahead, gaining 1,700 feet over 3.6 miles to Nordhoff Ridge. Atop the ridge are spectacular coastal and mountain views. Traversing the ridge is Nordhoff Ridge Road, a vehicle-restricted road. From the road, routes lead down the ridge into Horn Canyon and Sisar Canyon into Ojai Valley.

For now, go to the right on the West Fork Trail. Stay on the east side of the creek along the edge of the rocky hillside. Less than a half mile from the junction is West Fork Lion Camp. Rock hop up the narrow drainage a short distance past the camp to a beautiful waterfall and pool.

Return 0.4 miles to Four Points Trail Junction. Take the East Fork Lion Canyon Trail and enter the narrow canyon. Weave through the tall, reedy deer grass, used by the Chumash Indians to weave baskets. The canyon soon opens, with pockets of pines gracing the canyon slopes. Cross an ephemeral tributary to East Fork Lion Creek Camp at a half mile. Walk through the pine-dotted camp, passing a few metal grills and fire pits. Just past the camp, follow the creek, scrambling through the boulders to a box canyon and rock grotto with a waterfall and pool. Return by retracing your route. ▪

4. Piedra Blanca Formations

Piedra Blanca Camp and Twin Forks Camp

GENE MARSHALL — PIEDRA BLANCA
NATIONAL RECREATION TRAIL

Hiking distance: 6.4 miles round trip
(1.25 miles to Piedra Blanca formations)
Hiking time: 3.5 hours
Elevation gain: 600 feet
Maps: U.S.G.S. Lion Canyon
Sespe Wilderness Trail Map

**map
page 28**

Summary of hike: The magnificent Piedra Blanca Formations (meaning *white rock* in Spanish) are huge weather-sculpted sandstone outcrops carved by wind and water. The impressive formations stretch for over a mile, with rounded slopes, sheer cliffs, caves, and overhangs. You can easily spend the day exploring the trails around the unique rocks, cavities, and caves. The Gene Marshall-Piedra Blanca National Recreation Trail, a 17.7-mile trail in the Sespe Wilderness, weaves through these eroded monoliths en route to a series of wilderness campsites. This hike begins at Sespe Creek and winds through the formations, following Piedra Blanca Creek to Piedra Blanca Camp and Twin Forks Camp.

Driving directions: OJAI. From Ojai, drive 14.6 miles north on Highway 33 (Maricopa Highway) to the Rose Valley Road turnoff and turn right. Continue 4.8 miles to a road split. Take the left fork 0.9 miles down to the trailhead parking lot at the end of the road.

Hiking directions: From the signed path by the restrooms, walk towards the river gorge. Descend the slope through chaparral to an open flat. Cross the flat on the boulder-lined path to Lion Canyon Creek. Rock-hop over the creek to Sespe Creek at 0.3 miles. Wade across the river or use rocks as stepping-stones to a T-junction. The Sespe River Trail (Hike 5) goes to the right. Bear left on the Gene Marshall–Piedra Blanca National Recreation Trail, and head downstream a short distance. Curve right and climb the slope to great views of the Piedra Blanca rock outcrops straight ahead. Wind through scrub and chaparral to a posted junction. The Middle Sespe Trail bears left and heads 3.5 miles west to Rock Creek and another 3.5 miles west to Highway 33 by the abandoned Beaver Campground. Veer to the right, staying on the Marshall–Piedra Blanca Trail. Enter the Sespe Wilderness, reaching the Piedra Blanca formations at 1.25 miles. At the formations, leave the main trail and explore the area, choosing your own route.

To extend the hike, the Gene Marshall–Piedra Blanca National Recreation Trail winds through the stunning rock garden. Drop down the back side of the formations into a deep stream-fed ravine. Cross a tributary of Piedra Blanca Creek, and enter wide Piedra Blanca Canyon. Head north, parallel to Piedra Blanca Creek, following the west edge of the canyon through a pocket of oaks and exposed scrub. Traverse the lower slope, overlooking a few pools and small waterfalls. Loop around a side canyon, and drop into a circular flat with majestic oaks and boulders on the banks of Piedra Blanca Creek at 2.9 miles. Continue up-canyon and pass a five-foot waterfall by a rock-rimmed pool. Cross the creek on large boulders, and walk 50 yards to a signed junction.

The main trail continues straight ahead 3.3 miles to Pine Mountain Lodge, nestled in the conifers. For this hike, veer right 20 yards and cross the North Fork Piedra Blanca Creek. Climb another 20 yards to the Twin Forks Camp at 3.2 miles, a small campsite on a flat bench with scattered oaks above the creek. Return by retracing your steps. ■

5. Sespe River Trail

Hiking distance: 3.5 miles round trip
Hiking time: 2 hours
Elevation gain: 200 feet
Maps: U.S.G.S. Lion Canyon
Sespe Wilderness Trail Map

map
page 28

Summary of hike: Sespe Creek is a wide body of water that winds 55 miles through the Sierra Madre, from Potrero Seco to the Santa Clara River in Fillmore. The creek is formed by more than thirty tributary streams and appears more like a river than a creek. It is popular for whitewater rafting and kayaking. The Sespe River Trail stretches 17 miles along the Old Sespe Road, parallel to Sespe Creek. The trail leads to Sespe Hot Springs, a natural hot springs in the Los Padres National Forest with rock-lined soaking pools. This hike follows a portion of the trail into the Sespe Wilderness on a bluff above the creek to a scenic overlook. The trail parallels the creek past deep pools and sandy flats, crossing Piedra Blanca Creek and Trout Creek.

Driving directions: OJAI. From Ojai, drive 14.6 miles north on Highway 33 (Maricopa Highway) to the Rose Valley Road turnoff and turn right. Continue 4.8 miles to a road split. Take the left fork 0.9 miles down to the trailhead parking lot at the end of the road.

Hiking directions: From the signed path by the restrooms, walk towards the river gorge. Descend the slope through chaparral to an open flat. Cross the flat on the boulder-lined path to Lion Canyon Creek. Rock-hop over the creek to Sespe Creek at 0.3 miles. Wade across the creek or use rocks as stepping stones to a T-junction. The Gene Marshall-Piedra Blanca National Recreation Trail goes to the left (Hike 4). Take the right fork on the Sespe River Trail and head downstream, parallel to the northern banks of Sespe Creek. In a half mile, the trail crosses Piedra Blanca Creek. After crossing, the trail narrows as it enters a canyon. Past the canyon, the trail widens out again and crosses Trout Creek. Along the way, side paths lead down to

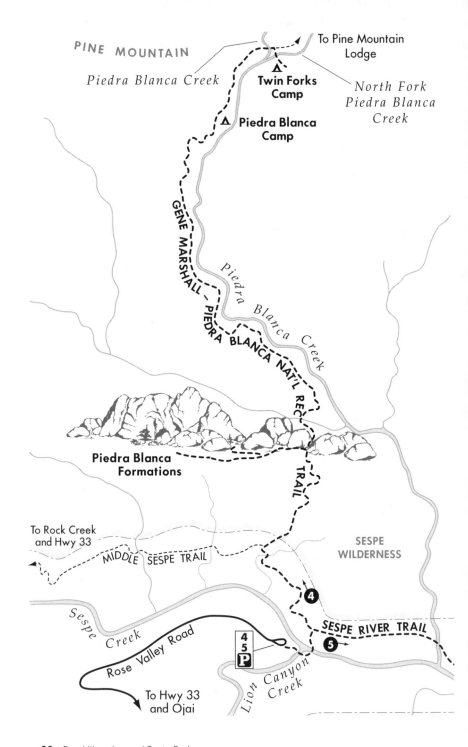

PINE MOUNTAIN

Piedra Blanca Creek

To Pine Mountain
Lodge

⚐ **Twin Forks
Camp**

*North Fork
Piedra Blanca
Creek*

⚐ **Piedra Blanca
Camp**

GENE MARSHALL - PIEDRA BLANCA NAT'L REC. TRAIL

Piedra Blanca Creek

**Piedra Blanca
Formations**

To Rock Creek
and Hwy 33

MIDDLE SESPE TRAIL

SESPE
WILDERNESS

Sespe Creek

Rose Valley Road

4

SESPE RIVER TRAIL

**4
5
P**

5

Lion Canyon Creek

To Hwy 33
and Ojai

the creek. A short distance ahead, enter the Sespe Wilderness and pass through a gate, gaining elevation to a vista overlooking the canyon. At the top of the ridge, the views open toward the mountains in the north. The ridge is the turn-around point.

To hike farther, the trail follows Sespe Creek downstream for miles, crossing the creek numerous times. The first crossing is at Bear Canyon, 4.5 miles from the trailhead. Sespe Hot Springs is another 10.5 miles past Bear Canyon. ■

HIKE 4
Piedra Blanca Formations
HIKE 5
Sespe River Trail

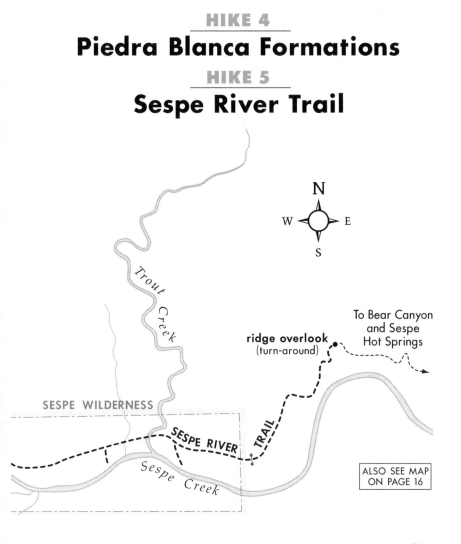

6. Wheeler Gorge Nature Trail

Hiking distance: 1-mile loop
Hiking time: 30 minutes
Elevation gain: 200 feet
Maps: U.S.G.S. Wheeler Springs
  Sespe Wilderness Trail Map

Summary of hike: Wheeler Gorge Nature Trail is an interpretive trail on the North Fork Matilija Creek near Wheeler Gorge Campground. The trail is an excellent introduction to the shaded creekside riparian habitats and arid chaparral plant communities that are so common throughout the area. The path winds through a small canyon gorge under sycamores, cottonwoods, willows and oaks, following the year-round creek past trickling waterfalls and bedrock pools. Free brochures from the Ojai Ranger Station correspond with numbered posts along the trail.

Driving directions: OJAI. From Ojai, drive 8 miles north on Highway 33 (Maricopa Highway) to the Wheeler Gorge Campground on the left. Continue on the highway another 0.5 miles to the posted nature trail on the left by a locked metal gate, just before crossing the bridge over the North Fork Matilija Creek.

Hiking directions: From the trailhead map panel, take the path to the right, following the North Fork Matilija Creek upstream. Cross under the Highway 33 bridge, passing cascades, small waterfalls, and pools. Rock hop to the north side of the creek, and climb up through chaparral dotted with oaks. Follow the watercourse, passing a 12-foot waterfall between signposts 7 and 8. Cross over a rock formation, and wind through a shady tunnel of tall chaparral. Climb rock steps to a vista of Dry Lakes Ridge to the north. Curve away from the creekside vegetation, and descend on the northern slope of the arid hillside. Curve left and parallel Highway 33 from above. Drop back down to the creek, completing the loop. Recross the creek and return to the trailhead. ■

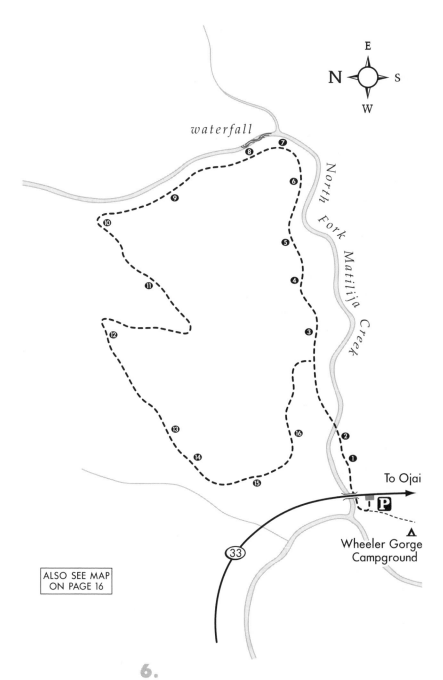

E
N — S
W

waterfall

North Fork Matilija Creek

⑧ ⑦
⑥
⑨
⑩ ⑤
④
⑪
③
⑫
⑬ ⑯
⑭ ②
⑮ ①

To Ojai

P

Wheeler Gorge
Campground

(33)

ALSO SEE MAP
ON PAGE 16

6.
Wheeler Gorge Nature Trail

7. Murietta Canyon

Hiking distance: 3.4 miles round trip
Hiking time: 1.5 hours
Elevation gain: 200 feet
Maps: U.S.G.S. Old Man Mountain and White Ledge Peak
Matilija and Dick Smith Wilderness Map Guide
Sespe Wilderness Trail Map

Summary of hike: San Antonio Creek, Coyote Creek, and Matilija Creek form the headwaters of the 31-mile long Ventura River. Matilija Creek, draining from the north, delineates the boundary between the Santa Ynez Mountains and the Topatopa Mountains. The diverse and wild landscape of the Matilija Creek watershed lies within the protected Matilija Wilderness. Hikes 7—9 explore the Matilija—Murietta Creek drainage.

The Murietta Trail begins in Matilija Canyon on the north side of Matilija Creek. The trail veers west into Murietta Canyon and follows Murietta Creek along the canyon bottom to a pristine trail camp. Murietta Camp sits on a shady wooded flat at the edge of the Murietta Creek by cascades and pools. The primitive camp rests under a forest canopy dominated by cedar and oak trees.

Driving directions: OJAI. From Ojai, drive 4.9 miles north on Highway 33 (Maricopa Highway) to Matilija Canyon Road and turn left. Continue 4.8 miles to the parking area on the left by the trailhead gate.

Hiking directions: Pass the trailhead gate and follow the paved road west. Enter the Matilija Canyon Ranch, a private wildlife refuge. Stay on the road along this forest service easement. Just past the refuge the pavement ends. Cross the creek two times to views up Murrieta Canyon, Old Man Canyon, and Matilija Canyon. At 0.5 miles, just past the second creek crossing, is the signed North Fork Matilija Creek Trail to the right (Hike 9). Instead, continue another 0.2 miles to the signed Murietta Trail on the left. Leave the road and head south on the footpath towards the mouth of Murietta Canyon. Proceed to a stream

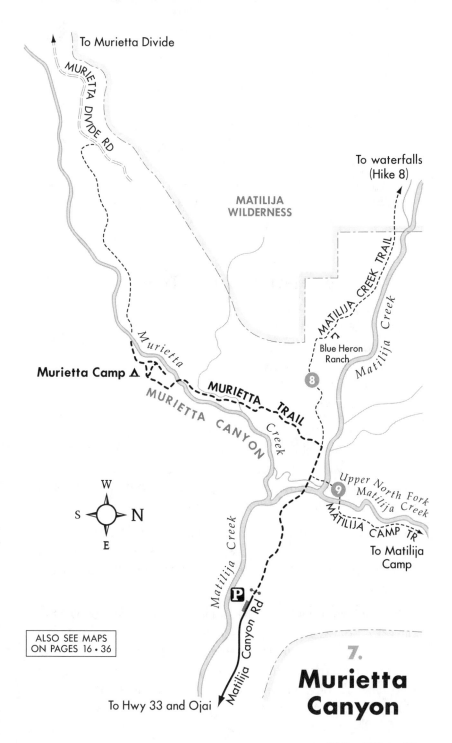

To Murietta Divide

MURIETTA DIVIDE RD

To waterfalls
(Hike 8)

MATILIJA
WILDERNESS

MATILIJA CREEK TRAIL

Matilija Creek

Murietta

Murietta Camp △

MURIETTA CANYON

MURIETTA TRAIL

Creek

Blue Heron
Ranch

8

Upper North Fork
Matilija Creek

9

MATILIJA CAMP TR

To Matilija
Camp

W
S ○ N
E

Matilija Creek

P

Matilija Canyon Rd

ALSO SEE MAPS
ON PAGES 16 • 36

7.
**Murietta
Canyon**

To Hwy 33 and Ojai

crossing by pools and cascades. Rock hop across the stream channels and up a small hill, heading deeper into the canyon. Follow the creek to Murietta Camp, perched on a flat at 1.7 miles. From the camp, several trails lead down to the stream. Return along the same path.

Up the canyon from the campground, the trail enters a dense forest with a tangle of vegetation and underbrush. This unmaintained trail becomes vague and hard to follow, but leads 0.8 miles to Murietta Divide Road. Murietta Divide Road—a dirt road—leads 2.4 miles west to the 3,443-foot divide, offering great views into the Santa Ynez River Valley. ■

8. Matilija Creek Trail

Hiking distance: 7 miles round trip
Hiking time: 3 hours
Elevation gain: 600 feet
Maps: U.S.G.S. Old Man Mountain
Matilija and Dick Smith Wilderness Map Guide
Sespe Wilderness Trail Map

map
page 36

Summary of hike: The Matilija Creek Trail heads up the main canyon of the Matilija Creek drainage to beautiful pools, cascades, and water slides. Large shale slabs border the creek for sunbathing beneath the steep canyon cliffs. Up the isolated and rugged canyon are several towering waterfalls.

Driving directions: OJAI. From Ojai, drive 4.9 miles north on Highway 33 (Maricopa Highway) to Matilija Canyon Road and turn left. Continue 4.8 miles to the parking area on the left by the trailhead gate.

Hiking directions: Pass the trailhead gate and follow the paved road west. Enter the Matilija Canyon Ranch, a private wildlife refuge. Stay on the road along this forest service easement. Just past the refuge the pavement ends. Cross the creek two times to views up Murrieta Canyon, Old Man Canyon, and Matilija Canyon. At 0.5 miles, just past the second creek crossing, is the signed North Fork Matilija Creek Trail to the right—Hike 9. Shortly after, a footpath on the left veers southwest along Murietta Creek—Hike 7. Stay on the main road to an intersection with another trail one mile from the trailhead. Take the right fork past a house on a Forest Service easement through the Blue Heron Ranch. For a short distance, the trail borders a beautiful, two-foot-high rock wall and fruit trees. As you approach the mountain range, cross a tributary stream at the mouth of Old Man Canyon and curve to the right. Follow the western edge of the deep, narrow canyon and cross another stream. Climb up a short hill to a perch overlooking the canyon. Take the left fork that curves around the gully, and hike down the rocky drainage. Near the canyon floor, the trail picks up again to the left. Hike parallel to the creek along its endless cascades, pools, and rock slabs. This natural playground is the destination. Return along the same path.

To hike farther, continue up-canyon, creating your own path. There are three waterfalls ahead. Two falls are located another mile up the main canyon. Another falls is in the canyon to the northeast. Hiking may be difficult due to slippery shale and an indistinct trail. ▪

9. North Fork Matilija Creek Trail
to Matilija Camp and Middle Matilija Camp

Hiking distance: 8 miles round trip
Hiking time: 4 hours
Elevation gain: 800 feet
Maps: U.S.G.S. Old Man Mountain and Wheeler Springs
      Matilija and Dick Smith Wilderness Map Guide
      Sespe Wilderness Trail Map

map
page 39

Summary of hike: The Upper North Fork of Matilija Creek forms on the southern slopes of Ortega Hill and flows year-round. The North Fork Matilija Creek Trail runs for 9 miles through the Matilija Wilderness along the Upper North Fork of Matilija Creek, from its confluence at Matilija Creek to Ortega Hill.

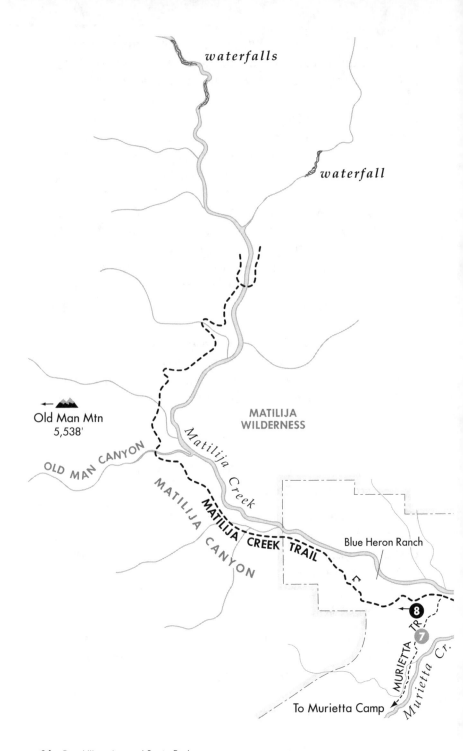

waterfalls

waterfall

← Old Man Mtn
5,538'

OLD MAN CANYON

MATILIJA
WILDERNESS

Matilija Creek

MATILIJA CANYON

MATILIJA CREEK TRAIL

Blue Heron Ranch

8

7

MURIETTA TR.

Murietta Cr.

To Murietta Camp

8.
Matilija Creek Trail

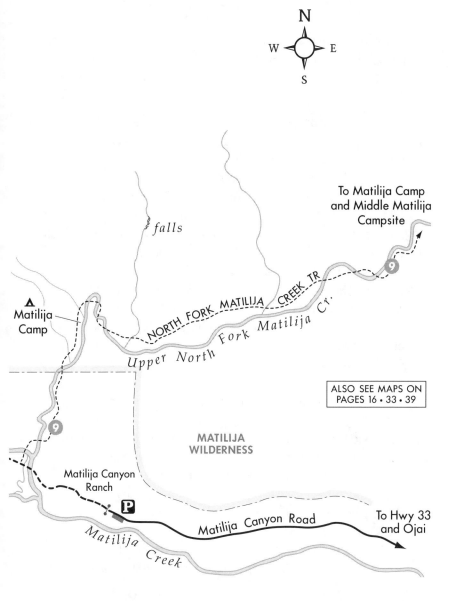

N
W ⟡ E
S

falls

To Matilija Camp
and Middle Matilija
Campsite

NORTH FORK MATILIJA CREEK TR.

▲
Matilija
Camp

Upper North Fork Matilija Cr.

ALSO SEE MAPS ON
PAGES 16 • 33 • 39

MATILIJA
WILDERNESS

Matilija Canyon
Ranch

P

Matilija Canyon Road

To Hwy 33
and Ojai

Matilija Creek

En route the trail passes pools, cascades, and waterfalls. This hike begins at the southern trailhead at Matilija Canyon Road and leads to Matalija Camp and Middle Matilija Camp, oak-shaded camps with large boulders, sandstone cliffs, swimming holes, and picnic areas. The easy trail winds through the lush canyon in the shade of oaks, alders, and sycamores, crossing the creek 14 times.

Driving directions: OJAI. From Ojai, drive 4.9 miles north on Highway 33 (Maricopa Highway) to Matilija Canyon Road and turn left. Continue 4.8 miles to the parking area on the left by the trailhead gate.

Hiking directions: Pass the trailhead gate and follow the paved road west. Enter the Matilija Canyon Ranch, a private wildlife refuge. Stay on the road along this forest service easement. Just past the refuge the pavement ends. Cross the creek two times to views up Murrieta Canyon, Old Man Canyon, and Matilija Canyon. At 0.5 miles, just past the second creek crossing, leave the road and take the North Fork Matilija Creek Trail to the right. Cross a rocky wash and head north up the narrow canyon floor between steep cliffs. Hop over the Upper North Fork Matilija Creek, enter the Matilija Wilderness, and follow the east canyon wall through a canopy of riparian growth. Cross the creek again by a rock wall and boulders forming a pool. At 1.3 miles, enter Matilija Camp, a group of campsites along the creek under a grove of oaks.

Just past the campsites, cross the creek as the canyon and trail curve to the east. Cross the creek three consecutive times, and slowly gain elevation as the canyon widens. Weave through an easy and uneventful stretch away from the creek. Return to the creek by another pool at 2.6 miles. Cross to the south side of the creek and continue upstream. Cross the creek two more times by a group of pools. Traverse the south canyon wall, and climb up two switchbacks to views across the length of the canyon to Old Man Mountain. Pass more pools, small waterfalls, and cascades. Curve left and cross a tributary stream, following the bends in the canyon. Cross the creek for the thirteenth time by another pool with a 4-foot waterfall. Make the final creek crossing and enter the Middle Matilija Campsite on a grassy flat with majestic oaks at 4 miles.

To extend the hike, the trail continues 1.6 miles north to Upper Matilija Camp, 3.4 miles to Maple Camp, and 5.1 miles to the upper trailhead at the south end of Cherry Creek Road. ■

To Upper Matilija Camp and Cherry Creek Road

falls

Middle Matilija Camp

Creek

MATILIJA WILDERNESS

falls

NORTH FORK MATILIJA CREEK TRAIL

Matilija

▲ **Matilija Camp**

Upper North Fork

N
W ⬥ E
S

7-8

Matilija Canyon Ranch

Matilija Canyon Road

To Hwy 33 and Ojai

ALSO SEE MAPS ON PAGES 16 • 36

Matilija Creek

9.

North Fork Matilija Creek Trail
to MATILIJA CAMP and MIDDLE MATILIJA CAMP

10. Rice Canyon—Wills Canyon Loop
VENTURA RIVER—RANCHO EL NIDO PRESERVE

Hiking distance: 4.8-mile loop
Hiking time: 2.5 hours
Elevation gain: 400 feet
Maps: U.S.G.S. Matilija
Matilija and Dick Smith Wilderness Map Guide
Ventura River-Rancho El Nido Trail Map

map
page 42

Summary of hike: The Ventura River-Rancho El Nido Preserve encompasses 1,591 acres on the western side of Ojai Valley. The sprawling preserve is bordered by the Los Padres National Forest and includes three miles of the Ventura River. The preserve, purchased and managed by the Ojai Valley Land Conservancy, was opened to the public in 2003.

This hike forms a loop through two creek-fed canyons. The trail heads up Rice Canyon, parallels Rice Creek, and returns along the banks of Wills Creek. En route, the trail weaves through the Los Padres National Forest, meanders through lush riparian habitats, and leads to overlooks of the surrounding mountains.

Driving directions: VENTURA. From Highway 101/Ventura Freeway in Ventura, drive 11.2 miles north on Highway 33 towards Ojai to Highway 150 (Baldwin Road). Turn left and go 0.2 miles to Rice Road, the third road on the right. Turn right and continue 2 miles to a junction with Fairview Road. Turn left—staying on Rice Road—and drive 0.1 mile to Meyer Road. Turn left and go 0.2 miles to the signed preserve entrance at Oso Road. Veer left through the entrance gate, and drive 0.1 mile to the Rice Canyon trailhead parking lot.

Hiking directions: Wade or rock-hop across the Ventura River (depending on the season) by a swimming hole. Curve up the hillside to the bluff. Follow the bluff, parallel to the historic orange grove, to a bridge over Rice Creek and a junction. Begin the loop to the right on the Rice Canyon Trail. Follow the north side of Rice Creek to Canal Road, a paved access road. Cross the road and a bridge over the canal to the mouth of Rice Canyon.

Drop into the shade of a sycamore, willow, and oak forest. Cross Rice Creek and head up the canyon. Cross the creek again and continue upstream through riparian vegetation. Merge with an old ranch road to a cattle gate at the Los Padres National Forest boundary. Enter the forest service land, and head uphill at a moderate grade. Follow the north canyon wall to an oak-rimmed meadow with a view of the surrounding hills. Continue west to a ridge overlooking the Ojai Valley and the Santa Ynez Mountains. Wend downhill into bucolic Wills Canyon. Pass through another cattle gate, reentering the Ojai Valley Land Conservancy tract. Continue downhill, cross El Nido Trail, and hop across Wills Creek. Veer left and follow the south edge of the creek to a junction with the Chaparral Crest Trail by the Wills Canyon footbridge.

Cross the bridge and slowly descend. Follow the course of the creek to the Fern Grotto Trail, a connector to the Chaparral Crest Trail. Stay on the Wills Canyon Trail, and steadily descend through an oak savanna. Cross Wills Creek to the mouth of the canyon and a trail junction by Canal Road. The right fork leads to the Riverview Trailhead (Hike 11). For this hike, cross Canal Road on the River Bluff Trail. Follow the east edge of the historic orange grove, parallel to the Ventura River. Cross a bridge over Rice Creek, completing the loop. Return to the trailhead, straight ahead. ■

coast live oak

Ventura River • Rancho El Nido Preserve

HIKE 10
Rice Canyon–Wills Canyon Loop

HIKE 11
Wills Canyon–Chaparral Crest Loop

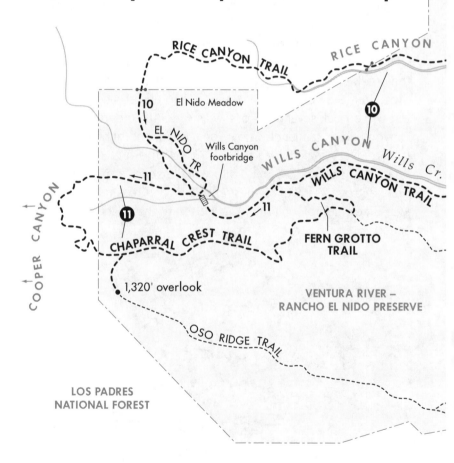

RICE CANYON TRAIL

RICE CANYON

10   El Nido Meadow

EL NIDO TR

Wills Canyon footbridge

WILLS CANYON

Wills Cr.

WILLS CANYON TRAIL

10

11

11

COOPER CANYON

CHAPARRAL CREST TRAIL

FERN GROTTO TRAIL

1,320' overlook

VENTURA RIVER – RANCHO EL NIDO PRESERVE

OSO RIDGE TRAIL

LOS PADRES NATIONAL FOREST

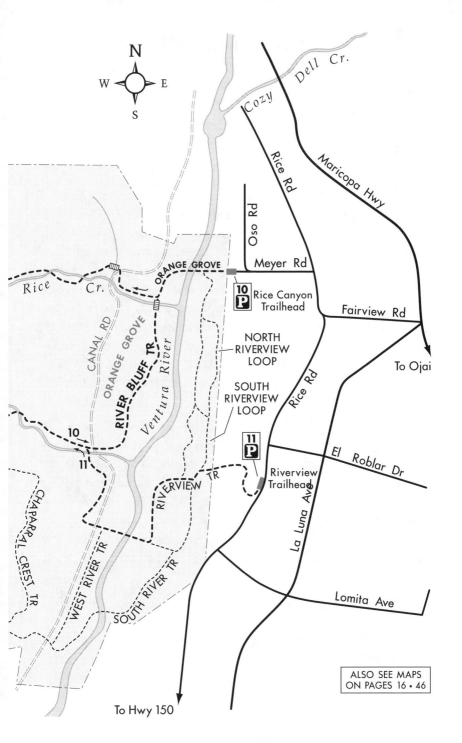

N
W   E
S

Cozy Dell Cr.

Cozy

Rice Rd

Maricopa Hwy

Oso Rd

Meyer Rd

ORANGE GROVE

Rice   Cr.

ORANGE GROVE

10 P
Rice Canyon
Trailhead

Fairview Rd

CANAL RD

ORANGE GROVE

RIVER BLUFF TR.

Ventura River

NORTH
RIVERVIEW
LOOP

SOUTH
RIVERVIEW
LOOP

Rice Rd

To Ojai

10

11

11 P

RIVERVIEW TR.

Riverview
Trailhead

El Roblar Dr

CHAPARRAL CREST TR.

WEST RIVER TR

SOUTH RIVER TR

La Luna Ave

Lomita Ave

ALSO SEE MAPS
ON PAGES 16 • 46

To Hwy 150

113 Great Hikes - **43**

11. Wills Canyon—Chaparral Crest Loop
VENTURA RIVER—RANCHO EL NIDO PRESERVE

Hiking distance: 5.6-mile loop

Hiking time: 3 hours

Elevation gain: 700 feet

Maps: U.S.G.S. Matilija

Matilija and Dick Smith Wilderness Map Guide

Ventura River-Rancho El Nido Trail Map

map page 42

Summary of hike: The Ventura River-Rancho El Nido Preserve is located in the Meiners Oaks area of Ojai Valley. The diverse topography includes open sandy terrain in the Ventura River basin, pockets of grasslands and meadows, chaparral hillsides exposed to the sun, riparian sycamore and willow groves, oak savanna, shaded creek-fed canyons, and year-round springs. This hike climbs through a stream-fed canyon under majestic coastal live oaks with an understory of native plants, including snowberries, Humboldt lilies, western raspberry, and hummingbird sage. The hike returns along a chaparral-covered ridge that offers exceptional vistas, including an overlook on the preserve's highest spot at 1,320 feet.

Driving directions: VENTURA. From Highway 101/Ventura Freeway in Ventura, drive 11.2 miles north on Highway 33 towards Ojai to Highway 150 (Baldwin Road). Turn left and go 0.2 miles to Rice Road, the third right turn. Turn right and continue 1.4 miles to the posted Riverview Trailhead parking lot on the left, directly across the street from the horse boarding facility. The parking lot is located between Lomita Avenue and just south of El Roblar Drive.

Hiking directions: Walk past the trailhead gate, and head down the slope on the Riverview Trail to the valley floor. Wind through the oak-dotted flatland with 360-degree vistas of the surrounding mountains. Cross the open terrain and several dry creekbeds to a posted trail split. The right fork leads to the Rice Canyon trailhead (Hike 10). Bear left for 20 yards, and curve right to another junction. Again, the right fork leads to the Rice Canyon trailhead. Bear left and head south to a fork. Go to the right, crossing rocky streambeds and passing pockets of bamboo to the Ventura River. Wade or rock-hop across the river (depending on the season) to Canal Road, a paved access road. Cross the road, staying on the trail, and curve right, parallel to the sycamore-lined stream. Follow the base of the oak-covered hillside to a junction by a bench and the historic orange grove at the mouth of Wills Canyon. The River Bluff Trail crosses Canal Road and heads north between the orange grove and the Ventura River to the Rice Canyon trailhead (Hike 10).

For this hike, bear left and head up Wills Canyon. Drop down and cross Wills Creek. Stroll through the pastoral oak savanna to the Fern Grotto Trail, a connector to the Chaparral Crest Trail. Begin the loop straight ahead, staying on the shaded canyon floor to the Wills Canyon footbridge. Cross the bridge to a posted junction with the Chaparral Crest Trail. Bear left and climb the north wall of the side canyon to a ridge with sweeping mountain vistas at the Los Padres National Forest boundary. Enter the Forest Service land, and traverse the ridge across the head of the canyon above Cooper Canyon on the right. Curve left and follow the south rim of Wills Canyon to a trail split. Detour right on the Oso Ridge Trail 220 yards to the preserve's highest point at the 1,320-foot overlook. From the summit are views of Lake Casitas, the coastal ridge, the Pacific Ocean, Ojai Valley, the Santa Ynez Mountains, the Topatopa Mountains, and Sulphur Mountain.

Return to the Chaparral Crest Trail and follow the ridge, steadily descending to a posted junction. Bear left on the Fern Grotto Trail, leaving the exposed ridge to the shade of the oaks. Complete the loop at Wills Creek. Bear right and retrace your steps along the creek, back to the trailhead. ▪

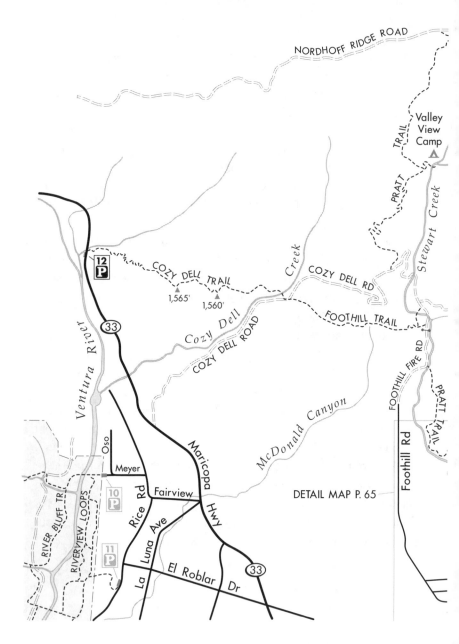

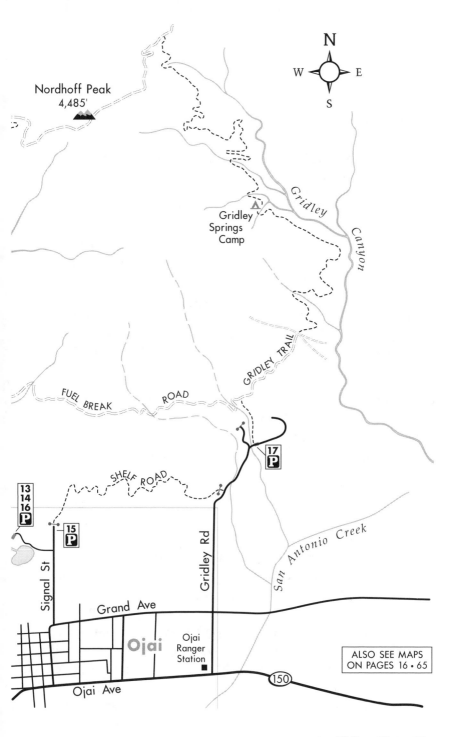

N
W E
S

Nordhoff Peak
4,485'

Gridley
Canyon

Gridley
Springs
Camp

GRIDLEY TRAIL

FUEL BREAK ROAD

17
P

SHELF ROAD

13
14
16
P

15
P

San Antonio Creek

Gridley Rd

Signal St

Grand Ave

Ojai

Ojai
Ranger
Station

ALSO SEE MAPS
ON PAGES 16 • 65

Ojai Ave

150

12. Cozy Dell Trail
to COZY DELL CANYON

Hiking distance: 4 miles round trip
Hiking time: 2 hours
Elevation gain: 700 feet
Maps: U.S.G.S. Matilija
Matilija and Dick Smith Wilderness Map Guide
Sespe Wilderness Trail Map

Summary of hike: The Cozy Dell Trail is on the west end of Ojai on the lower slopes of the Topatopa Mountains. The trail climbs up several switchbacks through a small, shaded canyon to vista points with panoramic views in every direction. There are great views into the Ojai Valley to the south and the surrounding peaks of the Santa Ynez and Topatopa Mountains. From the overlooks, the trail drops into the beautiful and forested Cozy Dell Canyon by Cozy Dell Creek. The trail ties in with the Foothill Trail and Cozy Dell Road. The hike can be extended with Hike 14 for a 7.2-mile loop hike.

Driving directions: OJAI. From Ojai, drive 3.4 miles north on Highway 33 (Maricopa Highway) to the Cozy Dell trailhead parking pullout on the left (west) side of the road. The pullout is located by a bridge, a packing house, and a Forest Service trailhead sign.

Hiking directions: From the parking area, cross the highway to the trailhead, which is south of the packing house along the right side of the metal railing. Take the well-defined trail east, and head up the canyon. A short distance ahead is a series of 18 switchbacks, gaining 600 feet up the south edge of the canyon. At one mile, the trail reaches its peak at a 1,565-foot saddle, giving way to an open area with breathtaking views. Proceed downhill towards Cozy Dell Canyon and back up to a second saddle with more outstanding views at 1,560 feet. Drop back into the oak trees, descending 200 feet into forested Cozy Dell Canyon, Cozy Dell Creek, and a T-junction with Cozy Dell Road. One hundred yards to the left (east) is a posted junction with

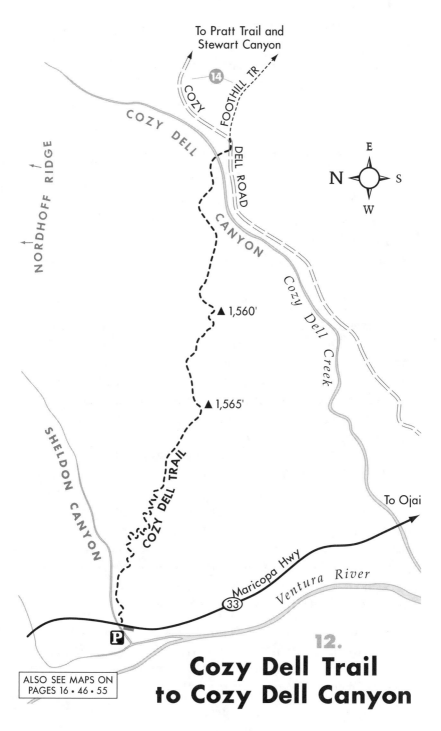

To Pratt Trail and
Stewart Canyon

14

COZY

FOOTHILL TR.

COZY DELL

DELL ROAD

CANYON

NORDHOFF RIDGE

Cozy Dell Creek

▲ 1,560'

▲ 1,565'

E
N ← → S
W

SHELDON CANYON

COZY DELL TRAIL

To Ojai

Maricopa Hwy

33

Ventura River

P

ALSO SEE MAPS ON
PAGES 16 • 46 • 55

12.
Cozy Dell Trail
to Cozy Dell Canyon

the Foothill Trail (Hike 15). This is the turn-around spot. Return by retracing your steps.

To hike farther, the fire road continues to the Pratt Trail and Foothill Fire Road at Stewart Canyon—Hikes 13 and 14. ■

13. Pratt Trail
Stewart Canyon to Valley View Camp
STEWART CANYON

Hiking distance: 6.6 miles round trip
Hiking time: 3.5 hours
Elevation gain: 2,000 feet
Maps: U.S.G.S. Ojai and Matilija
      Matilija and Dick Smith Wilderness Map Guide
      Sespe Wilderness Trail Map

Summary of hike: Stewart Canyon, at the north edge of downtown Ojai, is the gateway to a network of magnificent hiking trails in the Los Padres National Forest. The Pratt Trail heads up Stewart Canyon, leading 4.6 miles and gaining 3,000 feet in elevation to Nordhoff Ridge, one mile west of the old fire lookout tower. The lower canyon connects to several trails, including the Foothill Trail to Cozy Dell Canyon (Hike 14), the Cozy Dell Trail to Highway 33 (Hike 12), and the Ojai Fuel Break Road to Gridley Road (Hike 16). This hike winds up the lower canyon, following Stewart Creek for 1.3 miles through a eucalyptus grove, meadows, and landscaped rock gardens. The trail continues up the mountain slope to Valley View Camp, a beautiful forested camp in a serene grotto on the banks of Stewart Creek. The primitive camp sits beneath a vertical, moss-covered rock wall. Throughout the hike are vistas of picturesque Ojai Valley, but none are available at the aptly named camp

Driving directions: OJAI. From downtown Ojai, drive 0.8 miles north up Signal Street (on the west side of the arcade) to the Pratt/Foothill Trailhead sign by the water tower. Turn left and drive 0.2 miles to the parking area on the left.

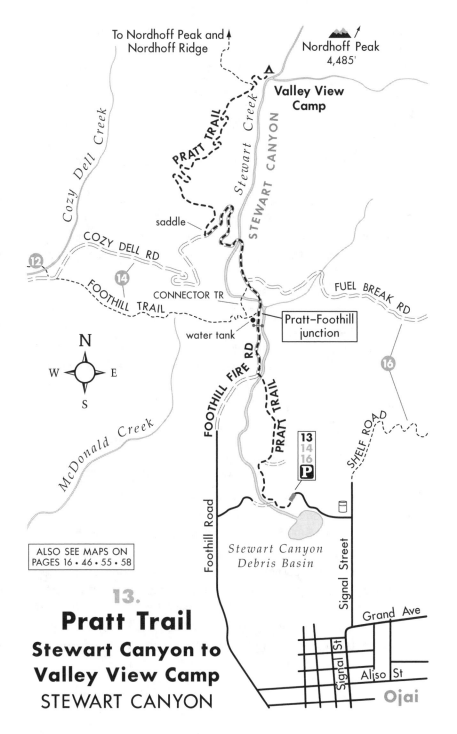

To Nordhoff Peak and
Nordhoff Ridge

Nordhoff Peak
4,485'

Valley View
Camp

Stewart Creek

STEWART CANYON

PRATT TRAIL

Cozy Dell Creek

saddle

COZY DELL RD

⑫

⑭

FOOTHILL TRAIL

CONNECTOR TR

FUEL BREAK RD

Pratt–Foothill
junction

water tank

⑯

N
W   E
S

FOOTHILL FIRE RD

PRATT TRAIL

SHELF ROAD

McDonald Creek

13
14
16
P

Foothill Road

Signal Street

ALSO SEE MAPS ON
PAGES 16 • 46 • 55 • 58

Stewart Canyon
Debris Basin

Grand Ave

Signal St

Aliso St

Ojai

13.
Pratt Trail
Stewart Canyon to
Valley View Camp
STEWART CANYON

Hiking directions: Take the posted Pratt Trail and curve north up Stewart Canyon. Parallel Stewart Creek, following the trail signs. Weave through the tall brush on the distinct rock-embedded path. Veer left and walk through a eucalyptus grove, following the east wall of Stewart Canyon to a plateau above the canyon with a picnic table. From this overlook are great views of the Ojai Valley and Sulphur Mountain. Descend into the canyon, staying on the rock-lined path past a few hillside homes, a creekside rock garden, and a paved road crossing. Cross Stewart Creek and take the Foothill Fire Road to the right, following the trail signs. Continue on the paved, narrow road along a beautiful rock wall. Pass a gate and water tank, where the pavement ends, to the posted Pratt and Foothill Trail junction on the left (Hike 14).

Stay on the Pratt Trail—straight ahead—climbing a quarter mile to a Y-fork on a wide, rounded flat at 1.3 miles. (Just shy of the Y-fork, the Foothill Connector Trail takes off to the left.) The Fuel Break Road, a connector trail to Gridley Road (Hike 16) curves to the right. Stay to the left and continue north, steadily climbing to a 2,050-foot saddle and a signed junction at 2 miles. Straight ahead, the trail descends into Cozy Dell Trail and leads 2.5 miles to Highway 33 (Hike 12). Bear sharply to the right on the footpath signed for Nordhoff Peak. Climb to views that span across Cozy Dell Canyon to Lake Casitas and the Pacific Ocean. Zigzag up four switchbacks, and follow the narrow path perched on the near-vertical cliffs. There is a spectacular bird's-eye view down Stewart canyon to Ojai and across Sulphur Mountain to Point Mugu in the Santa Monica Mountains. At 3.2 miles, on a left bend, is a unmarked but distinct Y-fork. The Pratt Trail continues to the left, leading another 1.4 miles and an additional thousand feet in elevation to Nordhoff Ridge. For this hike, veer right and descend 0.2 miles into the shady forest. Weave down five switchbacks to the end of the trail at Valley View Camp, a small primitive camp on the banks of Stewart Creek. Return by retracing your steps. ▪

14. Pratt Trail to
Foothill Trail—Cozy Dell Road Loop
STEWART CANYON • COZY DELL CANYON

Hiking distance: 5.8-mile loop
Hiking time: 3 hours
Elevation gain: 1,200 feet
Maps: U.S.G.S. Ojai and Matilija
    Matilija and Dick Smith Wilderness Map Guide
    Sespe Wilderness Trail Map

map
page 55

Summary of hike: This loop hike follows Stewart Creek up the canyon, passing meadows and rock gardens to the Foothill Trail. The route heads west through McDonald Canyon and drops into pastoral Cozy Dell Canyon by the creek. Cozy Dell Road winds up the forested canyon, climbing to sweeping overlooks beneath Nordhoff Peak.

Driving directions: OJAI. From downtown Ojai, drive 0.8 miles north up Signal Street (on the west side of the arcade) to the Pratt/Foothill Trailhead sign by the water tower. Turn left and drive 0.2 miles to the parking area on the left.

Hiking directions: Take the posted Pratt Trail and curve north up Stewart Canyon. Parallel Stewart Creek, following the trail signs. Weave through the tall brush on the distinct rock-embedded path. Veer left and walk through a eucalyptus grove, following the east wall of Stewart Canyon to a plateau above the canyon with a picnic table. From this overlook are great views of the Ojai Valley and Sulphur Mountain. Descend into the canyon, staying on the rock-lined path past a few hillside homes, a creekside rock garden, and a paved road crossing. Cross Stewart Creek and take the Foothill Fire Road to the right, following the trail signs. Continue on the paved, narrow road along a beautiful rock wall. Pass a gate and water tank, where the pavement ends, to the posted Pratt and Foothill Trail junction on the left.

Begin the loop to the left and climb rock steps, ascending the east-facing hillside to a trail split with the Foothill Connector Trail. Curve left and continue uphill along the short switchbacks, with great views down Stewart Canyon and across Ojai Canyon to Sulphur Mountain. Cross a saddle to views of Lake Casitas and the Santa Ynez Mountains. Drop into McDonald Canyon and cross another saddle. Descend a sloping meadow bordered by oaks. Head into Cozy Dell Canyon to the Cozy Dell Road. (A hundred yards to the left is the Cozy Dell Trail—Hike 12.) Bear right on the fire road towards the posted Pratt Trail, meandering through the rolling, forested glen. Steadily climb out of the canyon to a junction on a saddle. Bear left and continue uphill, curving right around the mountain to a posted junction with the Pratt Trail to Nordhoff Peak. Stay on the fire road to the right, and head downhill into Stewart Canyon to an open flat and road split. The left fork is the Fuel Break Road to Gridley Road (Hike 16). Descend to the right a quarter mile and complete the loop. Return down Stewart Canyon to the trailhead. ■

15. Shelf Road
STEWART CANYON • GRIDLEY CANYON

Hiking distance: 3.5 miles round trip
Hiking time: 1.5 hours
Elevation gain: 200 feet

map
page 58

Maps: U.S.G.S. Ojai
       Matilija and Dick Smith Wilderness Map Guide
       Sespe Wilderness Trail Map

Summary of hike: Shelf Road is an old, unpaved road that traverses the cliffs several hundred feet above the northern edge of Ojai. The road, connecting Signal Street with Gridley Road, is gated at both ends. The Los Padres National Forest is on the north side of the trail, and orange groves line the south side. It is a hiking, biking, and jogging path that is popular with the locals. The path has several scenic overlooks with great views of the city of Ojai, ten-mile long Ojai Valley, and Sulphur Mountain

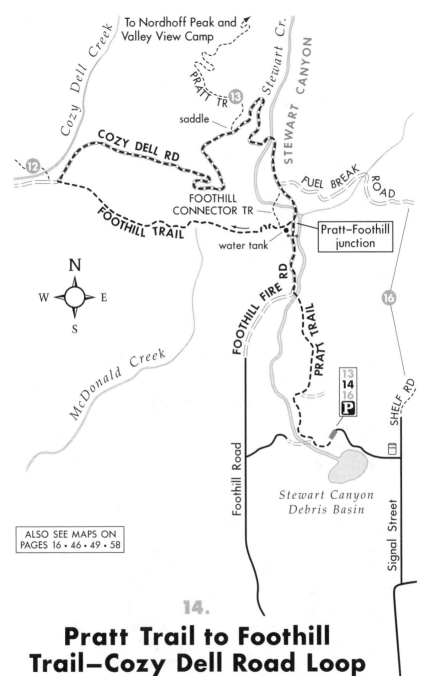

To Nordhoff Peak and
Valley View Camp

Cozy Dell Creek

Stewart Cr.

PRATT TR **13**

saddle

STEWART CANYON

COZY DELL RD

12

FOOTHILL
CONNECTOR TR

FUEL BREAK ROAD

FOOTHILL TRAIL

Pratt-Foothill
junction

water tank

N
W   E
S

FOOTHILL FIRE RD

PRATT TRAIL

16

McDonald Creek

13
14
16
P

SHELF RD

Foothill Road

Stewart Canyon
Debris Basin

Signal Street

ALSO SEE MAPS ON
PAGES 16 • 46 • 49 • 58

14.
Pratt Trail to Foothill
Trail–Cozy Dell Road Loop
STEWART CANYON • COZY DELL CANYON

across the valley. For a longer hike, Shelf Road can be combined with the Fuel Break Road—Hike 16—and the Pratt Trail for a 6.4-mile loop.

Driving directions: OJAI. From downtown Ojai, drive one mile north up Signal Street (on the west side of the arcade) to the trailhead gate at the end of the road. Park along the side of the road.

Hiking directions: Hike north past the gate and up the abandoned road. The road curves east, passing orange trees and avocado groves. Shelf Road follows the contours of the cliffs, snaking its way to the east above the city. At 1.7 miles, the trail ends at another entrance gate by Gridley Road. Return to the trailhead along the same route.

For the longer loop hike, continue north up Gridley Road and return on the Fuel Break Road, following the reverse directions for Hike 16. ■

16. Pratt Trail—Fuel Break Road— Shelf Road Loop
STEWART CANYON • GRIDLEY CANYON

Hiking distance: 6.4-mile loop
Hiking time: 3.5 hours
Elevation gain: 900 feet

map
page 58

Maps: U.S.G.S. Ojai and Matilija
Matilija and Dick Smith Wilderness Map Guide
Sespe Wilderness Trail Map

Summary of hike: The Fuel Break Road runs parallel to Ojai Valley a thousand feet above the city of Ojai. The views from above the valley are fascinating. The 1.5-mile fire road, built by the forest service in 1962, connects Stewart Canyon and the Pratt Trail on the west with Gridley Canyon on the east. This hike begins on the Pratt Trail and climbs up Stewart Canyon. The route then traverses the folded mountain layers on the Fuel Break Road to Gridley Road. The hike returns along Shelf Road, forming an easy, scenic loop. The Fuel Break Road is a backcountry hike while Shelf Road is more of an easy social stroll. Both fire roads are vehicle restricted.

Driving directions: OJAI. From downtown Ojai, drive 0.8 miles north up Signal Street (on the west side of the arcade) to the Pratt/Foothill Trailhead sign by the water tower. Turn left and drive 0.2 miles to the parking area on the left.

Hiking directions: Take the posted Pratt Trail and curve north up Stewart Canyon. Parallel Stewart Creek, following the trail signs. Weave through the tall brush on the distinct rock-embedded path. Veer left and walk through a eucalyptus grove, following the east wall of Stewart Canyon to a plateau above the canyon with a picnic table. From this overlook are great views of the Ojai Valley and Sulphur Mountain. Descend into the canyon, staying on the rock-lined path past a few hillside homes, a creekside rock garden, and a paved road crossing. Cross Stewart Creek and take the Foothill Fire Road to the right, following the trail signs. Continue on the paved, narrow road along a beautiful rock wall. Pass a gate and water tank, where the pavement ends, to the posted Pratt and Foothill Trail junction on the left (Hike 14). Stay on the Pratt Trail—straight ahead—climbing a quarter mile to a Y-fork on a wide, rounded flat at 1.3 miles. (Just shy of the Y-fork, the Foothill Connector Trail takes off to the left.) The Pratt Trail veers to the left and climbs to Valley View Camp and Nordhoff Ridge (Hike 13). For this hike, stay to the right on the Fuel Break Road.

Traverse the hillside on a winding course through the folded hills. Continue zigzagging eastward to a trail gate and posted junction on the right. The Gridley Trail (Hike 17) continues on the road to the left. Take the footpath to the right, and descend the narrow drainage 0.4 miles to the top of Gridley Road. Follow Gridley Road downhill one-third mile to the Shelf Road trailhead on the right. Take Shelf Road and head west 1.7 miles to the Signal Street gate. The trailhead turnoff is 0.2 miles ahead to the water tower. Bear right and complete the loop back at the trailhead parking area. ■

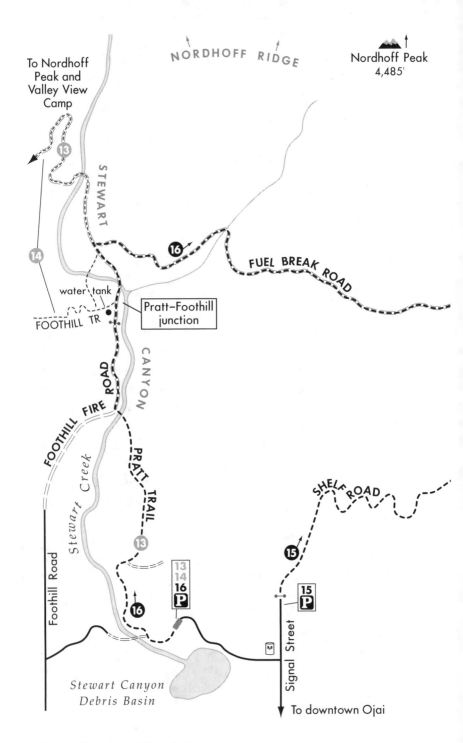

To Nordhoff
Peak and
Valley View
Camp

13

14

NORDHOFF RIDGE

Nordhoff Peak
4,485'

16

FUEL BREAK ROAD

STEWART

water tank

FOOTHILL TR

Pratt–Foothill
junction

CANYON

FOOTHILL FIRE ROAD

Stewart Creek

PRATT TRAIL

13

15

SHELF ROAD

Foothill Road

16

13
14
16
P

15
P

Signal Street

Stewart Canyon
Debris Basin

To downtown Ojai

HIKE 15
Shelf Road
HIKE 16
Pratt Trail–Fuel Break Road–
Shelf Road Loop
STEWART CANYON • GRIDLEY CANYON

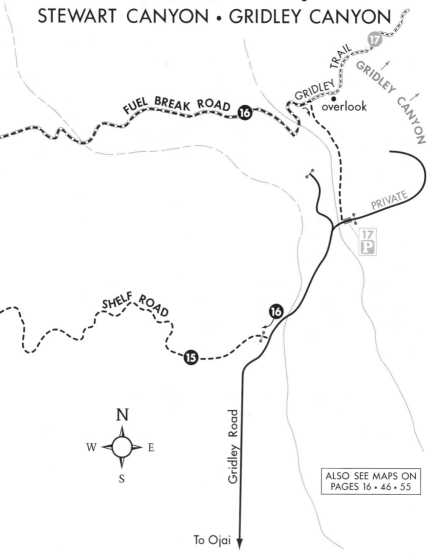

17. Gridley Trail
to Gridley Springs Camp

Hiking distance: 6 miles round trip
Hiking time: 3 hours
Elevation gain: 1,200 feet
Maps: U.S.G.S. Ojai
Matilija and Dick Smith Wilderness Map Guide
Sespe Wilderness Trail Map

Summary of hike: The Gridley Trail begins at the northern edge of Ojai in the foothills of the Topatopa Mountains. The trail follows a fire road into Gridley Canyon and climbs six miles to Gridley Saddle atop Nordhoff Ridge, 1.1 miles northeast of Nordhoff Peak and the lookout tower. This hike goes to Gridley Springs Camp, a primitive campsite by Gridley Springs and a stream halfway to the ridge. En route, the trail follows the shady northwest slope of the canyon.

Driving directions: OJAI. From downtown Ojai, drive one mile east on Highway 150 (Ojai Avenue) to Gridley Road and turn left. Continue 1.5 miles to the end of Gridley Road, and park by the signed trailhead on the left.

Hiking directions: Take the signed trail on the west up a draw through the tall, native brush. Continue up the footpath 0.4 miles to the Fuel Break Road (Hike 16). There is a beautiful overlook of the Ojai Valley and Sulphur Mountain on the right. The left fork leads 1.5 miles to the Pratt Trail in Stewart Canyon (Hike 13). Head to the right up the unpaved, vehicle-restricted fire road past avocado orchards on the steep slopes. The road curves around the contours of the mountain as the canyon narrows. Continue to a five-way junction of dirt ranch roads in Gridley Canyon. Take the center left fork, following the trail sign. At two miles, the trail is perched high above the deep canyon and enters a small side canyon at the confluence of two streams. Gridley Springs Camp is at the first sharp switchback by a horse watering trough. This is the turn-around spot.

To hike farther, the trail continues up switchbacks for three

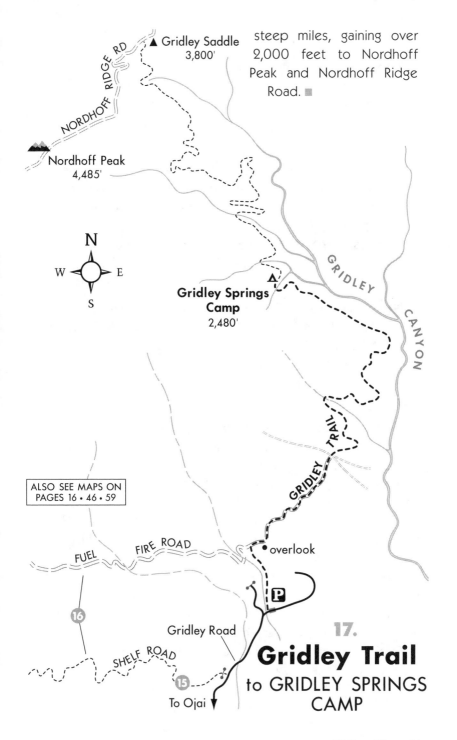

steep miles, gaining over 2,000 feet to Nordhoff Peak and Nordhoff Ridge Road. ■

NORDHOFF RIDGE RD

▲ Gridley Saddle
3,800'

▲▲ Nordhoff Peak
4,485'

N
W E
S

Gridley Springs
Camp
2,480'

GRIDLEY CANYON

GRIDLEY TRAIL

ALSO SEE MAPS ON
PAGES 16 • 46 • 59

FUEL FIRE ROAD

overlook

P

16

Gridley Road

SHELF ROAD

15

To Ojai

17.
Gridley Trail
to GRIDLEY SPRINGS
CAMP

18. Horn Canyon Trail

Hiking distance: 3 miles round trip
Hiking time: 1.5 hours
Elevation gain: 600 feet
Maps: U.S.G.S. Ojai
Sespe Wilderness Trail Map

Summary of hike: Horn Canyon is a stream-fed canyon northeast of Ojai in the Topatopa Mountains. The Horn Canyon Trail parallels Thacher Creek through a forested canyon that is lush with sycamores, alders, and oaks. The trail, which is partially a service road, crosses the creek four times to a rocky gorge. At the gorge, the trail is rugged and far less used, leading past a continuous series of cascades, pools, and small waterfalls.

Driving directions: OJAI. From downtown Ojai, drive 2.3 miles east on Highway 150 (Ojai Avenue) to Reeves Road and turn left. Continue 1.1 mile to McAndrew Road and turn left again. Drive one mile and enter the Thacher School grounds. The trailhead parking area is 0.4 miles ahead, bearing right at all three road splits.

Hiking directions: From the parking area, take the unpaved service road northeast past the gate and kiosk into Horn Canyon. There are two creek crossings in the first half mile. After the second crossing, the service road enters the forest and the trail narrows. At one mile, cross the creek again and climb up the west wall of the canyon while enjoying the great views of Horn Canyon and the creek below. Just before the fourth creek crossing, leave the main trail and take the left path, heading up Horn Canyon along the west side of the creek. The trail is replaced by faint paths that crisscross the creek in a scramble past pools, cascades, and small waterfalls. Choose your own turn-around spot, and return along the same path.

To hike farther, at the fourth creek crossing, continue on the Horn Canyon Trail across the creek. The trail steeply climbs out of the canyon to the Pines Campsite under the shade of Coulter pines, one mile ahead, and on to Sisar Road, 2.4 miles farther. ■

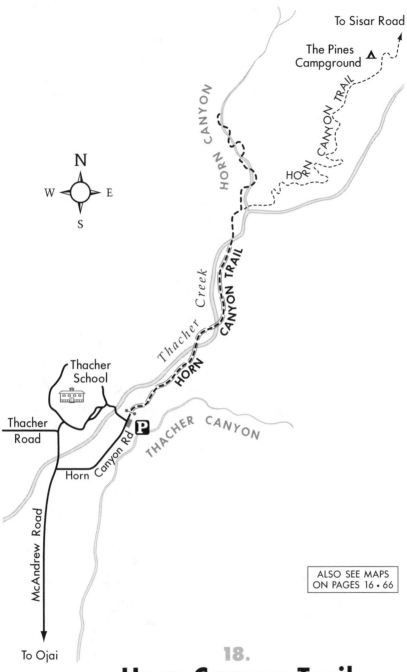

To Sisar Road

The Pines
Campground ▲

HORN CANYON TRAIL

HORN CANYON

HORN CANYON TRAIL

HORN

N
W · E
S

Thacher Creek

Thacher
School

Thacher
Road

Horn Canyon Rd

P

THACHER CANYON

McAndrew Road

To Ojai

ALSO SEE MAPS
ON PAGES 16 · 66

18.
Horn Canyon Trail

19. Sulphur Mountain Road Recreation Trail

Hiking distance: 10 miles one way (shuttle)
Hiking time: 4 hours
Elevation loss: 2,200 feet
Maps: U.S.G.S. Ojai and Matilija
Sespe Wilderness Trail Map

map page 66

Summary of hike: Sulphur Mountain rises 2,700 feet along the south side of Ojai, forming the southern border of Ojai Valley. The prominent 11-mile-long mountain stretches from the Ventura River on the west to Santa Paula Creek on the east. San Antonio Creek flows along the north base of the mountain. Sulphur Mountain Road—a gated hiking, biking, and equestrian road—follows the ridge across the length of Sulphur Mountain, connecting Highway 150 in upper Ojai Valley with Highway 33 in Casitas Springs.

This popular hike is a 10-mile downhill shuttle route from the eastern trailhead to the shuttle car near the confluence of San Antonio Creek and the Ventura River. The journey across the oak-dotted ridgeline has gorgeous alternating views. To the south and west are views of the Conejo Valley, Point Mugu, the Pacific Ocean, Lake Casitas, and the Channel Islands. To the north are views of the Ojai valley, the Topatopa Mountains, and the Los Padres National Forest.

Driving directions: SHUTTLE CAR: Leave a shuttle car at the end of the hike: From Highway 101/Ventura Freeway in Ventura, drive 7.5 miles north on Highway 33 towards Ojai to Sulphur Mountain Road and turn right. Continue 0.4 miles to the locked gate. Park the shuttle car alongside the road.

TRAILHEAD: Return to Highway 33 and continue north to Ojai. From downtown Ojai, drive 6.4 miles east on Highway 150 towards Santa Paula. Turn right on Sulphur Mountain Road, and continue 4.6 miles up the winding road to a locked gate at the trailhead.

Hiking directions: From the trailhead gate, head west on the paved, vehicle-restricted road. Follow the ridgetop road, which begins at an elevation of 2,600 feet. Enjoy the southwest views of Santa Paula and the Santa Clara River Valley. Continue along the shadeless ridge, overlooking Ojai Valley through open hills and meadows while slowly losing elevation. At 1.5 miles, the pavement ends and the well-graded dirt road meanders through pastureland with grazing cattle. Panoramic vistas span southward to the coastal foothills, the Oxnard Plain, the Pacific Ocean, and the Channel Islands. Gradually but steadily descend, staying atop the oak-dotted ridgecrest, to great views of Lake Casitas to the west. The final two miles are steeper, dropping 1,500 feet into an oak forest. As you near the trail's end, the serpentine road descends over a cattle guard and past a gate to the shuttle car parking area by the Casitas Springs trailhead. ∎

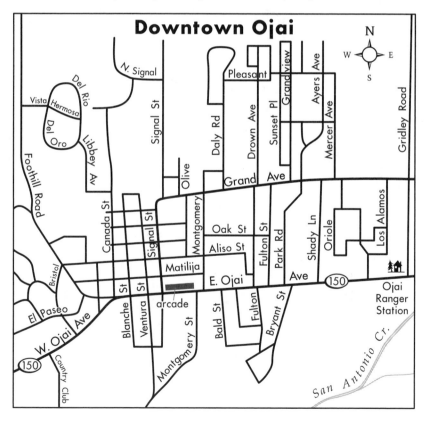

Downtown Ojai

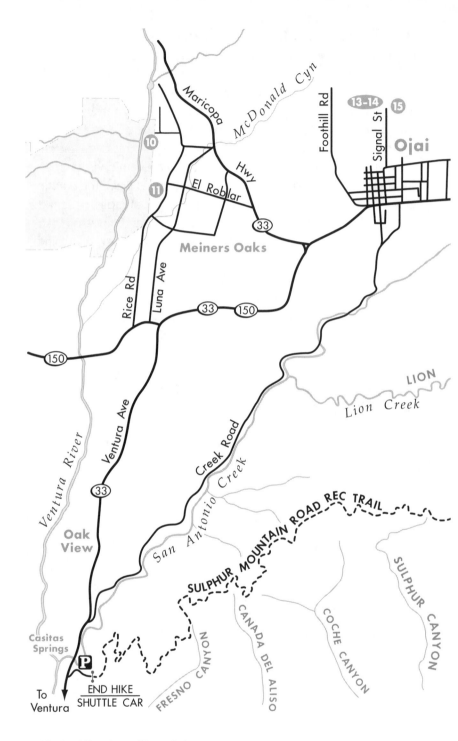

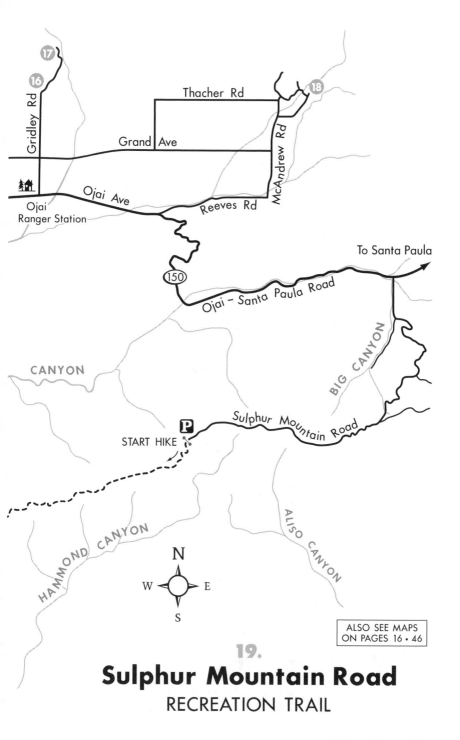

17
16

Gridley Rd

Thacher Rd

18

Grand Ave

McAndrew Rd

Ojai Ave

Reeves Rd

Ojai
Ranger Station

To Santa Paula

150

Ojai – Santa Paula Road

CANYON

BIG CANYON

START HIKE

P

Sulphur Mountain Road

HAMMOND CANYON

ALISO CANYON

N
W   E
S

ALSO SEE MAPS
ON PAGES 16 • 46

19.
Sulphur Mountain Road
RECREATION TRAIL

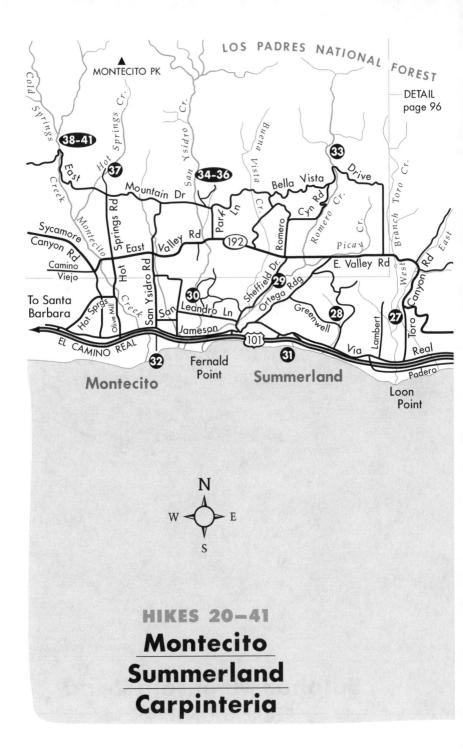

HIKES 20–41

Montecito
Summerland
Carpinteria

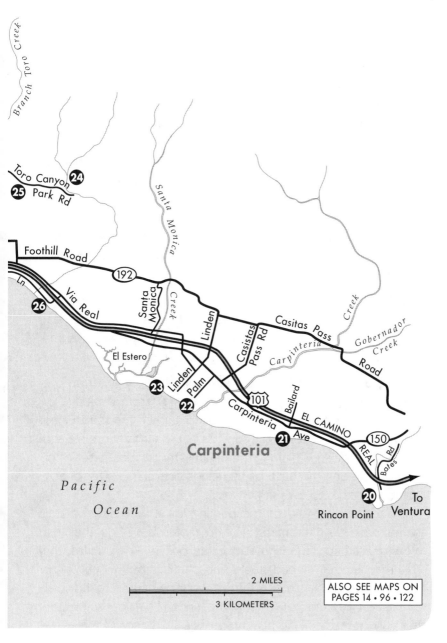

Branch Toro Creek

Toro Canyon ㉔
㉕ Park Rd

Santa Monica Creek

Foothill Road

Via Real

192

Santa Monica Creek

Linden

El Estero

Linden

㉓

Palm

㉒

101

Casitas Pass Rd

Casitas Pass

Carpinteria

Gobernador Creek

Road

Carpinteria Ave

Bailard

EL CAMINO

150

REAL

Bates Rd

Carpinteria

Ln

㉖

㉑

㉔

To
Ventura

Rincon Point

Pacific

Ocean

2 MILES

3 KILOMETERS

ALSO SEE MAPS ON
PAGES 14 • 96 • 122

20. Rincon Point and Rincon Beach Park

Hiking distance: 2 miles round trip
Hiking time: 1 hour
Elevation gain: 100 feet
Maps: U.S.G.S. White Ledge Peak

Summary of hike: Rincon Point (meaning *corner* in Spanish) straddles the Santa Barbara/Ventura County line three miles east of Carpinteria. It is considered to be one of the best places to surf in California. The point is bisected by Rincon Creek. The creek flows out of the mountains and carries rocks to the shoreline, forming a cobblestone beach with tidepools. Rincon Beach Park, located on the west side of the point in Santa Barbara County, has a large grassy picnic area atop the bluffs and great views of the coastline. A stairway leads to the 1,200 feet of beach frontage. A dirt path lined with eucalyptus trees and Monterey pines leads to the tidepools and the mouth of Rincon Creek, located on the east side of the point in Ventura County.

Driving directions: SANTA BARBARA. From Santa Barbara, drive southbound on Highway 101, and continue 3 miles past Carpinteria. Take the Bates Road exit to the stop sign. Park in either of the lots for Rincon Point or Rincon Park.

Hiking directions: WEST OF RINCON POINT: Begin from the Rincon Park parking lot on the right (west). From the edge of the cliffs, a long staircase and a paved service road both lead down the cliff face, providing access to the sandy shoreline and tidepools. Walk north along the beach, strolling past a series of tidepools along the base of the sandstone cliffs. After beachcombing, return to the parking lot.

From the west end of the parking lot, a well-defined trail heads west past the metal gate. The path is a wide shelf cut along the steep cliffs high above the ocean. At 0.3 miles, the trail reaches the railroad tracks and parallels the railroad right-of-way west to Carpinteria. Choose your own turn-around spot.

EAST OF RINCON POINT: From the Rincon Point parking lot on the east, take the wide beach access path. Descend through a shady, forested grove to the beach. Bear right on the rocky path to a small bay near the tree-lined point. This is an excellent area to explore the tidepools and watch the surfers. Return along the same route. ■

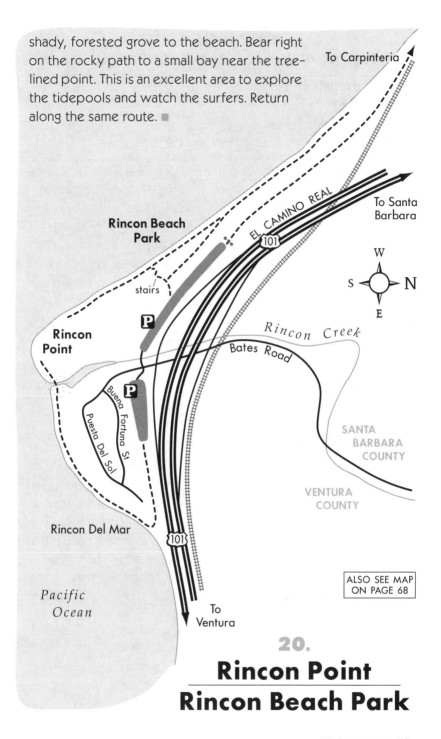

To Carpinteria

EL CAMINO REAL

101

To Santa Barbara

Rincon Beach Park

stairs

P

Rincon Point

Rincon Creek

Bates Road

P

Buena Fortuna St

Puesta Del Sol

SANTA BARBARA COUNTY

VENTURA COUNTY

Rincon Del Mar

101

Pacific Ocean

To Ventura

ALSO SEE MAP ON PAGE 68

20.
Rincon Point
Rincon Beach Park

21. Carpinteria Bluffs Nature Preserve and Seal Sanctuary

Hiking distance: 2 miles round trip
Hiking time: 1 hour
Elevation gain: Level
Maps: U.S.G.S. White Ledge Peak and Carpinteria

Summary of hike: The Carpinteria Bluffs and Seal Sanctuary encompass 52 oceanfront acres with grasslands, coastal sage, and eucalyptus groves. The area has panoramic views from the Santa Ynez Mountains to the islands of Anacapa, Santa Cruz, and Santa Rosa. At the cliff's edge, 100 feet above the ocean, is an overlook of the seal sanctuary. A community of harbor seals often plays in the water below, lounging and sunbathing on the rocks and shoreline. The sanctuary is a protected birthing habitat for harbor seals during the winter and spring from December 1 through May 31. Beach access is prohibited during these months, but the seals may be observed from the blufftop.

Driving directions: CARPINTERIA. From Highway 101 in Carpinteria, exit on Bailard Avenue. Drive one block south towards the ocean, and park at the road's end.

Hiking directions: From the end of the road, hike south on the well-worn path across the open meadow towards the ocean. As you near the ocean cliffs, take the pathway to the right, parallel to a row of stately eucalyptus trees. At the west end of the eucalyptus grove, bear left and cross the railroad tracks. The trail resumes across the tracks. For an optional side trip, take the beach access trail on the left down to the base of the cliffs.

Back on the main trail, continue west along the edge of the ocean bluffs to a bamboo fence—the seal sanctuary overlook. After enjoying the seals and views, return along the same path or explore the open space. ■

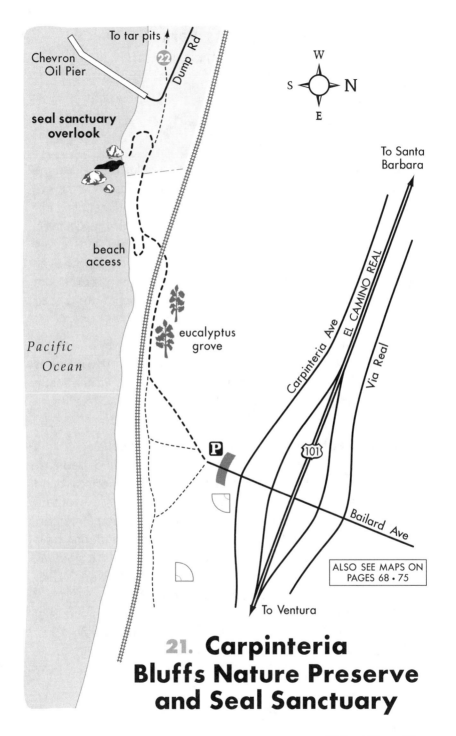

To tar pits

Chevron
Oil Pier

22 Dump Rd

seal sanctuary
overlook

beach
access

Pacific
Ocean

eucalyptus
grove

W

S ◇ N

E

To Santa
Barbara

Carpinteria Ave

EL CAMINO REAL

Via Real

P

101

Bailard Ave

ALSO SEE MAPS ON
PAGES 68 • 75

To Ventura

21. Carpinteria Bluffs Nature Preserve and Seal Sanctuary

22. Tarpits Park
CARPINTERIA STATE BEACH

Hiking distance: 1.5 miles round trip
Hiking time: 1 hour
Elevation gain: 50 feet
Maps: U.S.G.S. Carpinteria

Summary of hike: Tarpits Park is an 9-acre blufftop park at the east end of Carpinteria State Beach. The park was once the site of a Chumash Indian village. It is named for the natural tar (tarry asphaltum) that seeps up from beneath the soil. The Chumash used the tar for caulking canoes (called *tomols*) and sealing cooking vessels. Interconnecting trails cross the bluffs overlooking the steep, jagged coastline. Along Carpinteria Creek are riparian willow and sycamore woodlands. Benches are placed along the edge of the bluffs.

Driving directions: CARPINTERIA. From Highway 101 in Carpinteria, exit on Linden Avenue. Turn right and drive 0.5 miles south to 6th Street. Turn left and go 0.2 miles to Palm Avenue. Turn right and drive one block to the Carpinteria State Beach parking lot on the right. A parking fee is required.

Hiking directions: Two routes lead to Tarpits Park: follow the sandy beach east; or walk along the campground road east, crossing over Carpinteria Creek. At a half mile, the campground road ends on the grassy bluffs. From the beach, a footpath ascends the bluffs to the campground road. Several interconnecting paths cross the clifftop terrace. The meandering trails pass groves of eucalyptus trees and Monterey pines. A stairway leads down to the shoreline. As you near the Chevron Oil Pier, the bluffs narrow. This is a good turn-around spot.

To hike farther, cross the ravine and continue past the pier along the edge of the cliffs. The Carpinteria Bluffs and Seal Sanctuary (Hike 21) is a half mile ahead. ∎

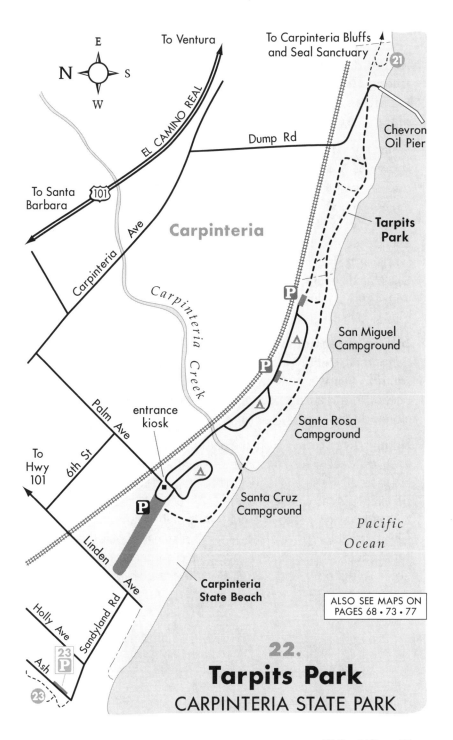

To Ventura

To Carpinteria Bluffs
and Seal Sanctuary

E
N — S
W

EL CAMINO REAL

Dump Rd

Chevron
Oil Pier

To Santa
Barbara

101

Carpinteria Ave

Carpinteria

Tarpits Park

Carpinteria Creek

San Miguel
Campground

Palm Ave

entrance
kiosk

Santa Rosa
Campground

To
Hwy
101

6th St

Santa Cruz
Campground

Pacific Ocean

Linden Ave

**Carpinteria
State Beach**

ALSO SEE MAPS ON
PAGES 68 · 73 · 77

Holly Ave

Sandyland Rd

Ash

23 P

23

22.
Tarpits Park
CARPINTERIA STATE PARK

23. Carpinteria Salt Marsh Nature Park

Hiking distance: 1 mile round trip
Hiking time: 30 minutes
Elevation gain: Level
Maps: U.S.G.S. Carpinteria

Summary of hike: The Carpinteria Salt Marsh, historically known as El Estero (*the estuary*), is one of California's last remaining wetlands. The area was once inhabited by Chumash Indians. The 230-acre estuary is fed by Franklin Creek and Santa Monica Creek. The reserve is a busy, healthy ecosystem with an abundance of sea and plant life. It is a nesting ground for thousands of migratory waterfowl and shorebirds. The Carpinteria Salt Marsh Nature Park sits along the east end of the salt marsh with a trail system, interpretive panels, and several observation decks.

Driving directions: CARPINTERIA. From Highway 101 in Carpinteria, exit on Linden Avenue. Turn right and drive 0.6 miles south to Sandyland Road, the last corner before reaching the ocean. Turn right and continue 0.2 miles to Ash Avenue. Park alongside the road by the signed park.

Hiking directions: From the nature trail sign, walk 20 yards to the west, reaching an observation deck. A boardwalk to the left leads to the ocean. Take the wide, meandering path to the right, parallel to Ash Avenue and the salt marsh. At the north end of the park, curve left to another overlook of the wetland. At the T-junction, the left fork leads a short distance to another observation deck. The right fork follows a pole fence along Franklin Creek to the trail's end. Return along the same path. ■

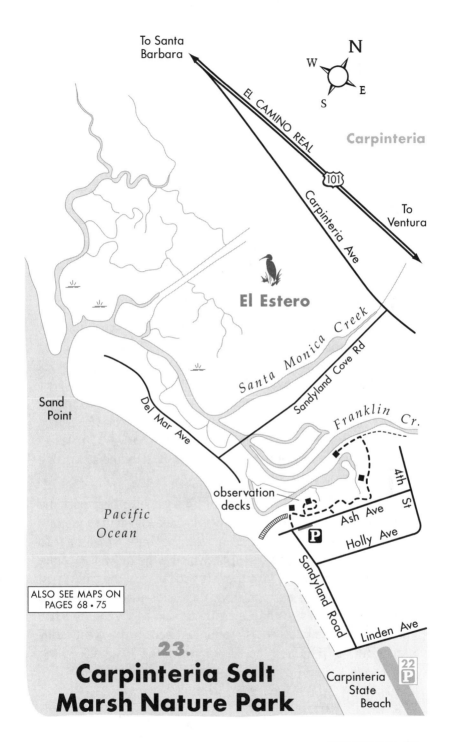

To Santa
Barbara

N
W
E
S

EL CAMINO REAL

Carpinteria

101

Carpinteria Ave

To
Ventura

El Estero

Santa Monica Creek

Sandyland Cove Rd

Sand
Point

Del Mar Ave

Franklin Cr.

4th St

observation
decks

Ash Ave

P

Holly Ave

*Pacific
Ocean*

ALSO SEE MAPS ON
PAGES 68 • 75

Sandyland Road

Linden Ave

**23.
Carpinteria Salt
Marsh Nature Park**

Carpinteria
State
Beach

22
P

24. Toro Canyon Park

Hiking distance: 1 mile round trip
Hiking time: 30 minutes
Elevation gain: 300 feet
Maps: U.S.G.S. Carpinteria
Santa Barbara Front Country and Paradise Road

Summary of hike: Toro Canyon Park is tucked into a rugged canyon in the foothills of the Santa Ynez Mountains between Carpinteria and Summerland. The secluded, dog-friendly county park includes 74 acres of oak woodland, native chaparral, stream-side vegetation, and sandstone outcroppings. There are shady picnic spots under the trees and along Arroyo Paredon Creek. The hike circles a knoll and climbs to a gazebo with panoramic 360-degree views of the coastline, mountains, and orchards.

Driving directions: SANTA BARBARA. From Santa Barbara, drive southbound on Highway 101 to Summerland, and exit on North Padaro Lane. (See map on page 89.) Drive north one block to Via Real and turn right. Continue 0.4 miles to Toro Canyon Road and turn left. Drive 1.3 miles to the signed Toro Canyon Park turnoff (Toro Canyon Park Road) and turn right. Proceed 1.1 mile to Toro Canyon Park on the left. Turn left and drive 0.2 miles to the trail sign at the upper end of the park. Park by the sandstone outcropping on the right.

Hiking directions: From the parking area, hike east past the trail sign and across the stream towards the prominent sandstone formation. From the outcropping, take the wide, uphill path to the right. At 0.3 miles is a trail split, which is the beginning of the loop. Hiking clockwise, take the left fork around the small knoll and up to a gazebo at the hilltop. The vistas extend across the Montecito foothills to the Carpinteria plain and Ventura. After enjoying the beautiful views, continue back to the west, completing the loop around the hill. Return to the left, back to the trailhead. ■

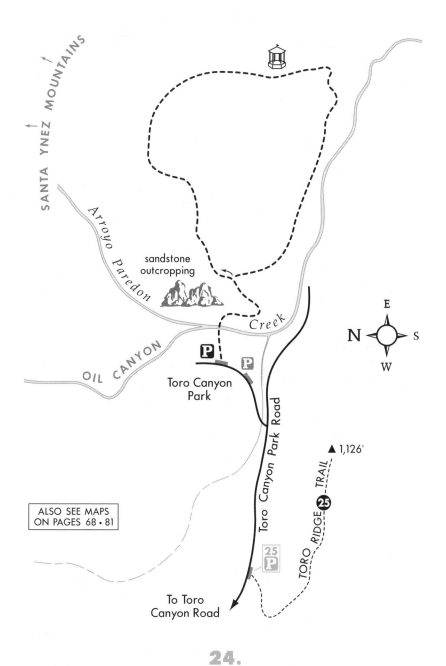

SANTA YNEZ MOUNTAINS

Arroyo Paredon

sandstone
outcropping

Creek

OIL CANYON

P

P

Toro Canyon
Park

Toro Canyon Park Road

▲ 1,126'

TORO RIDGE TRAIL

25

ALSO SEE MAPS
ON PAGES 68 • 81

25
P

To Toro
Canyon Road

N E S W

24.
Toro Canyon Park

25. Toro Ridge Trail

Hiking distance: 1.5 miles round trip
Hiking time: 1 hour
Elevation gain: 150 feet
Maps: U.S.G.S. Carpinteria
      Montecito Trails Foundation map
      Santa Barbara Front Country and Paradise Road

Summary of hike: The Toro Ridge Trail sits on the ocean-front hills between Summerland and Carpinteria in the Santa Ynez Mountains. The easy, near-level trail follows an old road, reclaimed by vegetation, along Toro Ridge. The path leads to the Toro Ridge bench sitting atop the 1,126-foot summit, where there are great views of the Pacific Ocean and the sweeping coastline. En route are vistas of the interior mountains. Due to a small, unmarked parking area and no visible trail sign, the trail is seldom hiked.

Driving directions: SANTA BARBARA. From Santa Barbara, drive southbound on Highway 101 to Summerland, and exit on North Padaro Lane. (See map on page 89.) Drive north one block to Via Real and turn right. Continue 0.4 miles to Toro Canyon Road and turn left. Drive 1.1 miles to the signed Toro Canyon Park turnoff (Toro Canyon Park Road) and turn right. Proceed 0.8 miles to the hard-to-spot trailhead on the right. It is located on the crest of the road. Park in the narrow pullout on the right side of the road.

Hiking directions: Walk over the metal trailhead bar and head up the hillside. Follow the narrow, rock-embedded path west through chaparral. Quickly gain elevation to overlooks of forested Toro Canyon and the Santa Ynez Mountains. The path levels out and traverses the south canyon wall just below the ridge. Weave through oak groves, with views of Toro Canyon Park and the gazebo (Hike 24). At 0.75 miles, the trail emerges atop Toro Ridge at the stone Toro Ridge bench, where the trail ends. From the overlook are sweeping vistas across Carpinteria and Summerland to the Pacific Ocean and the Channel Islands. ■

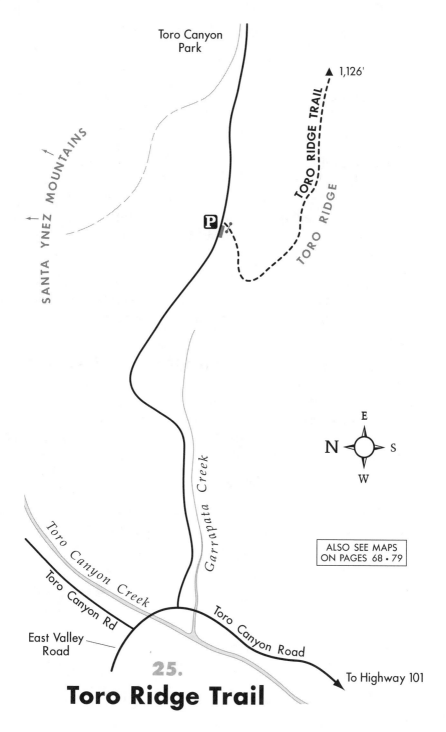

Toro Canyon
Park

▲ 1,126'

TORO RIDGE TRAIL

TORO RIDGE

P

SANTA YNEZ MOUNTAINS

Garrapata Creek

E
N ◇ S
W

ALSO SEE MAPS
ON PAGES 68 • 79

Toro Canyon Creek

Toro Canyon Rd

East Valley
Road

Toro Canyon Road

To Highway 101

25.
Toro Ridge Trail

26. Loon Point

Hiking distance: 3 miles round trip
Hiking time: 1.5 hours
Elevation gain: Near level
Maps: U.S.G.S. Carpinteria
                 Santa Barbara Front Country and Paradise Road

Summary of hike: Loon Point sits between Summerland and Carpinteria at the mouth of Toro Canyon Creek. Dense stands of sycamores, coastal oaks, Monterey cypress, and eucalyptus trees line the creek. The path to Loon Point follows an isolated stretch of coastline along the base of steep 40-foot sandstone cliffs.

Driving directions: SANTA BARBARA. From Santa Barbara, drive southbound on Highway 101 to Summerland, and exit on Padaro Lane south. Turn right and drive 0.2 miles to the signed Loon Point Beach parking lot on the left.

Hiking directions: Take the signed Loon Beach access trail parallel to the railroad tracks. Curve to the left, under the Padaro Lane bridge, past a grove of eucalyptus trees. The path descends through a narrow drainage between the jagged, weathered cliffs to the shoreline. Bear to the right on the sandy beach along the base of the sandstone cliffs. Loon Point can be seen jutting out to sea. Follow the shoreline, reaching large boulders at Loon Point in 1.5 miles. At high tide, the water level may be too high to reach the point. At a lower tide, the beach walk can be extended from Loon Point to Lookout Park (Hike 31), an additional 1.5 miles west. ∎

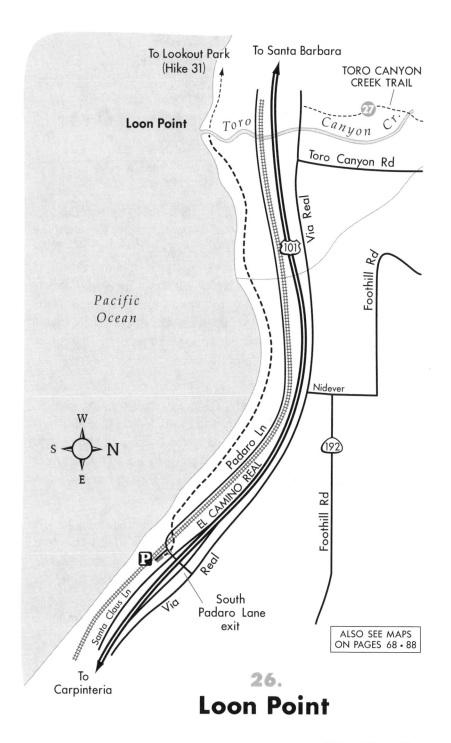

To Lookout Park
(Hike 31)

To Santa Barbara

TORO CANYON
CREEK TRAIL

Loon Point

Toro
Canyon Cr.

27

Toro Canyon Rd

Via Real

101

Foothill Rd

Pacific
Ocean

Nidever

192

Padaro Ln

EL CAMINO REAL

Foothill Rd

W
S — N
E

P

Santa Claus Ln

Via

Real

South
Padaro Lane
exit

ALSO SEE MAPS
ON PAGES 68 · 88

To
Carpinteria

26.
Loon Point

27. Polo Club Trail—
Toro Canyon Creek Trail

Hiking distance: 3.2 miles round trip
Hiking time: 1.5 hours
Elevation gain: 200 feet

map
page 89

Maps: U.S.G.S. Carpinteria
      Montecito Trails Foundation Trails Map
      Santa Barbara Front Country and Paradise Road

Summary of hike: The Montecito Trails Foundation preserves and maintains a vast network of trails throughout Montecito, Summerland, and Carpinteria. The Polo Club Trail and the Toro Canyon Creek Trail are two of these scenic routes that meander through the forested foothills of Summerland. The Toro Canyon Creek Trail follows the creek through an enchanting forest of oaks and sycamores. The Polo Club Trail connects Toro Canyon with Greenwell Road, climbing to a large lemon orchard with an overlook of Summerland, Carpinteria, and the Pacific Ocean.

Driving directions: SANTA BARBARA. From Santa Barbara, drive southbound on Highway 101 to Summerland, and exit on North Padaro Lane. Drive north one block to Via Real and turn right. Continue 0.4 miles to Toro Canyon Road and turn left. Continue 0.5 miles north to the posted trailhead on the left next to a private road and a utility pole. Park in the small pullouts on the side of the road.

Hiking directions: Head west on the signed trail along the left side of the gravel driveway. Follow the forested Polo Club Trail under the shade of oak trees, crossing Garrapato Creek. Merge with the gravel road for 40 yards, and return to the footpath on the left, crossing a rocky streambed to a trail split. Take Toro Canyon Creek Trail to the left, and curve around the Spanish-style stucco home. Head south through a large grove of sycamores and twisted oaks draped in vinca vines. The meandering path crosses Toro Canyon Creek twice and emerges from the forest to the polo field. Follow the east edge of the expansive lawn, parallel to Toro Canyon Creek. The trail ends by a bamboo grove at Via Real, just west of the Toro Canyon Creek bridge.

Return to the junction with the Polo Club Trail. Bear left on the Polo Club Trail, and skirt the north boundary of the horse ranch through a forest of oak and eucalyptus trees to Lambert Road. Bear left and follow the tree-lined road 200 yards to the posted trail on the right, just after crossing the stone bridge. Follow the fenced trail corridor through a horse ranch, and ascend the hillside into a lemon orchard. Follow the trail signs to the upper level of the orchard, weaving clockwise through the orchard to an unpaved road. Drop down to the Greenwell Preserve on Asegra Road by Greenwell Avenue and the Reservoir Trail (Hike 25). Return by retracing your steps or, for a longer hike, continue with Hike 28. ■

28. Reservoir Trail—Edison Trail Loop
SUMMERLAND GREENWELL PRESERVE

Hiking distance: 1.7-mile loop
Hiking time: 1 hour
Elevation gain: 300 feet
Maps: U.S.G.S. Carpinteria
       Montecito Trails Foundation Trails Map
       Santa Barbara Front Country and Paradise Road

**map
page 89**

Summary of hike: The Reservoir and Edison Trails, located in the Summerland Greenwell Preserve, climb a small stream-fed canyon to an overlook at the Ortega Reservoir. These two trails are part of a network of interwoven trails connecting the neighborhoods of Montecito, Summerland, and Carpinteria. The trail system is preserved and maintained by the Montecito Trails Foundation, supported entirely by membership dues and donations. (See page 315.)

Driving directions: SANTA BARBARA. From Santa Barbara, drive southbound on Highway 101 to Summerland, and exit on North Padaro Lane. Drive north one block to Via Real and turn left. Drive 0.5 miles to Greenwell Avenue and turn right. Continue 0.3 miles north to the Greenwell Preserve parking lot on the left by the railroad tie fence.

Hiking directions: Walk up the road past the block buildings to the large "Private Road" sign. Bear left on the gravel road to the posted footpath and trailhead gate. Head west up the draw on the tree-lined path to a trail split at 200 yards. Begin the loop on the Reservoir Trail to the right. Cross a seasonal stream through a willow thicket, and ascend the hillside on the north canyon wall. Climb to an overlook of the Pacific Ocean and the Channel Islands from atop Ortega Ridge. Drop down from the ridge at the south edge of the Ortega Reservoir, and climb two switch-backs to Hunt Drive. Bear left, follow the paved road around the reservoir, and descend to Ortega Ridge Road. (Across the road is the posted Valley Club Trail which drops down the hillside to Sheffield Drive and the Coffin Family Trail—Hike 29.) Bear left on Ortega Ridge Road, and walk 30 yards to the posted Edison Trail on the left. Descend on the wide gravel path, dropping into the canyon and completing the loop. ∎

29. Coffin Family Trail

Hiking distance: 1.8-mile loop
Hiking time: 1 hour
Elevation gain: 100 feet

map
page 88

Maps: U.S.G.S. Carpinteria
Santa Barbara Front Country and Paradise Road
Montecito Trails Foundation map

Summary of hike: The Coffin Family Trail (formerly Ketchum Trail) forms a loop around Montecito Valley Ranch between Sheffield Drive and Ortega Ridge Road. This easy and scenic hike begins and ends along Romero Creek, offering both coastal and mountain views. The Coffin Family Trail connects to the east with the Edison-Reservoir Loop (Hike 28) via the Valley Club Trail.

Driving directions: SANTA BARBARA. From Santa Barbara, drive southbound on Highway 101 to Montecito, and exit on Sheffield Drive. Cross under the freeway and curve right onto Sheffield Drive. Continue 0.9 miles north to a distinct pull-in parking area on the right under a grove of eucalyptus trees.

Hiking directions: From the north end of the parking area, descend on the footpath to Romero Creek. Cross the creek on boulders, just below the waterfall and pool. Head up the hill and curve right to the Montecito Valley Ranch horse corrals. Begin the loop to the left, curving left up the hillside to a T-junction and panoramic views of the Santa Ynez Mountains. The Valley Club Trail goes left, connecting with the Edison Trail (Hike 28). Go to the right, staying on the Coffin Family Trail. Traverse the hillside, with vistas across the ocean to the Channel Islands. Pass scattered pines and eucalyptus to a fenceline. Make a U-shaped left bend and weave up the hillside to Ortega Ridge Road, just north of Summerland Heights Lane. Bear right and walk 50 yards down Ortega Ridge Road to the signed trail on the right. Head downhill on the footpath under majestic oaks to the intersection of Ortega Hill Road and Sheffield Drive. Veer 100 yards to the right on the footpath along Sheffield Drive, and bear right on the posted Coffin Family Trail. Follow the 15-foot wide trail easement through Montecito Valley Ranch on the east edge of Romero Creek. Pass a trail on the left that crosses the creek. Stay straight, passing a few homes back to the horse corrals and the beginning of the loop. Return to the trailhead, straight ahead. ▪

HIKE 27
Polo Club Trail
Toro Canyon Creek Trail

HIKE 28
Reservoir Trail • Edison Trail

HIKE 29
Coffin Family Trail

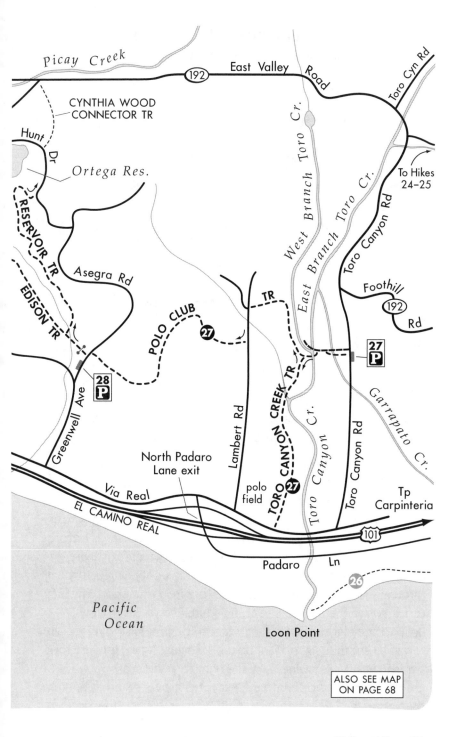

Picay Creek

East Valley Road

192

Toro Cyn Rd

CYNTHIA WOOD
CONNECTOR TR

Hunt Dr

Ortega Res.

RESERVOIR TR

EDISON TR

Asegra Rd

POLO CLUB

TR

27

28 P

Greenwell Ave

West Branch Toro Cr.

East Branch Toro Cr.

To Hikes
24–25

Toro Canyon Rd

Foothill

192

Rd

27 P

Lambert Rd

TORO CANYON CREEK TR

North Padaro
Lane exit

Via Real

EL CAMINO REAL

polo
field

27

Toro Canyon Cr.

Toro Canyon Cr.

Toro Canyon Rd

Garrapato Cr.

Tp
Carpinteria

101

Padaro Ln

26

*Pacific
Ocean*

Loon Point

ALSO SEE MAP
ON PAGE 68

30. Ennisbrook Trail
ENNISBROOK NATURE PRESERVE

Hiking distance: 2.4 miles round trip
Hiking time: 1.4 hours
Elevation gain: Near level
Maps: U.S.G.S. Carpinteria
      Montecito Trails Foundation Trails Map

Summary of hike: The Ennisbrook Nature Preserve is a 44-acre oasis located at the base of the mountains in the heart of Montecito. The preserve contains oak, olive, sycamore, and eucalyptus woodlands along San Ysidro Creek. Old stone bridges span the creek, and clusters of migrating monarch butterflies winter in the eucalyptus grove. The Ennisbrook Trail meanders through pastoral open space, exploring all of the preserve's lush habitats.

Driving directions: SANTA BARBARA. From Santa Barbara, drive southbound on Highway 101 to Montecito, and exit on San Ysidro Road. Drive one block north to San Leandro Lane and turn right. Continue 0.7 miles to the parking pullout on the left by the trailhead sign and white picket fence. En route to the trailhead, San Leandro Lane jogs to the left and back again to the right.

Hiking directions: Pass the trailhead sign and walk through the gate in the white picket fence. Stroll under a shaded oak canopy to an old stone bridge. Cross the bridge over San Ysidro Creek and veer left. Follow the east side of the creek to Ennisbrook Drive at 0.4 miles. Follow the road for one hundred yards before dropping back down into the forest and the creek. Cross another stone bridge over San Ysidro Creek, continuing upstream through the bay, oak, and sycamore forest to a junction. The left fork leads to the cul-de-sac at the south end of East Valley Lane. Bear to the right, crossing a stream through a lush, overgrown forest to another signed junction at 1.2 miles. Again, the left fork leads to East Valley Lane. Take the right fork and cross San Ysidro Creek. Climb the slope into a eucalyptus grove, where monarch butterflies gather when migrating. Weave through the riparian ferns and vine-strewn forest to the end of the trail at private property. Retrace your steps back to the trailhead. ■

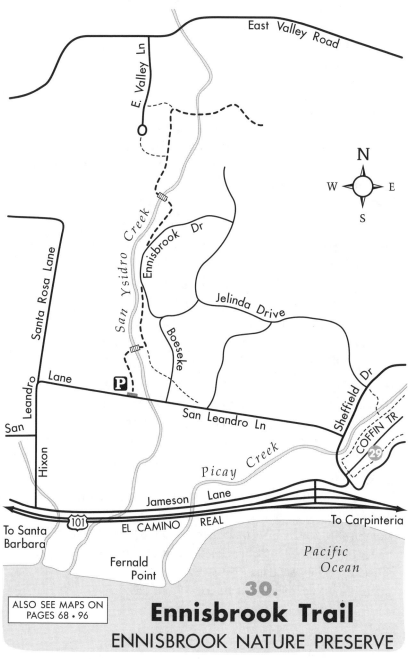

N
W ◇ E
S

30.
Ennisbrook Trail
ENNISBROOK NATURE PRESERVE

ALSO SEE MAPS ON
PAGES 68 • 96

31. Summerland Beach • Lookout Park

Hiking distance: 1-mile loop
Hiking time: 30 minutes
Elevation gain: 50 feet
Maps: U.S.G.S. Carpinteria
  Santa Barbara Front Country and Paradise Road
  Montecito Trails Foundation map

Summary of hike: Lookout Park is a beautiful grassy flat along the oceanfront cliffs in Summerland. From the four-acre park perched above the sea, paved walkways and natural forested trails lead down to a sandy beach, creating a one-mile loop. There are tidepools and coves a short distance up the coast from the beach.

Driving directions: SANTA BARBARA. From Santa Barbara, drive southbound on Highway 101 and take the Summerland exit. Turn right (south), crossing the railroad tracks in one block, and park in the Lookout Park parking lot.

From the south, heading northbound on Highway 101, take the Evans Avenue exit and turn left. Cross Highway 101 and the railroad tracks to Lookout Park.

Hiking directions: From the parking lot, head left (east) through the grassy flat along the cliff's edge to an open gate. A path leads through a shady eucalyptus forest. Cross a wooden bridge and head to the sandy shoreline. At the shore, bear to the right, leading to the paved walkways that return up to Lookout Park.

To extend the walk, continue along the coastline to the west. At low tide, the long stretch of beach leads to coves, rocky points, and tidepools. The beach continues west past charming beachfront homes, reaching Eucalyptus Lane and the Hammonds Meadow Trailhead (Hike 32) at 2 miles. From Lookout Park, the beach heads 1.5 miles east to Loon Point (Hike 26). ■

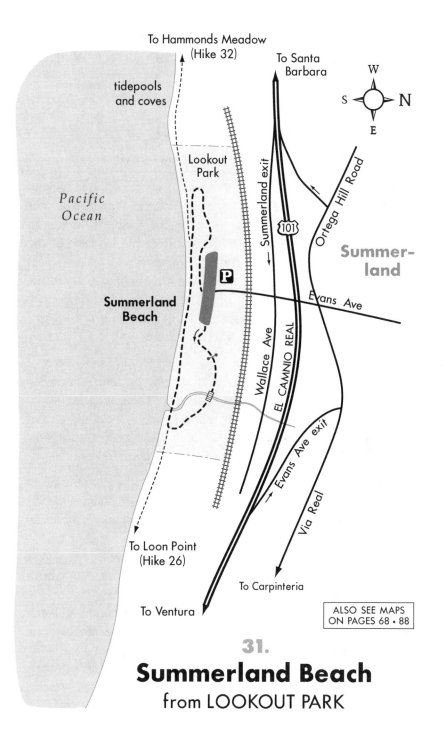

To Hammonds Meadow
(Hike 32)

To Santa
Barbara

W
S — N
E

tidepools
and coves

Lookout
Park

Pacific
Ocean

Summerland exit

Summerland

Ortega Hill Road

101

Summer-
land

P

Evans Ave

Summerland
Beach

Wallace Ave

EL CAMNIO REAL

To Loon Point
(Hike 26)

Evans Ave exit

Via Real

To Carpinteria

To Ventura

ALSO SEE MAPS
ON PAGES 68 · 88

31.
Summerland Beach
from LOOKOUT PARK

32. Hammonds Meadow Trail
MIRAMAR BEACH • HAMMONDS BEACH • BUTTERFLY BEACH

Hiking distance: 2 miles round trip
Hiking time: 1 hour
Elevation gain: Level
Maps: U.S.G.S. Santa Barbara
The Thomas Guide—Santa Barbara and Vicinity

Summary of hike: The Hammonds Meadow Trail strolls through a forest of palm and eucalyptus trees with high hedges and flowering bougainvillea bushes in the town of Montecito. Hammonds Beach sits near the foot of Eucalyptus Lane at the trailhead. The pastoral path connects Miramar Beach, Hammonds Beach, and Butterfly Beach, linking the old Miramar Hotel to the Biltmore Hotel. The walking path passes beautiful homes to a bridge crossing over Montecito Creek. Trails on both sides of the creek provide access to the beachfront.

Driving directions: SANTA BARBARA. From Santa Barbara, drive southbound on Highway 101 to Montecito, and exit on San Ysidro Road south. Turn right on Eucalyptus Lane, and drive south 0.1 mile (towards the ocean) to a small parking lot at the end of the road, just past Bonnymede Drive. If the lot is full, additional parking is located on Humphrey Road, the first street north.

Hiking directions: A short detour straight ahead to the south leads down a few steps to coastal access at Miramar Beach. Return to the trailhead and take the signed Hammonds Meadow Trail to the west. The path traverses through a beautiful forested lane surrounded by every color of flowering bougainvillea. At 0.2 miles, a bridge crosses Montecito Creek. Along both sides of the creek are coastal access paths. Cross the bridge and parallel the west side of the creek to Hammonds Beach. Follow the shoreline to the west for a quarter mile, reaching the Biltmore Hotel at the east end of Butterfly Beach. Continue along the coastline west on Butterfly Beach below the bluff terrace. Several staircases lead up to Channel Drive, the turn-around point. After beach combing, return along the same path. ■

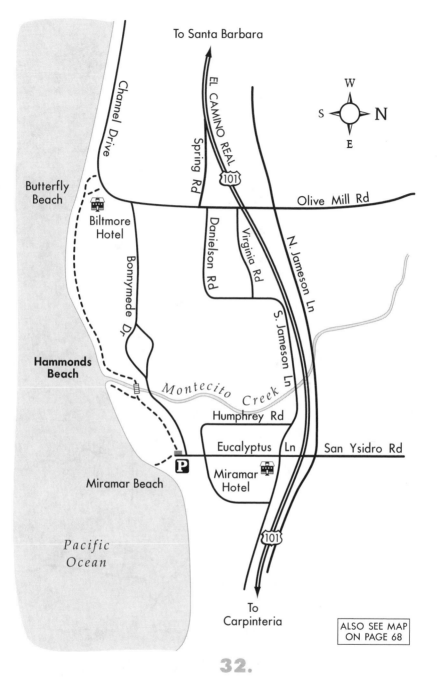

To Santa Barbara

EL CAMINO REAL

Spring Rd

101

Channel Drive

Butterfly
Beach

Biltmore
Hotel

Olive Mill Rd

Danielson Rd

Virginia Rd

N. Jameson Ln

Bonnymede Dr

S. Jameson Ln

Hammonds
Beach

Montecito Creek

Humphrey Rd

Eucalyptus Ln

San Ysidro Rd

P

Miramar Beach

Miramar
Hotel

101

*Pacific
Ocean*

To
Carpinteria

W
S ✦ N
E

ALSO SEE MAP
ON PAGE 68

32.

Hammonds Meadow Trail

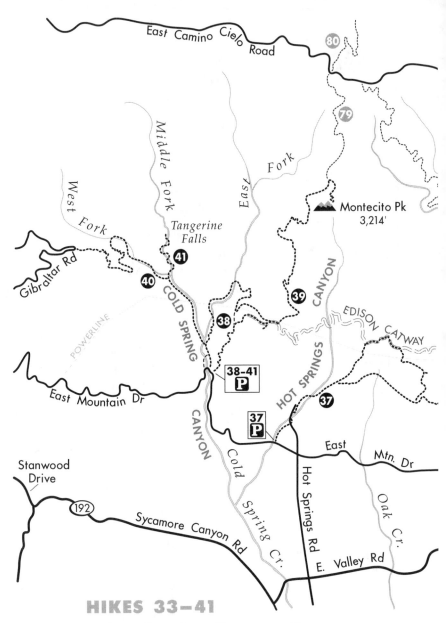

HIKES 33–41

Santa Barbara Front Range (EAST)

Romero Canyon • San Ysidro Canyon
Hot Springs Canyon • Cold Spring Canyon

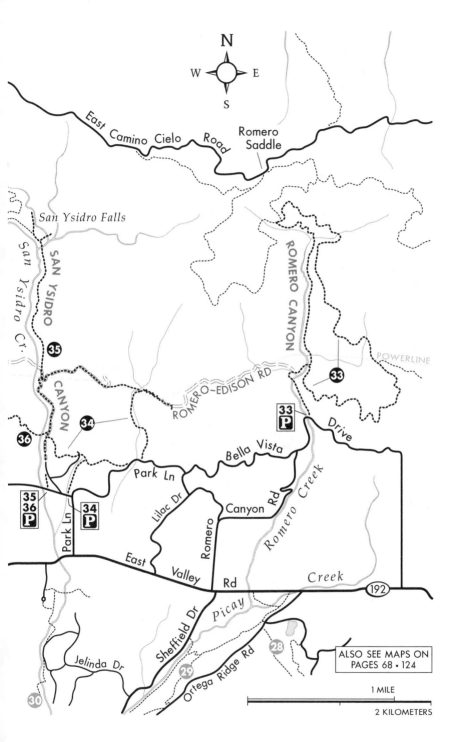

N
W E
S

East Camino Cielo Road

Romero Saddle

San Ysidro Falls

San Ysidro Cr.

SAN YSIDRO

San Ysidro

CANYON

ROMERO CANYON

POWERLINE

35

ROMERO-EDISON RD.

33

33 P

34

36

Drive

35 36 P

34 P

Park Ln

Park Ln

Lilac Dr

Bella Vista

Canyon Rd

Romero

Romero Creek

East

Valley

Rd

Creek

192

Sheffield Dr

Picay

Jelinda Dr

28

29

Ortega Ridge Rd

30

ALSO SEE MAPS ON
PAGES 68 • 124

1 MILE

2 KILOMETERS

33. Romero Canyon Loop

Hiking distance: 6-mile loop
Hiking time: 3 hours
Elevation gain: 1,400 feet
Maps: U.S.G.S. Carpinteria
　　　　Santa Barbara Front Country and Paradise Road
　　　　Montecito Trails Foundation map

Summary of hike: Romero Canyon is a popular hiking and biking area in the mountains above Montecito. The Romero Canyon Trail follows cascading Romero Creek up a narrow, shady, secluded canyon past pools and a waterfall. The lush canyon contains groves of oaks, sycamores, and alders, with an understory of ferns, dewy grass, and exposed tree roots. The hike returns on scenic Romero Canyon Road, an abandoned road with dramatic vistas that overlook the canyon, Montecito, and the coastline.

Driving directions: SANTA BARBARA. From Santa Barbara, drive southbound on Highway 101 to Montecito, and exit on Sheffield Drive. Cross under the freeway, and curve right onto Sheffield Drive. Continue 1.3 miles to East Valley Road. Turn left and quickly turn right on Romero Canyon Road. Continue 1.5 miles (bearing right at 0.4 miles) to Bella Vista Drive and turn right. Drive a quarter mile to a horseshoe bend in the road. The trailhead is at the bend, on the left by a steel gate.

Hiking directions: Hike past the gate on Old Romero Road along the east side of Romero Creek. After a quarter mile, cross the wide concrete bridge over the creek. At 0.4 miles is a second creek crossing and a junction. The left fork (the Romero–Edison Road) leads west to San Ysidro Canyon (Hikes 34—36). Head right on the main trail to another creek crossing a hundred yards ahead. After crossing, begin the loop. Leave the main trail and take the left fork, following the trail sign up the secluded Romero Canyon drainage. The trail runs parallel to the creek, crossing boulders by pools and a waterfall at 1.3 miles. A short distance ahead, two streams converge and the trail crosses the

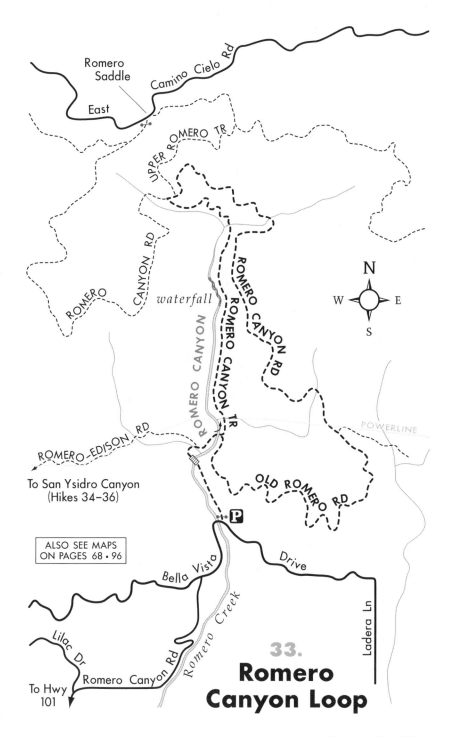

Romero
Saddle

Camino Cielo Rd

East

UPPER ROMERO TR

CANYON RD

ROMERO

waterfall

ROMERO CANYON

ROMERO CANYON TR

ROMERO CANYON RD

N
W   E
S

POWERLINE

ROMERO-EDISON RD

To San Ysidro Canyon
(Hikes 34–36)

OLD ROMERO RD

P

ALSO SEE MAPS
ON PAGES 68 • 96

Bella Vista   Drive

Ladera Ln

Romero Creek

Lilac Dr

Romero Canyon Rd

To Hwy
101

33.
**Romero
Canyon Loop**

east stream. At 1.7 miles, switchbacks lead up to Romero Canyon Road. Take the road to the right, and begin a four-mile descent while enjoying the dramatic views across the canyon and coast. Complete the loop at the canyon junction and creek crossing. Retrace your steps back to the trailhead. ■

34. Wiman—Old Pueblo— Buena Vista Loop
to BUENA VISTA OVERLOOK

Hiking distance: 5.8-mile loop
Hiking time: 3 hours
Elevation gain: 1,100 feet
Maps: U.S.G.S. Carpinteria
Santa Barbara Front Country and Paradise Road map
Montecito Trails Foundation map

Summary of hike: This hike follows a group of five trails which form a loop on the lower slopes of the Santa Ynez Mountains in the Montecito foothills. The hike covers a variety of habitats that include forested riparian canyons with creeks, waterfalls, pools, exposed slopes with tunnels of chaparral, sandstone outcroppings, scrub-covered ridges, and coastal overlooks.

The hike begins on the Wiman Trail and climbs up a small stream-fed canyon. (The trail is named for Charles Wiman, who bought 23 acres at the upper end of Park Lane in 1932.) The hike continues west on the Old Pueblo Trail into San Ysidro Canyon and parallels San Ysidro Creek past waterfalls and pools. The Buena Vista Connector Trail traverses the oceanfront mountains and drops into Buena Vista Canyon. The loop returns through the sandstone canyon under a canopy of sycamores. En route, a side path climbs to the Buena Vista Overlook above Romero Canyon, with stunning views across Montecito to the Channel Islands.

Driving directions: SANTA BARBARA. From Santa Barbara, drive southbound on Highway 101 to Montecito, and exit on San

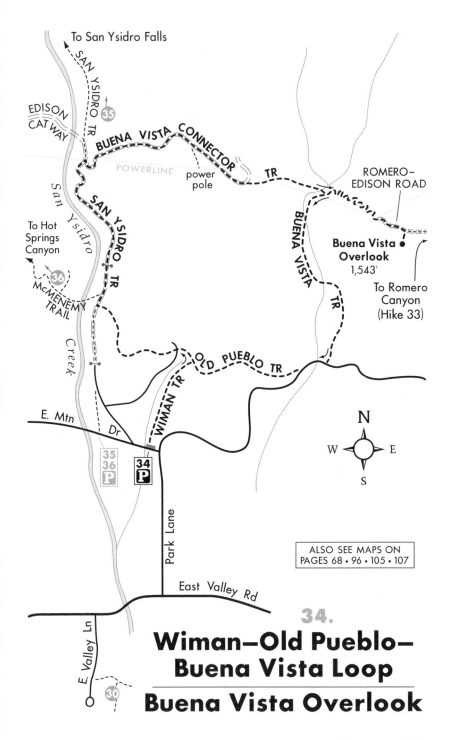

To San Ysidro Falls

SAN YSIDRO TR

EDISON CATWAY

35

BUENA VISTA CONNECTOR

POWERLINE   power pole   TR

SAN YSIDRO TR

ROMERO–
EDISON ROAD

BUENA VISTA

San Ysidro

Creek

To Hot Springs Canyon

36

McMENEMY TRAIL

**Buena Vista
Overlook**
1,543'

BUENA VISTA TR

To Romero
Canyon
(Hike 33)

OLD PUEBLO TR

WIMAN TR

E. Mtn   Dr

35
36
P

34
P

N
W — E
S

Park Lane

ALSO SEE MAPS ON
PAGES 68 • 96 • 105 • 107

East Valley Rd

E. Valley Ln

30

34.

Wiman–Old Pueblo–
Buena Vista Loop
Buena Vista Overlook

Ysidro Road. Drive one mile north to East Valley Road and turn right. Continue 0.9 miles to Park Lane and turn left. Drive 0.4 miles and veer left on East Mountain Drive. Immediately park in the small pullout on the right by the signed trailhead.

Hiking directions: Walk past the trailhead sign, and enter a riparian forest of bay laurel, sycamores, oaks, and maples. Follow the east side of a stream on the gently rolling terrain. At a half mile, leave the stream and climb to a junction with the Old Pueblo Trail. Begin the loop to the left, hiking clockwise. Traverse the hillside while overlooking the Pacific Ocean and the Channel Islands. Continue to a paved access road for a private home. Cross the road, staying on the trail, and pass sandstone outcrops, large cacti, and great vistas. Curve right and descend on the east slope of San Ysidro Canyon to a T-junction with the San Ysidro Trail (Hike 35). Bear right and follow the watercourse of San Ysidro Creek upstream, passing small waterfalls and pools to a posted junction with the McMenemy Trail (Hike 36). Stay straight on the San Ysidro Trail, steadily climbing 0.6 miles to the Buena Vista Connector Trail, a utility access road on the right.

Bear sharply right on the old dirt road and head uphill, climbing out of the canyon to a Y-fork at a coastal overlook. The right fork leads to a power pole. Stay to the left and continue uphill, with spectacular views of Santa Barbara, the coastline, and marina. Continue to a posted trail on the right as the road curves left. Descend on the footpath—the Buena Vista Trail—into the shade of the forest. Zigzag 0.4 miles downhill into the upper end of Buena Vista Canyon, reaching the creek on the canyon floor. Cross the creek and walk twenty yards to a signed junction. The right fork, straight ahead, is the return route.

To visit the Buena Vista Overlook and extend the hike an additional mile (and gain another 500 feet), detour left towards Romero Canyon. Weave up the lush trail on the serpentine path, which zigzags up 21 switchbacks to the Romero-Edison Road, a dirt road by a utility tower. Follow the catway 0.1 mile to the summit, straddling Romero Canyon and Buena Vista Canyon. At the top, a narrow side path veers to the right through tall oak scrub 130 yards to The Chair, a wooden, hand-made memorial bench atop Peak 1,543. The magnificent vistas extend across Santa Barbara, Montecito, Summerland, and Carpinteria to Point Mugu and the Channel Islands.

Return a half mile back down the switchbacks to the junction with the Buena Vista Trail. Head downhill to the left along the east canyon wall. Cross Buena Vista Creek two times, and pass sandstone outcroppings and a waterfall on the right. Wind down the canyon to the trailhead on Park Lane. Bear right and walk 150 yards on Park Lane to the Old Pueblo Trail sign. Veer right, leaving Park Lane on the paved driveway to another trail sign. Take the Old Pueblo Trail and continue downhill, completing the loop at a Y-fork with the Wiman Trail by a chain-link fence. Retrace your steps back to the trailhead. ∎

35. San Ysidro Canyon to San Ysidro Falls

Hiking distance: 3.7 miles round trip
Hiking time: 2 hours
Elevation gain: 1,200 feet

**map
page 105**

Maps: U.S.G.S. Carpinteria and Santa Barbara
Santa Barbara Front Country and Paradise Road
Montecito Trails Foundation map

Summary of hike: San Ysidro Canyon is a lush, stream-fed canyon in the mountains above Montecito. The San Ysidro Trail heads up the picturesque San Ysidro Canyon along the cascading creek. The steep, narrow, upper canyon is filled with small waterfalls, continuous cascades, and pools. This hike leads to San Ysidro Falls, a beautiful 60-foot waterfall that pours over a fern-covered rock wall and into a shallow pool below.

Driving directions: SANTA BARBARA. From Santa Barbara, drive southbound on Highway 101 to Montecito, and exit on San Ysidro Road. Drive one mile north to East Valley Road and turn right. Continue 0.9 miles to Park Lane and turn left. Drive 0.4 miles and veer left on East Mountain Drive. The trailhead is 0.2 miles ahead on the right. Park along East Mountain Drive.

Hiking directions: The signed trail heads to the right (north), parallel to a wooden fence. Proceed on the tree-covered lane past a few homes to a paved road. Follow the road 100 yards uphill to an unpaved road. Take the dirt road and drop into the cool and lush San Ysidro Canyon. At a half mile is a trail junction with the Old Pueblo Trail on the right, ascending east (Hike 34). Soon after is the McMenemy Trail on the left (Hike 36). Continue up the canyon on the fire road past another gate and a large eroded sandstone wall on the left. A hundred yards beyond the rock wall, power lines cross high above the trail near another junction. The Buena Vista Connector Trail, a utility access road, bears sharply to the right (Hike 34). Stay left on the San Ysidro Trail a short distance to a junction with the Edison Catway on the left.

Take the footpath bearing to the right, leaving the fire road. The trail gains elevation up the canyon past continuous cascades and pools. Several side paths lead to the left down to San Ysidro Creek. At 1.5 miles, a switchback and metal railing marks the beginning of the steeper ascent up-canyon. Cross a stream at 1.8 miles. To the right is a short side scramble up the narrow canyon to various pools, falls, and cascades. Back on the main trail, continue 100 yards to a trail fork. The right fork leads to the base of San Ysidro Falls. This is the turn-around spot.

To hike farther, the left fork climbs out of the canyon to East Camino Cielo Road, gaining 1,800 feet in 2.5 miles. ■

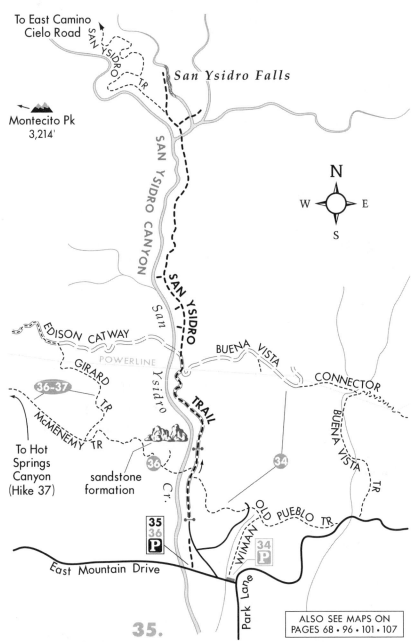

To East Camino Cielo Road

San Ysidro Falls

Montecito Pk 3,214'

SAN YSIDRO TR

SAN YSIDRO CANYON

San Ysidro TR

N
W E
S

EDISON CATWAY

POWERLINE

GIRARD TR

36-37

McMENEMY TR

To Hot Springs Canyon (Hike 37)

sandstone formation

36

San Ysidro Cr.

SAN YSIDRO TRAIL

BUENA VISTA

CONNECTOR

BUENA VISTA TR

34

35 36 P

34 P

OLD PUEBLO TR

WIMAN

East Mountain Drive

Park Lane

ALSO SEE MAPS ON
PAGES 68 • 96 • 101 • 107

35.
San Ysidro Canyon
San Ysidro Falls

36. McMenemy Trail Loop
from SAN YSIDRO CANYON

Hiking distance: 5 miles round trip
Hiking time: 3 hours
Elevation gain: 1,000 feet
Maps: U.S.G.S. Carpinteria and Santa Barbara
       Santa Barbara Front Country and Paradise Road
       Montecito Trails Foundation map

Summary of hike: The McMenemy Trail is a connector trail linking San Ysidro Canyon and Hot Springs Canyon. This hike begins in the picturesque San Ysidro Canyon. The trail crosses over the ridge between the canyons to meadows and scenic overlooks at 1,250 feet. It then descends into Hot Springs Canyon below Montecito Peak. The return loop leads past beautiful sandstone formations. Hike 37 accesses this loop from the Hot Springs Canyon drainage.

Driving directions: SANTA BARBARA. From Santa Barbara, drive southbound on Highway 101 to Montecito, and exit on San Ysidro Road. Drive one mile north to East Valley Road and turn right. Continue 0.9 miles to Park Lane and turn left. Drive 0.4 miles and veer left on East Mountain Drive. The trailhead is 0.2 miles ahead on the right. Park along East Mountain Drive.

Hiking directions: The signed trail heads to the right (north), parallel to a wooden fence. Proceed on the tree-covered lane past a few homes to a paved road. Follow the road 100 yards uphill to an unpaved road. Take the dirt road and drop into San Ysidro Canyon. At a half mile is a trail junction with the Old Pueblo Trail on the right (Hike 34). Soon after is the signed McMenemy Trail on the left.

Go left on the McMenemy Trail, rock hopping across San Ysidro Creek into a eucalyptus woodland. Head up a short hill to another junction. Take the left fork up to a meadow overlooking the ocean. Switchbacks lead up to a trail split. Both trails lead up McMenemy Hill to a ridge with a rock bench on a 1,250-foot

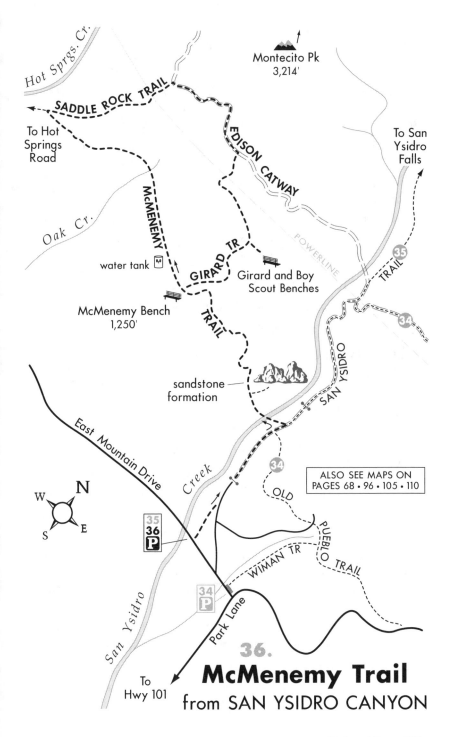

Hot Sprgs. Cr.

Montecito Pk
3,214'

SADDLE ROCK TRAIL

To Hot
Springs
Road

EDISON CATWAY

To San
Ysidro
Falls

McMENEMY

Oak Cr.

water tank

GIRARD TR

Girard and Boy
Scout Benches

POWERLINE

TRAIL

35

TRAIL

McMenemy Bench
1,250'

34

SAN YSIDRO

sandstone
formation

East Mountain Drive

Creek

34

OLD

ALSO SEE MAPS ON
PAGES 68 • 96 • 105 • 110

N
W   E
S

35
36
P

PUEBLO TRAIL

WIMAN TR

San Ysidro

34
P

Park Lane

To
Hwy 101

36.
McMenemy Trail
from SAN YSIDRO CANYON

perch. There are first-class views up and down the coastline from the Colonel McMenemy Bench.

From the meadow, the Girard Trail heads north to the Edison Catway. Instead, proceed downhill on the McMenemy Trail past a water tank and rock outcroppings. Cross a small stream near a 40-foot seasonal waterfall, and head to a signed junction on a ridge near a majestic oak tree. The right fork—the Saddle Rock Trail—leads a short distance up to a garden of large sandstone boulders, then joins with the Edison Catway. This route can be combined with the Girard Trail, forming a loop back to the McMenemy Bench. The left fork at the oak tree trail junction leads 0.2 miles down to Hot Springs Creek (Hike 37). ■

37. Hot Springs—Saddle Rock— Girard—McMenemy Loop
from HOT SPRINGS CANYON

Hiking distance: 4.2-mile loop
Hiking time: 2.5 hours
Elevation gain: 1,000 feet

map page 110

Maps: U.S.G.S. Santa Barbara
      Montecito Trails Foundation map
      Santa Barbara Front Country and Paradise Road map

Summary of hike: The Hot Springs, Saddle Rock, Girard, and McMenemy trails form a loop on the ridge between San Ysidro Canyon and Hot Springs Canyon. This diverse hike begins in Hot Springs Canyon and follows a small stream up the canyon. The route climbs to Saddle Rock, a group of gorgeous sandstone formations located on a ridge with great coastal views of the Santa Barbara coastline. The trail loops up and around on the Edison Catway on the Girard Trail and the McMenemy Trail, passing hand-crafted memorial benches that overlook the Pacific Ocean, the Channel Islands, and the Santa Ynez Mountains.

Driving directions: SANTA BARBARA. From Santa Barbara, drive southbound on Highway 101 to Montecito. Take the Hot

Springs Road exit and turn left. Drive 0.1 mile to Hot Springs Road and turn left again. Continue 2.2 miles to East Mountain Drive and turn left. Drive 0.2 miles to the signed trailhead and parking spaces on the right.

Hiking directions: Walk past the trailhead sign and through a fenced corridor among large boulders, cacti, and oaks. Follow the east side of Hot Springs Creek to Hot Springs Road. Cross the paved road and stay on the footpath, quickly returning to the road. Walk up Hot Springs Road, crossing over the creek to a property entrance gate. Take the path on the right side of the gate, parallel to Hot Springs Creek. Continue on the dirt road, and curve right onto the footpath. Cross over Hot Springs Creek, and climb rock and wooden steps. Steadily weave up the hillside to a junction at a majestic oak at 0.75 miles.

The McMenemy Trail—our return route—veers off to the right (east). Begin the loop to the left (north) on the Saddle Rock Trail. Climb the sandstone-lined path to coastal overlooks at the sculpted rock outcroppings, reaching a circular flat with spectacular views. A short distance ahead, pass under the powerlines to the Edison Catway at 1.5 miles. To the left, the dirt road leads into upper Hot Springs Canyon. Go to the right and traverse the hillside to the east—savoring the vistas along the way—to a Y-fork. The left fork continues on the Edison Catway and drops into San Ysidro Canyon (Hike 35).

Veer right on the signed Girard Trail and head downhill. The descent overlooks San Ysidro Canyon and the Santa Ynez Mountains. At a junction, detour 40 yards on the left fork. Descend steps to rock outcrops and two benches on a sandstone ridge. The Edward "Bud" Girard Bench is formed in the sandstone rock and overlooks the ocean and the Channel Islands. The Boy Scout Bench, made with rocks and mortar, faces the mountains.

After enjoying the overlooks, return to the Girard Trail. Continue to a T-junction with the McMenemy Trail and the Colonel McMenemy Bench, a rock bench with additional coastal vistas on a grass-covered ridge. The left fork descends into San Ysidro Canyon. (Hike 35 accesses this beautiful loop from its eastern access in San Ysidro Canyon.) Bear right, pass a water tank on the left, and cross the headwaters of Oak Creek just above a rock-walled, 40-foot seasonal waterfall. Zigzag uphill and complete the loop in Hot Springs Canyon. Retrace your steps on the Hot Springs Trail, 0.75 miles to the left. ■

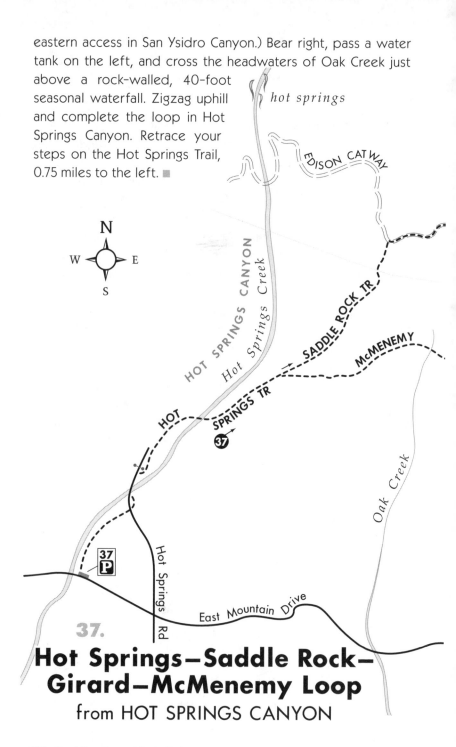

hot springs

EDISON CAT WAY

HOT SPRINGS CANYON

Hot Springs Creek

SADDLE ROCK TR.

McMENEMY

HOT SPRINGS TR.

37

Oak Creek

37 P

Hot Springs Rd

East Mountain Drive

37.

Hot Springs–Saddle Rock–Girard–McMenemy Loop
from HOT SPRINGS CANYON

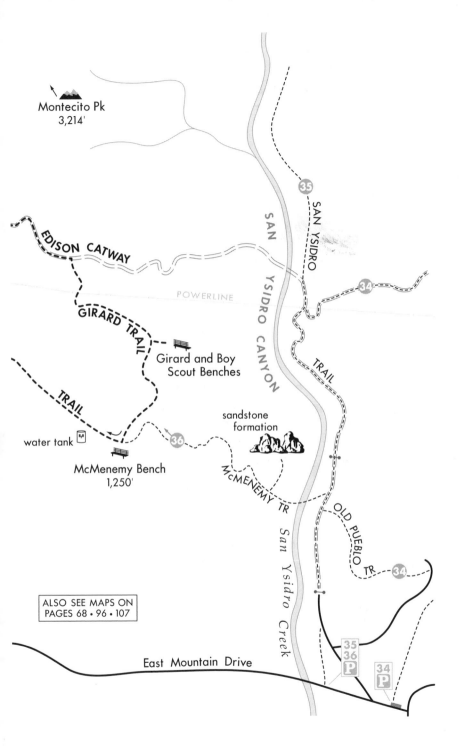

Montecito Pk
3,214'

EDISON CATWAY

SAN YSIDRO CANYON

SAN YSIDRO

35

34

POWERLINE

GIRARD TRAIL

Girard and Boy
Scout Benches

TRAIL

TRAIL

water tank

36

sandstone
formation

McMenemy Bench
1,250'

McMENEMY TR

OLD PUEBLO TR

34

ALSO SEE MAPS ON
PAGES 68 • 96 • 107

San Ysidro Creek

East Mountain Drive

35
36
P

34
P

38. East Fork—Cold Spring Ridge Loop to Montecito Overlook
COLD SPRING CANYON

Hiking distance: 3-mile loop
Hiking time: 2 hours
Elevation gain: 900 feet
Maps: U.S.G.S. Santa Barbara
   Montecito Trails Foundation map
   Santa Barbara Front Country and Paradise Road map

Summary of hike: Cold Spring Canyon divides into three forks: the East Fork, Middle Fork, and West Fork. Hikes 38—41 explore these three stream-fed canyons. All the hikes begin on the main Cold Spring Trail, then head into different directions after 0.75 miles.

This hike forms a loop along the East Fork drainage and Cold Spring Ridge. The East Fork Cold Spring Trail follows the shaded creek up the canyon, climbing the east canyon wall to the Edison Catway and the Montecito Overlook. From the overlook are sweeping vistas of Santa Barbara, the chain of connecting coastal towns, the Pacific Ocean, and the Channel Islands. From the overlook, the Ridge Trail zigzags across the exposed hillside, offering more outstanding views across the canyon and down to the ocean.

Driving directions: SANTA BARBARA. From Santa Barbara, drive southbound on Highway 101 to Montecito. Take the Hot Springs Road exit and turn left. Drive 0.1 mile to Hot Springs Road and turn left again. Continue 2.2 miles to East Mountain Drive and turn left. Drive 1.1 mile to the Cold Spring trailhead on the right, located where the creek flows across the paved road. Park along the road.

Hiking directions: From the east side of Cold Spring Creek, head up Cold Spring Canyon along the cascading, rock-filled creek. Walk up the trail under the shade of oaks, alders, and sycamores, passing water shoots, small falls, and pools. At a

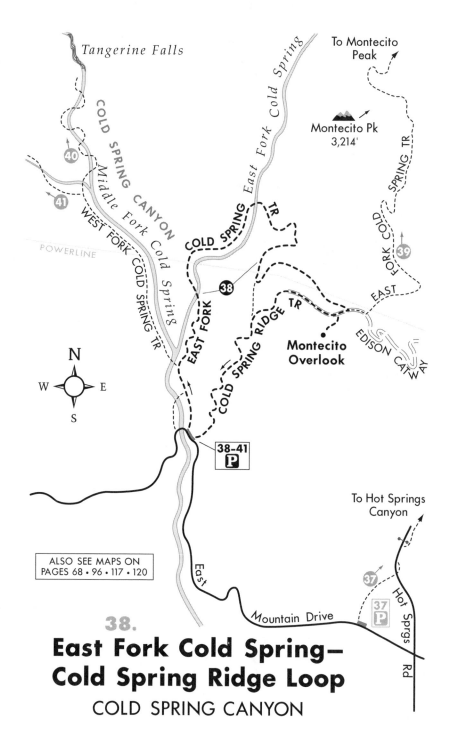

Tangerine Falls

To Montecito Peak

Montecito Pk
3,214'

COLD SPRING CANYON

East Fork Cold Spring

Middle Fork Cold Spring

WEST FORK COLD SPRING TR

COLD SPRING TR

EAST FORK COLD SPRING TR

40

41

POWERLINE

38

39

EAST FORK

COLD SPRING RIDGE TR

EAST

EDISON CAT'WAY

Montecito Overlook

N
W   E
S

38-41
P

ALSO SEE MAPS ON
PAGES 68 • 96 • 117 • 120

To Hot Springs Canyon

37

37
P

Hot Sprgs Rd

East

Mountain Drive

38.

East Fork Cold Spring—
Cold Spring Ridge Loop
COLD SPRING CANYON

quarter mile is a posted junction with the West Fork Cold Spring Trail. The junction is located by a waterfall, pool, and bench near the confluence of the Middle Fork and East Fork. The West Fork Cold Spring Trail (Hikes 40 and 41) crosses the creek to the left.

Continue straight on the East Fork Trail and head up-canyon, zigzagging up four switchbacks to a creek crossing at 0.6 miles. Rock-hop over the creek, then loop around the hillside back to the creek, passing waterfalls and pools. Cross the creek a second time and curve right. Leave the sound of the cascading water, and enter the quiet of the forest. Ascend the mountain to a trail split at 1.2 miles. A connector to the Ridge Trail goes straight ahead (for a shorter 2.4-mile loop). For this hike, bear left and continue uphill to views of the upper East Fork and Montecito Peak. Climb to the end of the footpath at 1.5 miles, reaching the Edison Road, a dirt utility road known as the Catway. To the left, the Catway leads to Hot Springs Canyon and San Ysidro Canyon (Hikes 34—38). Hike 39—to Montecito Peak—heads north 100 yards ahead.

Instead, take the road a short distance to the right to the Montecito Overlook on a knoll. After enjoying the views, continue to the west. Walk parallel to the powerlines for a short distance to the end of the road. Pick up the Cold Spring Ridge Trail, a narrow footpath, and weave steeply down the hillside to a T-junction with the connector trail. Bear left, staying on the Ridge Trail, and slowly lose elevation. Enter a forest canopy, and wend your way down the hill back to the trailhead on East Mountain Drive. ▪

39. East Fork Cold Spring to Montecito Peak

COLD SPRING CANYON

Hiking distance: 7 miles round trip
Hiking time: 4.5 hours
Elevation gain: 2,450 feet
Maps: U.S.G.S. Santa Barbara
Montecito Trails Foundation map
Santa Barbara Front Country and Paradise Road map

map
page 117

Summary of hike: From nearly anywhere along the Santa Barbara–Montecito coastline, Montecito Peak looks like a rounded dome jutting out from the mountains. The prominent 3,214-foot peak rises between Cold Spring Canyon and San Ysidro Canyon. The East Fork Cold Spring Trail climbs up the Santa Ynez Mountains to Montecito Peak, then continues to East Camino Cielo atop the ridge. From the peak are sweeping coastal panoramas that stretch from Point Mugu to Gaviota. The trail begins in Cold Spring Canyon and weaves between the steep canyon walls through a lush hardwood forest, passing deep pools and waterfalls.

Driving directions: SANTA BARBARA. From Santa Barbara, drive southbound on Highway 101 to Montecito. Take the Hot Springs Road exit and turn left. Drive 0.1 mile to Hot Springs Road and turn left again. Continue 2.2 miles to East Mountain Drive and turn left. Drive 1.1 mile to the Cold Spring trailhead on the right, located where the creek flows across the paved road. Park along the road.

Hiking directions: From the east side of Cold Spring Creek, head up Cold Spring Canyon along the cascading, rock-filled creek. Walk up the trail under the shade of oaks, alders, and sycamores, passing water shoots, small falls, and pools. At a quarter mile is a posted junction with the West Fork Cold Spring Trail. The junction is located by a waterfall, pool, and bench near the confluence of the Middle Fork and East Fork. The West Fork

Cold Spring Trail (Hikes 40 and 41) crosses the creek to the left.

Continue straight on the East Fork Trail and head up-canyon, zigzagging up four switchbacks to a creek crossing at 0.6 miles. Rock-hop over the creek, then loop around the hillside back to the creek, passing waterfalls and pools. Cross the creek a second time and curve right. Leave the sound of the cascading water, and enter the quiet of the forest. Ascend the mountain to a trail split at 1.2 miles. A connector to the Ridge Trail goes straight ahead. For this hike, bear left and continue uphill to views of the upper East Fork and Montecito Peak. Climb to the end of the footpath at 1.5 miles, reaching the Edison Road, a dirt utility road known as the Catway. The right fork leads to the Montecito Overlook and Cold Spring Ridge Trail (Hike 38).

Follow the Catway 100 yards to the left, reaching the upper section of the East Fork Cold Spring Trail on the left. The Edison Catway continues to Hot Springs Canyon and San Ysidro Canyon (Hikes 34—38). Instead, bear left on the signed East Fork Cold Spring Trail, and continue climbing towards Montecito Peak. Wind up the steep, rocky path through dense chaparral, pausing to enjoy the great coastal views. Skirt the west side of Montecito Peak to a steep, narrow path on the right at 3.6 miles. (Watch for the path as you wind past the peak.) Take a sharp right and head up to a ridge. From here, it is a short, but steep, scramble on shale to the 3,514-foot summit. Careful footing is a must! At the summit is a sign-in log book, where you can proclaim you made it to the top. Return by retracing your route.

To extend the hike, the trail continues 1.4 miles up to East Camino Cielo Road (Hike 79). ■

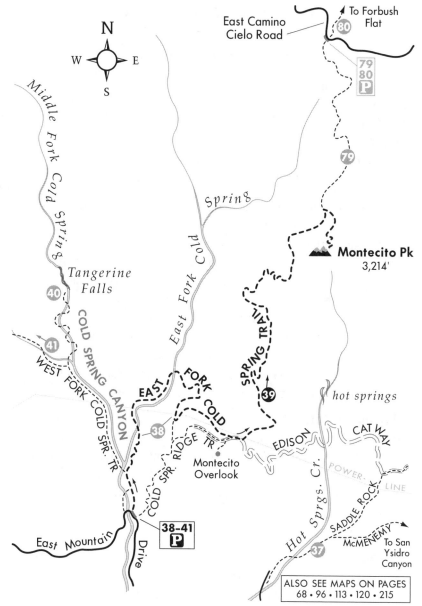

39. **East Fork Cold Spring to Montecito Peak**
COLD SPRING CANYON

40. West Fork Cold Spring to Tangerine Falls

COLD SPRING CANYON

Hiking distance: 2.6 miles round trip
Hiking time: 2 hours
Elevation gain: 800 feet
Maps: U.S.G.S. Santa Barbara
Montecito Trails Foundation map
Santa Barbara Front Country and Paradise Road map

**map
page 120**

Summary of hike: Tangerine Falls is located in a narrow, rocky gorge on the Middle Fork of Cold Spring Canyon. The fall, named for the tangerine-colored rock walls, tumbles 100 feet into a shallow pool. The vertical sandstone walls are layered with maidenhair ferns and green moss. This forested hike continuously parallels the creek under a canopy of California bays, sycamores, and alders. The trail passes sandstone formations, cascades, pools, and waterfalls. The last quarter mile to the scenic area at the base of the cataract is not an official trail. It is a rock-hop and scramble, with many creek crossings, in a cool, shady gorge. The hike to the falls is also a great side trip for Hike 41.

Driving directions: SANTA BARBARA. From Santa Barbara, drive southbound on Highway 101 to Montecito. Take the Hot Springs Road exit and turn left. Drive 0.1 mile to Hot Springs Road and turn left again. Continue 2.2 miles to East Mountain Drive and turn left. Drive 1.1 mile to the Cold Spring trailhead on the right, located where the creek flows across the paved road. Park along the road.

Hiking directions: From the east side of Cold Spring Creek, head up Cold Spring Canyon along the cascading, rock-filled creek. Walk up the trail under the shade of oaks, alders, and sycamores, passing water shoots, small falls, and pools. At a quarter mile is a posted junction with the West Fork Cold Spring Trail by a waterfall, pool, and bench near the confluence of the East Fork and Middle Fork. The East Fork Cold Spring Trail (Hikes 38—39) continues straight ahead.

For this hike, bear left on the West Fork Cold Spring Trail, and rock-hop over the creek. Continue up-canyon on the west side of the creek. Steadily climb amid large sandstone boulders, perched on the canyon wall high above the tumbling creek. Curve left into the West Fork Canyon and a trail split. The main trail continues up-canyon to the historic 1905 Cold Spring Water Tunnel and Gibraltar Road (Hike 41). For this hike, go to the right, crossing over the creek. Continue up the Middle Fork of Cold Spring Canyon. Follow the creek past pools and waterfalls, working your way to the base of Tangerine Falls. This unmaintained path is a scramble over boulders and old water pipes in a steep but beautiful canyon. Use caution! ▪

41. West Fork Cold Spring to Gibraltar Road

COLD SPRING CANYON

Hiking distance: 4 miles round trip
Hiking time: 2.5 hours
Elevation gain: 1,200 feet
Maps: U.S.G.S. Santa Barbara
       Montecito Trails Foundation map
       Santa Barbara Front Country and Paradise Road map

map page 120

Summary of hike: The West Fork Cold Spring Trail begins in the main Cold Spring drainage, then veers off to the west, crossing the main fork of the creek by a waterfall and pool. The two-mile trail climbs up the canyon under sycamores, alders, and bays through the narrow riparian corridor. The trail passes a historic water tunnel, then leaves the creek and climbs up the south canyon wall to Gibraltar Road. Although the trail gains 1,200 feet over two miles, it is rarely steep. The coastal vistas along the upper section of the trail are beautiful.

Driving directions: SANTA BARBARA. From Santa Barbara, drive southbound on Highway 101 to Montecito. Take the Hot Springs Road exit and turn left. Drive 0.1 mile to Hot Springs Road and turn left again. Continue 2.2 miles to East Mountain Drive and turn left. Drive 1.1 mile to the Cold Spring trailhead on the right, located where the creek flows across the paved road. Park along the road.

Hiking directions: From the east side of Cold Spring Creek, head up Cold Spring Canyon along the cascading, rock-filled creek. Walk up the trail under the shade of oaks, alders, and sycamores, passing water shoots, small falls, and pools. At a quarter mile is a posted junction with the West Fork Cold Spring Trail by a waterfall, pool, and bench near the confluence of the East Fork and Middle Fork. The East Fork Cold Spring Trail (Hikes 38–39) continues straight ahead.

For this hike, bear left on the West Fork Cold Spring Trail, and rock-hop over the creek. Continue up-canyon on the west side

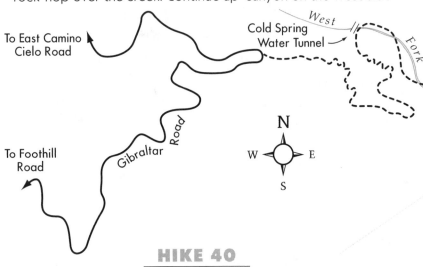

HIKE 40
West Fork Cold Spring
to Tangerine Falls

HIKE 41
West Fork Cold Spring
to Gibraltar Road
COLD SPRING CANYON

of the creek. Steadily climb amid large sandstone boulders, perched on the canyon wall high above the tumbling creek. Curve left into the West Fork Canyon and a trail split. The right fork crosses over the creek and scrambles up the Middle Fork to Tangerine Falls. (See Hike 40 for this side trip.)

Continue straight, staying in the narrow West Fork Canyon. Follow the course of the water, rock-hopping over the creek four times. At the fourth crossing is the historic Cold Spring Water Tunnel, built in 1905. After crossing, leave the riparian creekside habitat and begin a steeper ascent, gaining 700 feet over 0.75 miles with the help of 25 switchbacks. At the eighth switchback is a great view down the canyon to the ocean. En route, the trail crosses a minor draw. Near the top are coastal vistas that extend across Santa Barbara, Montecito, and Carpinteria to Point Mugu. The trail levels out and emerges from the forest to Gibraltar Road at a horseshoe bend in the road. Return along the same route. ▧

ALSO SEE MAPS ON
PAGES 68 • 96 • 117 • 133

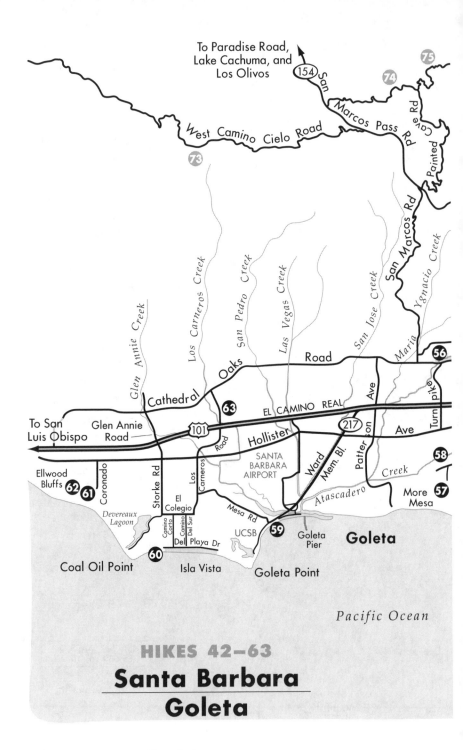

To Paradise Road,
Lake Cachuma, and
Los Olivos

154 San Marcos Pass Rd

75

74

West Camino Cielo Road

Cave Rd

Pointed

73

San Marcos Rd

Glen Annie Creek

Los Carneros Creek

San Pedro Creek

Las Vegas Creek

San Jose Creek

Maria Ygnacio Creek

Road

56

Oaks

Cathedral

63

EL CAMINO REAL

Ave

Turnpike

To San
Luis Obispo

Glen Annie
Road

101

Hollister

217

Ave

Patter on

58

Coronado

Storke Rd

Los Carneros Road

SANTA
BARBARA
AIRPORT

Ward Mem. Bl.

Creek

Ellwood
Bluffs

62 61

El
Colegio

Atascadero

More
Mesa

57

Devereaux
Lagoon

Camino Corto

Camino Del Sur

Mesa Rd

UCSB

59

Goleta
Pier

Goleta

60

Del Playa Dr

Coal Oil Point

Isla Vista

Goleta Point

Pacific Ocean

HIKES 42–63

Santa Barbara
Goleta

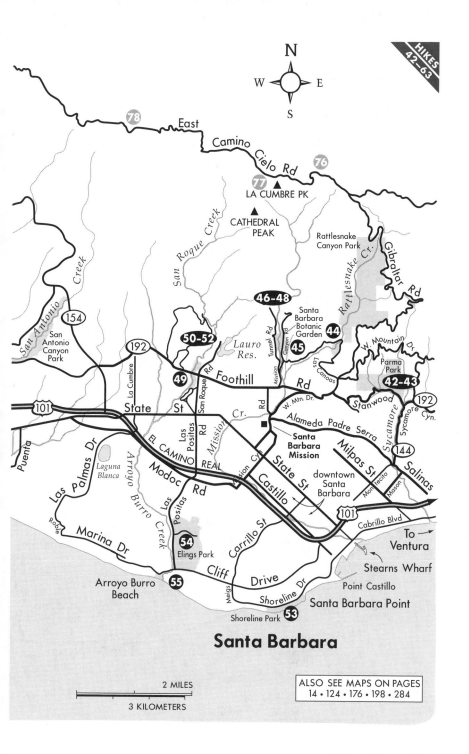

HIKES 42-63

East Camino Cielo Rd

78
76
77 LA CUMBRE PK

CATHEDRAL PEAK

San Roque Creek

Rattlesnake Canyon Park

Rattlesnake Cr.

Gibraltar Rd

46-48

San Antonio Creek

154

San Antonio Canyon Park

192

50-52

Lauro Res.

Tunnel Rd

Santa Barbara Botanic Garden

Canyon

44
45

W. Mountain Dr.

E. Camino Cielo Rd

Parma Park

42-43

La Cumbre

49

Foothill Rd

Mission Cr.

Rd

W. Mtn. Dr.

Stanwood

Sycamore

Sycamore Cyn.

192

101

State St

San Roque Rd

Mission Cyn.

Alameda Padre Serra

144

Puente

Las Palmas Dr

Laguna Blanca

Arroyo Burro Creek

EL CAMINO REAL

Modoc Rd

Las Positas Rd

Las Positas Rd

Santa Barbara Mission

downtown Santa Barbara

Milpas St

Montecito

Mason

Salinas

101

Marina Dr

Roble

54

Elings Park

Carrillo St

Castillo St

State St

Cabrillo Blvd

To Ventura

Stearns Wharf

Cliff Drive

55

Arroyo Burro Beach

Meigs

Shoreline Dr

Point Castillo

Santa Barbara Point

53

Shoreline Park

Santa Barbara

2 MILES

3 KILOMETERS

ALSO SEE MAPS ON PAGES
14 • 124 • 176 • 198 • 284

HIKES 42–52

Santa Barbara Front Range (WEST)

Rattlesnake Canyon
Mission Canyon
San Roque Canyon

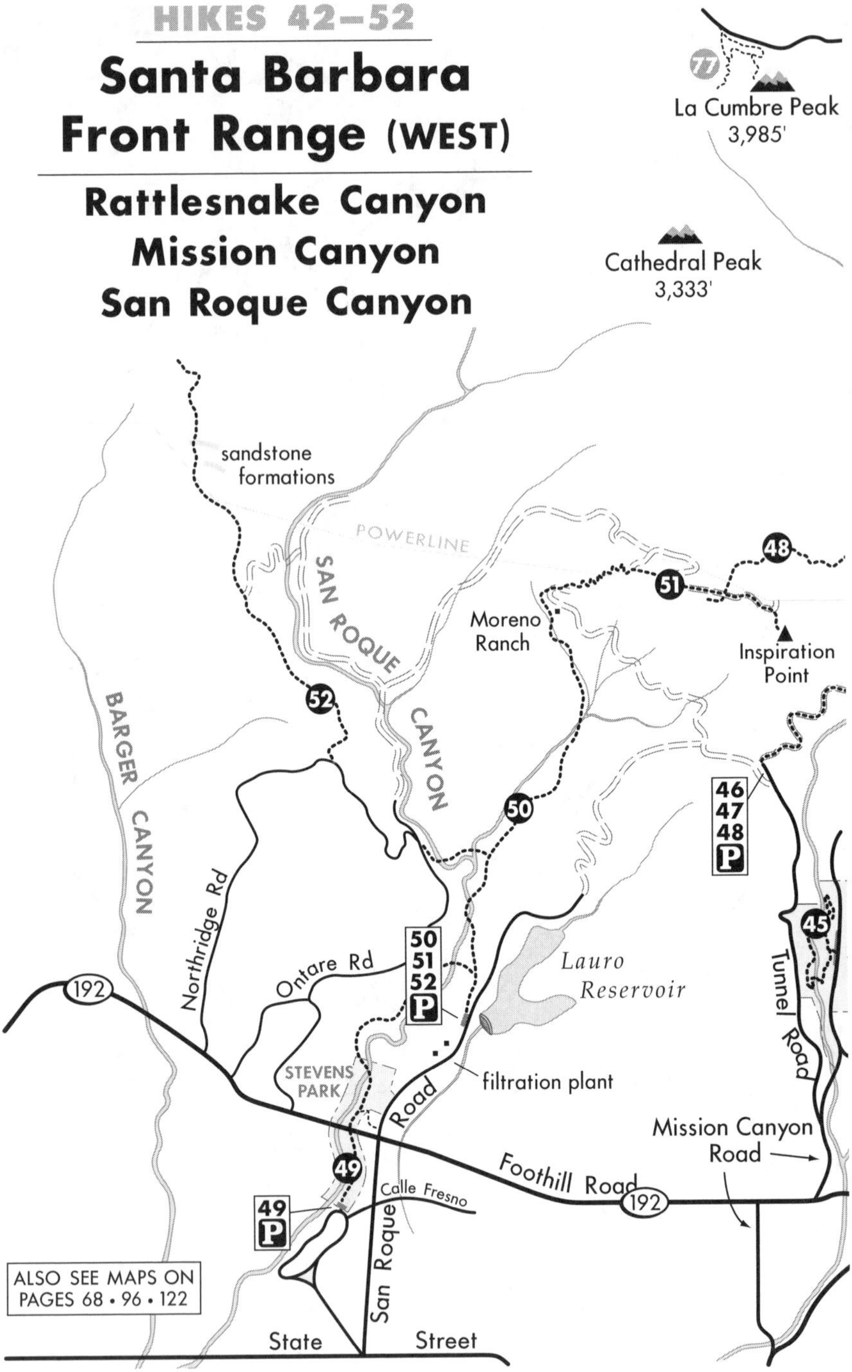

77
La Cumbre Peak
3,985'
Cathedral Peak
3,333'
sandstone formations
POWERLINE
SAN ROQUE
CANYON
48
51
Moreno Ranch
Inspiration Point
52
BARGER
CANYON
50
46
47
48
P
Northridge Rd
45
50
51
52
P
Ontare Rd
Lauro Reservoir
Tunnel Road
192
STEVENS PARK
filtration plant
Road
Mission Canyon Road
Foothill Road
192
49
Calle Fresno
49
P
San Roque
ALSO SEE MAPS ON PAGES 68 • 96 • 122
State
Street

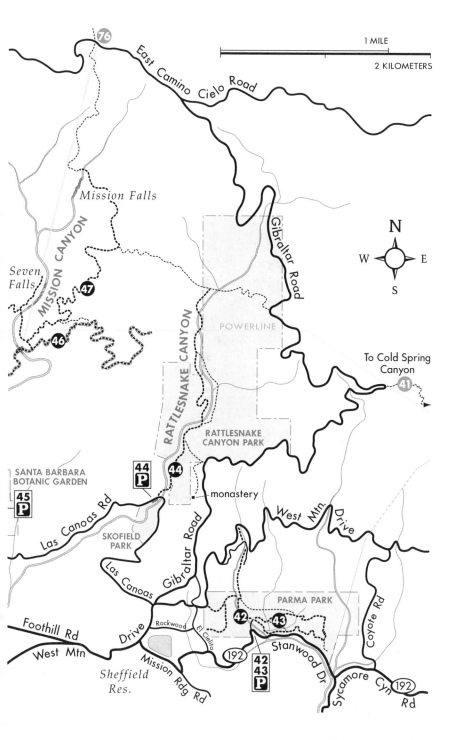

1 MILE

2 KILOMETERS

East Camino Cielo Road

76

Mission Falls

MISSION CANYON

Seven Falls

47

46

RATTLESNAKE CANYON

Gibraltar Road

POWERLINE

N
W   E
S

To Cold Spring Canyon

41

RATTLESNAKE CANYON PARK

SANTA BARBARA BOTANIC GARDEN

45
P

44
P

44

monastery

Las Canoas Rd

SKOFIELD PARK

West Mtn. Drive

Las Canoas

Gibraltar Road

Drive

Rockwood

El Cielito

PARMA PARK

42

43

Coyote Rd

Foothill Rd

West Mtn

Mission Rdg Rd

Sheffield Res.

192

42
43
P

Stanwood Dr

Sycamore Cyn Rd

192

42. Parma Park—East Trails

Hiking distance: 2.5-mile loop
Hiking time: 1.5 hour
Elevation gain: 300 feet
Maps: U.S.G.S. Santa Barbara
      Santa Barbara Front Country and Paradise Road map
      Montecito Trails Foundation map

map
page 128

Summary of hike: Parma Park is an undeveloped 200-acre park in the foothills below Sycamore Canyon at the northeast end of Santa Barbara. Coyote Creek, Sycamore Creek, and seasonal feeder streams flow through the park. The natural area, burned in the Tea Fire of 2008, includes forested canyons, grassy knolls overlooking the surrounding hills, and exposed, chaparral-clad hillsides. The hiking, biking, and equestrian trails are intentionally unmarked.

This hike forms a loop through the eastern portion of the park. The loop follows the chaparral-covered Rowe Trail—with sweeping vistas—and returns through a riparian oak woodland on the Parma Fire Road. Dogs are allowed in the park.

Driving directions: SANTA BARBARA. In Santa Barbara, take Sycamore Canyon Road north to Stanwood Drive. Turn left and drive 0.7 miles to Parma Park on the right. Park across the road in the parking pullouts.

Hiking directions: Cross Stanwood Drive, and walk through the park gate at the entrance sign. Cross an old stone bridge to the end of the paved road at an open, oak-lined picnic area and a four-way junction. The left fork follows Sycamore Creek and connects with trails leading to West Mountain Drive and El Cielito Road (Hike 43). For this hike, begin the loop to the right and head downhill on the Rowe Trail. Cross a fork of Sycamore Creek, and climb to the ridge above Stanwood Drive. Head east along the ridge, parallel to the road below. At the east end, curve left and climb to the Parma Fire Road on a knoll overlooking Parma Park, the Santa Ynez Mountains, the ocean, and the Channel Islands. Atop the knoll is a picnic bench and plaque honoring

Rowe McMullin for his dedication to the park and equestrian community. Bear left, returning along the ridge on the fire road. Descend to a series of knolls, and meander through an ancient oak woodland in the canyon, parallel to a fork of Sycamore Creek. Cross the East Fork of Sycamore Creek, and complete the loop at the picnic area. ■

43. Parma Park — West Trails

Hiking distance: 1.8 miles round trip
Hiking time: 1 hour
Elevation gain: 300 feet
Maps: U.S.G.S. Santa Barbara
      Santa Barbara Front Country and Paradise Road map
      Montecito Trails Foundation map

**map
page 128**

Summary of hike: Parma Park was owned by the Parma family from the 1890s until 1973. In 1973, the Parma brothers, Harold and John, donated the 200-acre parkland to Santa Barbara. The city's largest undeveloped open space is located in a crevice of hills between Stanwood Drive and West Mountain Drive. The scenic park includes creekside habitats; a mosaic of wooded canyons; vista points; grassy knolls; brushy, chaparral slopes; vista overlooks; and a maze of hiking, biking, and equestrian trails. This hike follows a combination of paths on the western side of the natural area. The route follows Sycamore Canyon up to West Mountain Road and climbs to the upper meadows near El Cielito Road. Dogs are allowed in the park.

Driving directions: SANTA BARBARA. In Santa Barbara, take Sycamore Canyon Road north to Stanwood Drive. Turn left and drive 0.7 miles to Parma Park on the right. Park across the road in the parking pullouts.

Hiking directions: Cross Stanwood Drive, and walk through the park gate at the entrance sign. Cross an old stone bridge to the end of the paved road at an open, oak-lined picnic area and a four-way junction. The Parma Fire Road continues straight ahead, and the Rowe Trail crosses a branch of Sycamore Creek to the

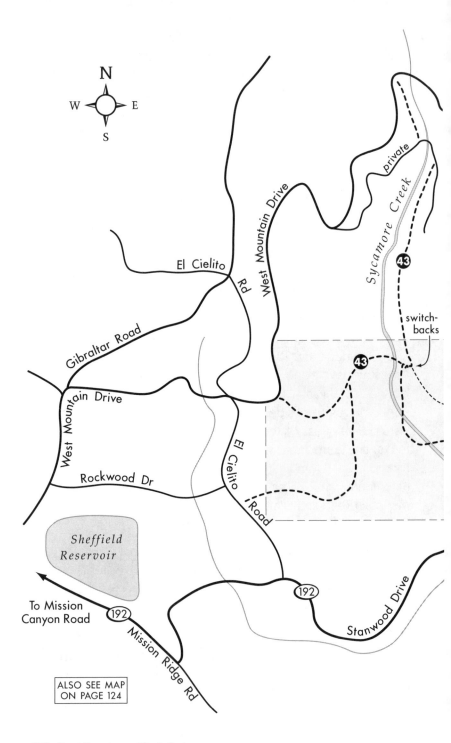

N
W E
S

West Mountain Drive

El Cielito

Sycamore Creek

private

43

switch-backs

Gibraltar Road

43

West Mountain Drive

El Cielito Road

Rockwood Dr

Sheffield Reservoir

To Mission Canyon Road

192

192

Stanwood Drive

Mission Ridge Rd

ALSO SEE MAP
ON PAGE 124

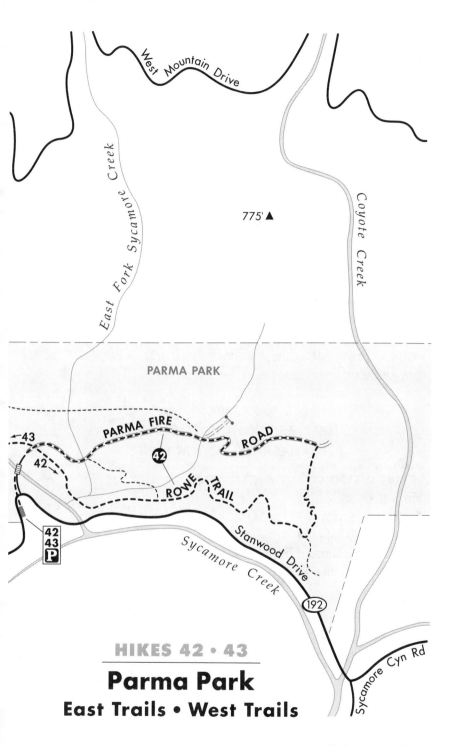

West Mountain Drive

East Fork Sycamore Creek

Coyote Creek

775' ▲

PARMA PARK

PARMA FIRE **42** ROAD

←**43**

42→

ROWE TRAIL

Stanwood Drive

Sycamore Creek

42
43
P

192

Sycamore Cyn Rd

HIKES 42 • 43

Parma Park
East Trails • West Trails

right (Hike 42). Bear left and take the footpath along Sycamore Creek. Follow the east edge of the creek under a canopy of oaks. Rock-hop two times over the creek to a trail fork.

For now, cross the creek on the left fork and weave up the slope to a Y-fork. The right fork climbs the rolling hillside a quarter mile to West Mountain Drive. The left fork traverses the hillside and cuts through a large sloping meadow a quarter mile to El Cielito Road, just below Rockwood Drive. Both routes offer views across the undeveloped park and the Santa Ynez Mountains.

Return to the trail fork at Sycamore Creek. Wind up the hillside on four switchbacks to a T-junction. The right fork traverses the open grassy slope and descends to the Parma Fire Road. Bear left and follow the east wall of the Sycamore Creek drainage under old, stately oaks. Continue north, steadily gaining elevation, to a privately owned dirt road. Cross over Sycamore Creek on the road and veer right, returning to the footpath. Walk 100 yards uphill, topping off at the end of the trail onto West Mountain Drive. Return down-canyon to the trailhead. ■

44. Rattlesnake Canyon Trail
RATTLESNAKE CANYON PARK

Hiking distance: 3.5 miles round trip
Hiking time: 2 hours
Elevation gain: 1,000 feet

map page 132

Maps: U.S.G.S. Santa Barbara
Santa Barbara Front Country and Paradise Road map
Montecito Trails Foundation map

Summary of hike: The trail up Rattlesnake Canyon is one of Santa Barbara's most popular trails. The shady trail follows the creek up the winding canyon through a lush riparian forest with alders, bays, oaks, big leaf maples, and sycamores. The path meanders past pools, cascades, small waterfalls, stream crossings, a grotto, and beautiful sandstone formations to a wildflower-filled meadow. From the meadow is a panoramic vista overlooking the Pacific Ocean and the Channel Islands. Rattlesnake Canyon is named for the serpentine canyon and not for an abundance of snakes.

Driving directions: SANTA BARBARA. From the Santa Barbara Mission, take Mission Canyon Road north towards the mountains for 0.6 miles to Foothill Road—turn right. Drive 0.2 miles to Mission Canyon Road and turn left. Continue 0.5 miles to Las Conoas Road and turn sharply to the right, following the Skofield Park sign. Take this winding road 1.2 miles to the trailhead, located by a beautiful stone bridge over Rattlesnake Creek. Park in the pull-outs along the right side of the road or a short distance ahead in Skofield Park.

Hiking directions: Head north past the trail sign along the west side of the stone bridge. Rock hop across the creek to a wide trail. Head to the left another half mile to a trail split. The right fork connects to Gibraltar Road. Continue straight ahead on the narrower trail, staying in the canyon and creek. Descend to the cascading Rattlesnake Creek and recross to the west side of the creek. The trail climbs out of the canyon via switchbacks.

At 1.3 miles is the first of two successive creek crossings. Between these crossings are cascades, small waterfalls, pools, flat sunbathing boulders, and a rock grotto. Back on the west side of the watercourse, the trail climbs to Tin Can Flat, a large, grassy meadow with views of the surrounding mountains. Just beyond the meadow is a junction with the Tunnel Connector Trail to Mission Canyon. This is the turn-around spot. Return along the same path.

To hike farther, the right fork leads up switchbacks to Gibraltar Road, gaining 600 feet in 0.7 miles. To the left, the Tunnel Connector Trail also climbs 600 feet in 0.7 miles to the Tunnel Trail in Mission Canyon (Hike 47). ▪

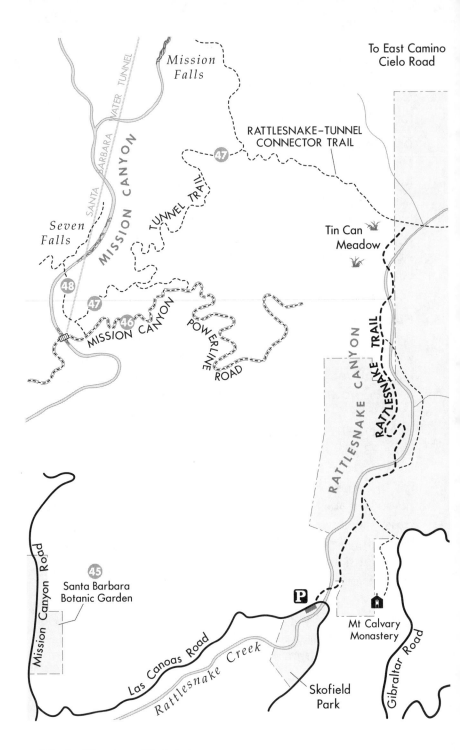

Mission Falls

To East Camino
Cielo Road

RATTLESNAKE–TUNNEL
CONNECTOR TRAIL

SANTA BARBARA WATER TUNNEL

MISSION CANYON

TUNNEL TRAIL

47

Seven
Falls

Tin Can
Meadow

48

47

46

MISSION CANYON

POWERLINE
ROAD

RATTLESNAKE CANYON

RATTLESNAKE TRAIL

Mission Canyon Road

45

Santa Barbara
Botanic Garden

P

Mt Calvary
Monastery

Gibraltar Road

Las Canoas Road

Rattlesnake Creek

Skofield
Park

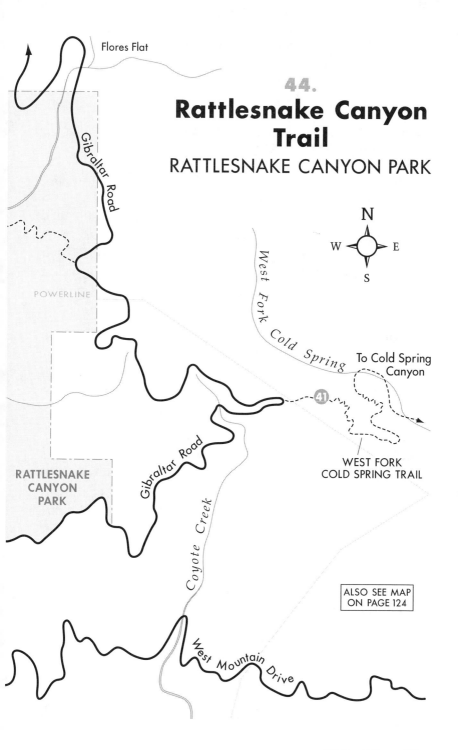

44.
Rattlesnake Canyon Trail
RATTLESNAKE CANYON PARK

Flores Flat

Gibraltar Road

N
W ⊕ E
S

West Fork Cold Spring

POWERLINE

To Cold Spring Canyon

WEST FORK COLD SPRING TRAIL

Gibraltar Road

RATTLESNAKE CANYON PARK

Coyote Creek

West Mountain Drive

ALSO SEE MAP ON PAGE 124

45. Santa Barbara Botanic Garden

Hiking distance: 2-mile loop (variable)
Hiking time: 2 hours
Elevation gain: 50 feet
Maps: Santa Barbara Botanic Garden Visitors Map
Guide to the Santa Barbara Botanic Garden

Summary of hike: The Santa Barbara Botanic Garden has several looping nature trails totaling 5.5 miles. The trails cover a wide variety of habitats on the 65-acre grounds. Through the heart of the garden flows Mission Creek. The trails pass through a canyon, a redwood forest, over bridges, past a waterfall, and across a historic dam built in 1906. This hike is only a suggested route. Many other paths can be chosen to view areas of your own interests.

Driving directions: SANTA BARBARA. From the Santa Barbara Mission, take Mission Canyon Road north towards the mountains for 0.6 miles to Foothill Road—turn right. Drive 0.2 miles to Mission Canyon Road and turn left. Continue 0.9 miles to the botanic garden parking lot on the left at 1212 Mission Canyon Road. An entrance fee is required.

Hiking directions: From the entrance, head to the right past a pond and through a meadow. Past the meadow is the Redwood Forest. (The Woodland Trail is a side loop to the east.) The trail leads downhill towards Mission Creek before looping back to the south under the forested canopy. Cross Mission Dam and continue parallel to the creek. (The Pritchett Trail is a hillside loop to the west.) Campbell Bridge crosses the creek to the left, returning to the entrance. For the longer loop hike, continue south to the island section. Take the Easton–Aquaduct Trail loop around the hillside, and descend to the creek at Stone Creek Crossing. Once across, head up the rock steps into the Manzanita Section, and return to the garden entrance. ■

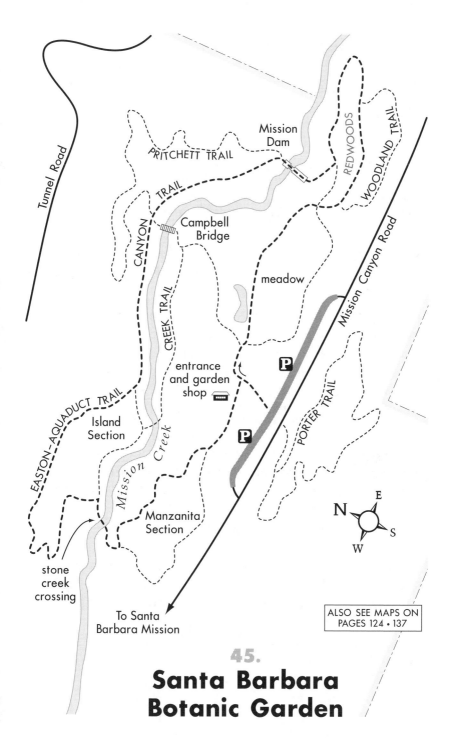

Tunnel Road

Mission Dam

PRITCHETT TRAIL

REDWOODS

WOODLAND TRAIL

CANYON TRAIL

Campbell Bridge

Mission Canyon Road

meadow

CREEK TRAIL

EASTON–AQUADUCT TRAIL

entrance and garden shop

P

P

PORTER TRAIL

Island Section

Mission Creek

Manzanita Section

N E S W

stone creek crossing

To Santa Barbara Mission

ALSO SEE MAPS ON PAGES 124 • 137

45.

Santa Barbara Botanic Garden

46. Mission Canyon Powerline Road
EDISON CATWAY from MISSION CANYON

Hiking distance: 5.6 miles round trip
Hiking time: 2.5 hours
Elevation gain: 1,300 feet
Maps: U.S.G.S. Santa Barbara
Santa Barbara Front Country and Paradise Road map

Summary of hike: The Mission Canyon Powerline Road is a utility easement road also referred to as the Edison Catway. The trail is a steady, but not steep, uphill climb that follows the contours of the hillside. The hike leads to a hilltop overlook of Rattlesnake Canyon and offers great views of Santa Barbara, the coastline, and the Channel Islands.

Driving directions: SANTA BARBARA. From the Santa Barbara Mission, take Mission Canyon Road north towards the mountains for 0.6 miles to Foothill Road—turn right. Drive 0.2 miles to Mission Canyon Road and turn left. Continue 0.3 miles and bear left at a road split onto Tunnel Road. Drive 1.1 mile on Tunnel Road, and park along the right side of the road near the road's end.

Hiking directions: Walk to the end of Tunnel Road and past the trailhead gate. Head uphill and wind around the hillside, with great downward views of the city and ocean. At 0.7 miles, cross a bridge over Mission Creek and Little Fern Canyon Falls. Arrive at a trail split, where the paved trail ends. Bear to the right, staying on the unpaved road as it gains elevation along the contours of the hills. At 1.4 miles is a junction on the left with a connector trail to the Tunnel Trail (Hike 47). Stay to the right, entering a shady, forested area. The grade gets steeper as you near the upper end of the utility road. The road/trail ends on the hilltop by utility poles overlooking Rattlesnake Canyon (Hike 44). To return, reverse your route. ■

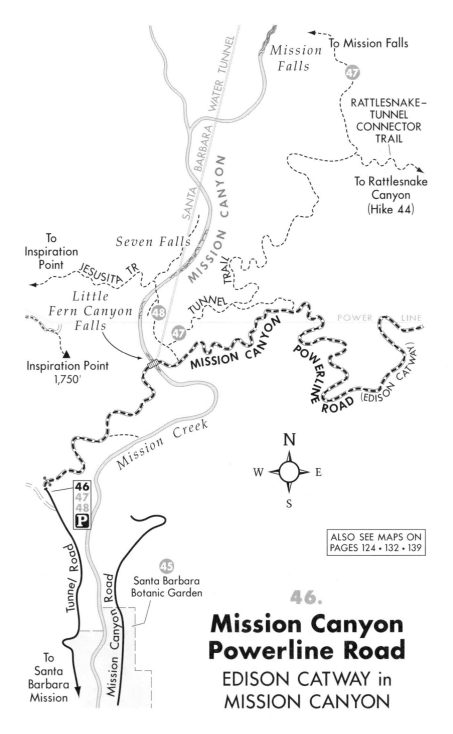

Mission Falls

To Mission Falls

47

RATTLESNAKE–
TUNNEL
CONNECTOR
TRAIL

To Rattlesnake
Canyon
(Hike 44)

Seven Falls

To
Inspiration
Point

JESUSITA TR

*Little
Fern Canyon
Falls*

48

TUNNEL TRAIL

MISSION CANYON

47

Inspiration Point
1,750'

POWER LINE

MISSION CANYON

POWERLINE ROAD (EDISON CATWAY)

Mission Creek

N
W · E
S

46
47
48
P

Tunnel Road

Mission Canyon Road

45
Santa Barbara
Botanic Garden

ALSO SEE MAPS ON
PAGES 124 • 132 • 139

To
Santa
Barbara
Mission

46.

Mission Canyon
Powerline Road
EDISON CATWAY in
MISSION CANYON

47. Tunnel Trail to Mission Falls
MISSION CANYON

Hiking distance: 5.8 miles round trip
Hiking time: 3 hours
Elevation gain: 1,800 feet
Maps: U.S.G.S. Santa Barbara
Santa Barbara Front Country and Paradise Road map

Summary of hike: The Tunnel Trail is a historic and popular trail in the front country above Santa Barbara. The trail is named for a diversion tunnel built at the turn of the century that brings fresh water to Santa Barbara from the Gibraltar Reservoir. The four-mile trail climbs the Santa Ynez Mountains to East Camino Cielo Road on the mountain crest. This hike follows the first 2.9 miles to an overlook atop the ephemeral 200-foot Mission Falls. The panoramic views span across Santa Barbara and the Channel Islands. En route, the trail climbs the eastern wall of Mission Canyon past beautiful, weathered sandstone outcroppings.

Driving directions: SANTA BARBARA. From the Santa Barbara Mission, take Mission Canyon Road north towards the mountains for 0.6 miles to Foothill Road—turn right. Drive 0.2 miles to Mission Canyon Road and turn left. Continue 0.3 miles and bear left at a road split onto Tunnel Road. Drive 1.1 mile on Tunnel Road, and park on the right side of the road near the road's end.

Hiking directions: Walk to the end of Tunnel Road and past the trailhead gate. Head uphill and wind around the hillside, with great downward views of the city and ocean. At 0.7 miles, cross a bridge over Mission Creek and Little Fern Canyon Falls. Arrive at a trail split, where the paved trail ends. Bear left on the Jesusita Trail for 150 yards to the Tunnel Trail junction on the right. Take this footpath through the brush to a junction at 1.2 miles with a connector trail to the Mission Canyon Powerline Road. Cross the road, picking up the trail again. The steady, uphill trail passes the signed Rattlesnake Canyon–Tunnel Connector Trail at 2.3 miles on the right; stay left. Mission Falls can be seen across the canyon just before reaching this junction. Continue 0.7 miles to the creek crossing above the falls. It is a difficult scramble to see the waterfall up close, but it is possible to sit among the large sandstone boulders above the falls and marvel at the views. Return along the same route.

To continue hiking, it is another 1.2 miles north to East Camino Cielo Road. ■

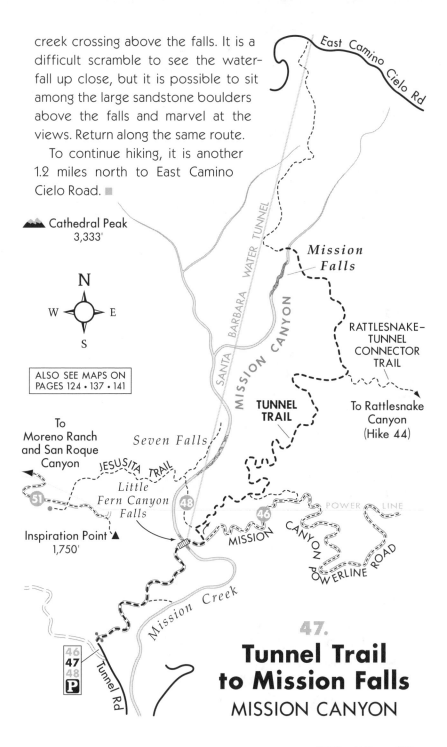

Cathedral Peak
3,333'

N
W — E
S

ALSO SEE MAPS ON
PAGES 124 • 137 • 141

To
Moreno Ranch
and San Roque
Canyon

JESUSITA TRAIL

Little
Fern Canyon
Falls

Inspiration Point
1,750'

Seven Falls

East Camino Cielo Rd

SANTA BARBARA WATER TUNNEL

Mission
Falls

MISSION CANYON

RATTLESNAKE-
TUNNEL
CONNECTOR
TRAIL

TUNNEL
TRAIL

To Rattlesnake
Canyon
(Hike 44)

POWER LINE

MISSION

CANYON

POWERLINE ROAD

Mission Creek

46
47
48
P

Tunnel Rd

47.
Tunnel Trail
to Mission Falls
MISSION CANYON

48. Seven Falls and Inspiration Point
MISSION CANYON

Hiking distance: 3.7 miles round trip
Hiking time: 2.5 hours
Elevation gain: 800 feet
Maps: U.S.G.S. Santa Barbara
　　　　Santa Barbara Front Country and Paradise Road map

Summary of hike: Seven Falls is in a stunning, sculpted gorge in Mission Canyon. Mission Creek cascades down the canyon and over boulders, creating more than a dozen waterfalls. The waterfalls drop into smooth bowls carved into the sandstone rock, forming deep, rock-rimmed pools. One mile beyond Seven Falls is Inspiration Point, a 1,750-foot scenic overlook with sweeping vistas of the Pacific Ocean, the Channel Islands, Santa Barbara, and Goleta.

Driving directions: SANTA BARBARA. From the Santa Barbara Mission, take Mission Canyon Road north towards the mountains for 0.6 miles to Foothill Road—turn right. Drive 0.2 miles to Mission Canyon Road and turn left. Continue 0.3 miles and bear left at a road split onto Tunnel Road. Drive 1.1 mile on Tunnel Road, and park on the right side of the road near the road's end.

Hiking directions: Walk to the end of Tunnel Road and past the trailhead gate. Head uphill and wind around the hillside, with great downward views of the city and ocean. At 0.7 miles, cross a bridge over Mission Creek and Little Fern Canyon Falls. Arrive at a trail split, where the paved trail ends. The right fork is the powerline access road (Hike 46). Bear left on the Jesusita Trail into Mission Canyon. In 150 yards is a footpath heading off to the right, which is the Tunnel Trail (Hike 47). Continue straight and descend into the forest to Mission Creek. Once across the creek, leave the Jesusita Trail for now, which leads to Inspiration Point. Instead, take the narrow path to the right up the west side of the canyon and parallel to the creek. Be careful! This trail is not maintained and can be very challenging. Boulder climbing

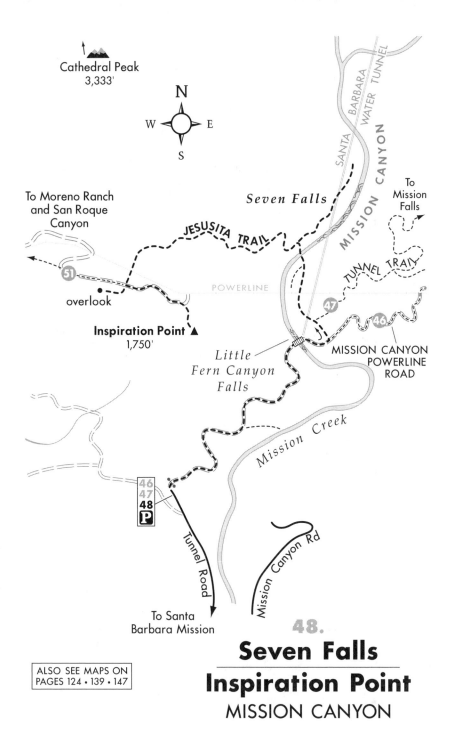

Cathedral Peak
3,333'

N
W   E
S

To Moreno Ranch
and San Roque
Canyon

Seven Falls

SANTA BARBARA WATER TUNNEL

MISSION CANYON

To
Mission
Falls

JESUSITA TRAIL

TUNNEL TRAIL

51

overlook

POWERLINE

47

46

Inspiration Point ▲
1,750'

Little
Fern Canyon
Falls

MISSION CANYON
POWERLINE
ROAD

Mission Creek

46
47
48
P

Tunnel Road

Mission Canyon Rd

To Santa
Barbara Mission

ALSO SEE MAPS ON
PAGES 124 • 139 • 147

48.
Seven Falls
Inspiration Point
MISSION CANYON

and branch dodging will be involved as you slowly work your way up the narrow gorge past an endless display of waterfalls, cascades, and pools. Choose your own swimming hole and turn-around spot. There are additional waterfalls and pools down canyon from the main trail.

To continue to Inspiration Point, follow the main Jesusita Trail from Mission Creek. The trail switchbacks one mile up the chaparral-covered canyon wall past sandstone outcroppings. At the summit is a T-junction with a powerline service road. Cross the road and curve right to the south edge of the ridge to an inspirational point, but not *the* Inspiration Point. Return to the power pole road, and walk a short distance east. Watch for a footpath on the right leading into the brush. This narrow path ends 300 yards ahead at Inspiration Point on a jumble of sand-stone boulders directly below Cathedral Peak. Return along the same route.

The Jesusita Trail continues 3 miles west into San Roque Canyon. Hike 50 climbs to Inspiration Point from the opposite direction, beginning in San Roque Canyon. ■

49. Stevens Park

Hiking distance: 1.8 miles round trip
Hiking time: 1 hour
Elevation gain: 150 feet
Maps: U.S.G.S. Santa Barbara

Summary of hike: Stevens Park is a beautiful oak-shaded park at the bottom of San Roque Canyon. San Roque Creek flows down the forested canyon through the length of Stevens Park. An easy creekside nature trail winds through the park past bed-rock mortars, ancient holes worn into the rock by Chumash Indians from grinding acorns into meal. The trail continues from the north end of the park, connecting to the Jesusita Trail (Hikes 50—52). The Jesusita Trail links San Roque Canyon with Mission Canyon. Stevens Park can be used an an alternative (and longer) trailhead for Hikes 50—52.

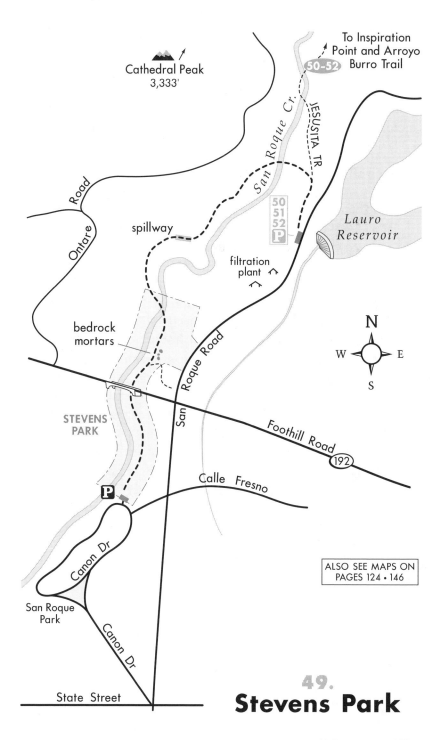

To Inspiration
Point and Arroyo
Burro Trail

50-52

Cathedral Peak
3,333'

San Roque Cr.

JESUSITA TR.

Road

Ontare

spillway

50
51
52
P

*Lauro
Reservoir*

filtration
plant

bedrock
mortars

San Roque Road

N

W ⊹ E

S

STEVENS
PARK

Foothill Road

192

P

Calle Fresno

ALSO SEE MAPS ON
PAGES 124 • 146

Canon Dr

San Roque
Park

Canon Dr

State Street

49.
Stevens Park

Driving directions: SANTA BARBARA. From Highway 101 in Santa Barbara, exit on Las Positas Road. Drive 1.2 miles north to Calle Fresno on the left, shortly after crossing State Street. (Las Positas Road becomes San Roque Road after crossing State Street.) Turn left one block to Canon Drive. Turn right and quickly turn right again into the posted park entrance. Park in the spaces 0.1 mile ahead.

Hiking directions: Walk to the upper (north) end of the parking lot and take the footpath along the east side of San Roque Creek. Enter the shady woodland and cross under the towering Foothill Road bridge. Pass through an oak and sycamore grove to an open grassy meadow on the right with views of Cathedral Peak. At the trail split, the right fork curves around the meadow and up the hill to San Roque Road, just north of Foothill Road. Go left and follow San Roque Creek upstream, passing a sandstone rock on the right with five bedrock mortars. Descend and cross the creek to an oak glen and a circle of large boulders overlooking the creek. Leave the creek and curve up the hillside. Cross over the ridge and continue to a second ridge at a concrete spillway outside the park boundary. Cross the spillway and follow the wide path along the left (west) side of the creek. Curve right and drop down to the banks of the creek again. Cross the creek, picking up the trail upstream. Climb the hill to a T-junction with the Jesusita Trail. The right fork leads 140 yards to the trailhead on San Roque Road. The left fork continues to the Arroyo Burro Trail, Moreno Ranch, and Inspiration Point (Hikes 50—52). Return to Stevens Park along the same route or hike a loop, returning on San Roque Road and Calle Fresno. ◼

50. Jesusita Trail in Lower San Roque Canyon

Hiking distance: 2.5 miles round trip
Hiking time: 1.5 hours
Elevation gain: 700 feet
Maps: U.S.G.S. Santa Barbara
       Santa Barbara Front Country and Paradise Road map

map
page 146

Summary of hike: The Jesusita Trail is a 4.5-mile trail that connects San Roque Canyon to Mission Canyon. This hike starts at Lauro Reservoir and heads up lower San Roque Canyon on the first 1.25 miles of the trail, parallel to a tributary of San Roque Creek. The trail winds through open, grassy meadows and lush, riparian habitat under the shade of oaks, sycamores, cottonwoods, and willows. There are numerous creek crossings.

Driving directions: SANTA BARBARA. From Highway 101 in Santa Barbara, exit on Las Positas Road. Drive 2 miles north to the posted trailhead parking area on the left, just beyond the filtration plant. (Las Positas Road becomes San Roque Road after crossing State Street.) The trailhead is located one mile above (north of) State Street.

Hiking directions: Take the posted trail downhill (north) into San Roque Canyon. Pass a junction on the left leading to Stevens Park (Hike 49). Traverse the east canyon wall above San Roque Creek. Descend and rock hop over the creek a couple of times. Follow the lazy watercourse upstream, winding through a shaded grove of twisted oaks, to a signed Y-fork at a half mile. To the left is the Arroyo Burro Trail (Hike 52).

Curve right—staying on the Jesusita Trail—and ascend a small hill. Emerge from the forest to a large open meadow. Pass through the grassy plateau, and descend back into the forest to the creek. Cross to the west side of the creek by a pool at one mile. Cross the creek three more times in quick succession, reaching the Moreno Ranch entrance at a private, unpaved road.

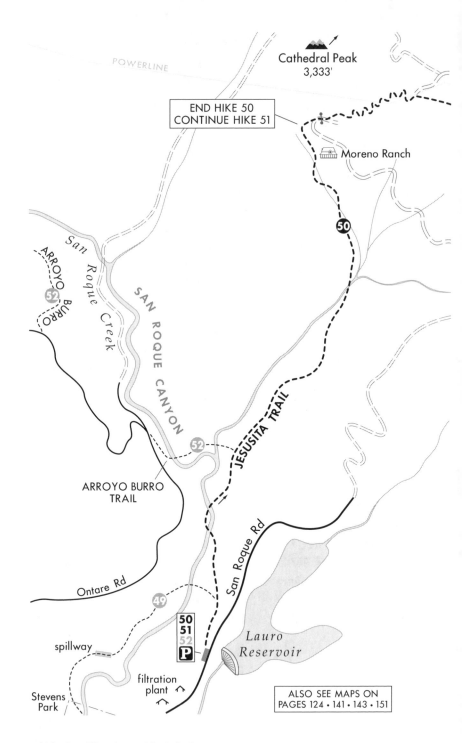

POWERLINE

Cathedral Peak
3,333'

END HIKE 50
CONTINUE HIKE 51

Moreno Ranch

50

San Roque Creek

ARROYO BURRO

52

SAN ROQUE CANYON

JESUSITA TRAIL

52

ARROYO BURRO
TRAIL

San Roque Rd

Ontare Rd

49

50
51
52
P

Lauro
Reservoir

spillway

filtration
plant

Stevens
Park

ALSO SEE MAPS ON
PAGES 124 • 141 • 143 • 151

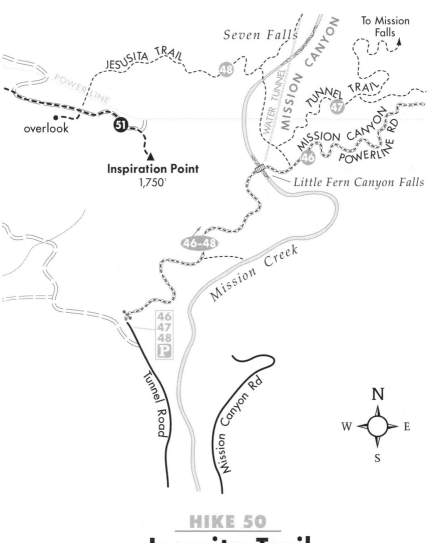

Seven Falls

To Mission Falls

JESUSITA TRAIL

POWERLINE

overlook

51

Inspiration Point
1,750'

WATER TUNNEL

MISSION CANYON

TUNNEL TRAIL

47

MISSION CANYON

POWERLINE RD

46

Little Fern Canyon Falls

46-48

Mission Creek

46
47
48
P

Tunnel Road

Mission Canyon Rd

N
W E
S

HIKE 50

Jesusita Trail
to Moreno Ranch

HIKE 51

Jesusita Trail
to Inspiration Point
from SAN ROQUE CANYON

This is the end of the lower canyon and our turn-around spot. The Jesusita Trail continues another 1.7 miles to Inspiration Point (Hike 51), then connects to Mission Canyon (Hikes 46—48). ■

51. Jesusita Trail to Inspiration Point
from SAN ROQUE CANYON

Hiking distance: 6 miles round trip
Hiking time: 3 hours
Elevation gain: 1,300 feet
Maps: U.S.G.S. Santa Barbara
      Santa Barbara Front Country and Paradise Road map

**map
page 146**

Summary of hike: The climb to Inspiration Point leads to the 1,750-foot perch below Cathedral Peak, with sweeping views of Santa Barbara, Goleta, the Pacific Ocean, and the Channel Islands. The point is accessed from the Jesusita Trail, which connects San Roque Canyon with Mission Canyon. This hike heads up the stream-fed San Roque Canyon through a shaded woodland, and traverses a ridge east of the canyon to Inspiration Point.

Driving directions: SANTA BARBARA. From Highway 101 in Santa Barbara, exit on Las Positas Road. Drive 2 miles north to the posted trailhead parking area on the left, just beyond the filtration plant. (Las Positas Road becomes San Roque Road after crossing State Street.)

Hiking directions: Reference Hike 50—follow the hiking directions to the Moreno Ranch entrance. From the ranch, walk up the unpaved road 50 yards and curve right, following the trail sign. Pass through a trail gate, and continue to the east on the unpaved road. Cross a stream and pick up the posted footpath on the left. Traverse the north slope of the rock-walled canyon. Cross over to the south canyon wall and climb a series of 12 switchbacks out of the canyon to a magnificent vista of Santa Barbara and the coastline. Head east through the chaparral, zig-zagging up the mountain while overlooking the city and ocean. Pass large sculpted sandstone formations on the right. Cross under power lines to the ridge at a junction with the power pole road. Bear left 50 yards along the road to footpaths on both the left and right. To the left, the Jesusita Trail descends from the ridge into Mission Canyon and Seven Falls (Hike 48). The right path curves along the south edge of the ridge to what many believe is Inspiration Point, and it certainly is inspirational. After resting and savoring the views, return to the power pole road. A short distance east, the road begins dropping slightly. Watch for a narrow footpath on the right that leads into the chaparral. Take the side path 300 yards to the actual Inspiration Point, located at a jumble of sandstone boulders directly beneath Cathedral Peak. Return along the same route back to the trailhead. ∎

52. Arroyo Burro Trail
SAN ROQUE CANYON

Hiking distance: 6 miles round trip
Hiking time: 3.5 hours
Elevation gain: 1,250 feet

**map
page 151**

Maps: U.S.G.S. Santa Barbara
Santa Barbara Front Country and Paradise Road map

Summary of hike: The Arroyo Burro Trail is one of Santa Barbara's historic trails. It was once a Chumash Indian route from the coast to the Santa Ynez Valley and the San Rafael Range. Prospectors later used it as a route to the quicksilver mines. For years, the route was closed to public use due to a three-mile section that ran through the San Roque Ranch. After decades, the ranch allowed a trail easement and access has been restored.

The trail leads six miles from the base of the Santa Ynez Mountains to the 3,400-foot ridge at East Camino Cielo Road. The Arroyo Burro Trail then continues north of East Camino Cielo Road all the way to the Santa Ynez River (Hike 76). This hike follows the first half of the lower trail in San Roque Canyon, gaining 1,250 feet to the upper knolls above Barger Canyon and an overlook atop weather-carved, sandstone Sespe formations. From the perch are sweeping vistas of the Goleta coastline. Part of the trail has been lost due to development and now includes a couple of sections of paved and dirt roads.

Driving directions: SANTA BARBARA. From Highway 101 in Santa Barbara, exit on Las Positas Road. Drive 2 miles north to the posted trailhead parking area on the left, just beyond the filtration plant. (Las Positas Road becomes San Roque Road after crossing State Street.) The trailhead is located one mile above (north of) State Street.

Hiking directions: Take the posted trail downhill (north) into San Roque Canyon. Pass the junction on the left leading to Stevens Park (Hike 49). Traverse the east canyon wall above San Roque Creek. Descend and rock hop over the creek a couple of times. Follow the watercourse upstream, winding through a shaded grove of twisted oaks to a signed Y-fork at a half mile. The Jesusita Trail veers right (Hikes 50—51).

Take the Arroyo Burro Trail to the left, and cross San Roque Creek. Weave through the oaks at an easy uphill grade 200 yards to a paved private road and trail easement. Follow the road uphill, with great vistas of the Santa Ynez Mountains, Santa Barbara, Goleta, the ocean, and the Channel Islands. Atop the ridge, between San Roque Canyon and Barger Canyon, is a road split and a sign for the public trail. Take the footpath and veer right, staying in San Roque Canyon. Traverse the hillside—with city, ocean, and mountain views—to a saddle with an unpaved road on San Roque Ranch lands. Take the dirt road to the left, following the trail signs. Climb the steep hill, passing water tanks on the right. Meander up and down the undulating ridge road to the powerpoles. At the second tower is a signed footpath on the right. Weave through the chaparral to gorgeous red sandstone outcroppings jutting above the scrub. Meander up the formations, passing small caves, overhangs, and perches. This is the turn-around point and a perfect place to rest and take in the surrounding vistas.

To extend the hike, the trail climbs another steep 700 feet through tall chaparral to the white-colored Coldwater Sandstone formations, then another steep 900 feet, reaching East Camino Cielo Road at 6 miles. ■

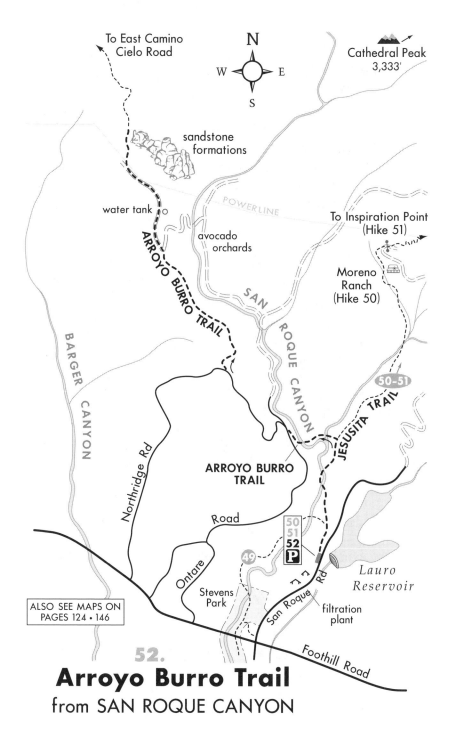

To East Camino
Cielo Road

N
W · E
S

Cathedral Peak
3,333'

sandstone
formations

POWERLINE

water tank

avocado
orchards

To Inspiration Point
(Hike 51)

ARROYO BURRO TRAIL

SAN ROQUE CANYON

Moreno
Ranch
(Hike 50)

BARGER CANYON

JESUSITA TRAIL

50-51

Northridge Rd

ARROYO BURRO
TRAIL

Road

50
51
52
P

49

Ontare

Lauro
Reservoir

ALSO SEE MAPS ON
PAGES 124 · 146

Stevens
Park

San Roque Rd

filtration
plant

Foothill Road

52.

Arroyo Burro Trail
from SAN ROQUE CANYON

53. Shoreline Park

Hiking distance: 1—2 miles round trip
Hiking time: 30 minutes—1 hour
Elevation gain: Level
Maps: U.S.G.S. Santa Barbara

Summary of hike: Shoreline Park is a long and narrow 15-acre park along La Mesa Bluff. From the landscaped bluffs are panoramic vistas of Leadbetter Beach, the Santa Barbara Harbor, Stearns Wharf, the Channel Islands, and the Santa Ynez Mountains. The grassy park hugs the ocean bluffs on the west side of Santa Barbara Point. This paved, level path is an easy stroll along the marine terrace. A stairway leads down to the shore for a sandy beach stroll at the base of the cliffs.

Driving directions: SANTA BARBARA. From Stearns Wharf at the south end of State Street in Santa Barbara, drive 1.4 miles west on Cabrillo Boulevard (which becomes Shoreline Drive) to the first Shoreline Park parking lot on the left.

Hiking directions: The paved path heads west along the oceanfront bluffs between the cliff's edge and Shoreline Drive. At 0.3 miles, a stairway leads down to the sandy beach and shoreline. Along the way are benches and information stations about the Chumash Indians, the Channel Islands, gray whales, and dolphins. A half mile ahead, at the west end of the park, is a picnic area and another parking lot. From the east end of the park, a steep path descends through cypress trees to Leadbetter Beach and tidepools.

To continue hiking along the shoreline, return to the stairway and descend to the beach. Stroll along the sand beneath the cliffs. ■

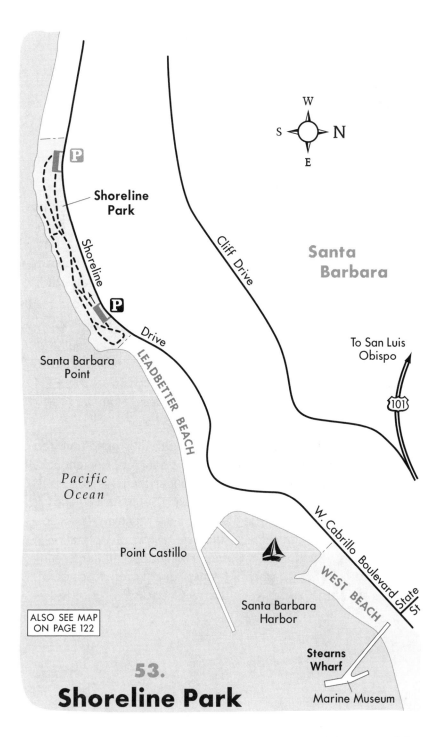

W N S E

P

Shoreline Park

Shoreline

P

Drive

Cliff Drive

Santa Barbara

To San Luis Obispo

101

Santa Barbara Point

LEADBETTER BEACH

Pacific Ocean

Point Castillo

W. Cabrillo Boulevard

State St

WEST BEACH

Santa Barbara Harbor

ALSO SEE MAP ON PAGE 122

Stearns Wharf

Marine Museum

53.
Shoreline Park

54. Elings Park
THE SIERRA CLUB TRAIL

Hiking distance: 1.3-mile loop
Hiking time: 40 minutes
Elevation gain: 300 feet
Maps: U.S.G.S. Santa Barbara
Santa Barbara Front Country and Paradise Road map

Summary of hike: Elings Park (formerly Las Positas Friendship Park) is a 236-acre hilltop park with a developed north side that includes baseball and soccer fields, gazebos, picnic areas, a war memorial, and an amphitheater. The natural south side of the park has nature trails leading up to a ridge overlooking Santa Barbara, with 360-degree views of the ocean harbor, the Channel Islands, and the Santa Ynez Mountains.

Driving directions: SANTA BARBARA. From Highway 101 in Santa Barbara, exit on Las Positas Road. Drive 1.2 miles south (toward the ocean) to the Elings Park entrance on the left at 1298 Las Positas Road. Take the park road—Jerry Harwin Parkway—0.4 miles to the signed trailhead on the right across from the soccer fields. Park in the lots on the left or straight ahead.

Hiking directions: Cross the park road to the signed trailhead and a junction. Take the right fork up a series of switchbacks. Various side paths may be confusing, but all the trails lead up to Vanyo Point, the hilltop perch overlooking South Park and Jesuit Hill. At the top, the 360-degree views are stunning. The Sierra Club Trail follows the ridge to the east before sharply curving back to the west. This begins the winding descent, completing the loop back at the trailhead. A steep, direct route leads down the center of the hill between the switchbacks. ■

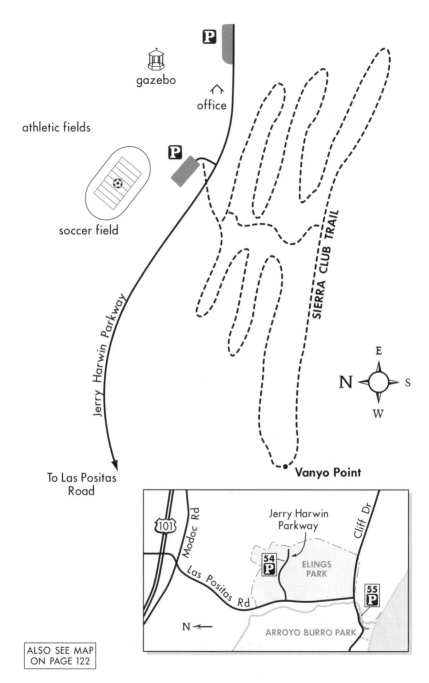

gazebo

office

P

P

athletic fields

soccer field

Jerry Harwin Parkway

To Las Positas
Road

SIERRA CLUB TRAIL

● **Vanyo Point**

N

E
S
W

Jerry Harwin
Parkway

101

Modoc Rd

Cliff Dr

Las Positas Rd

54 P

ELINGS
PARK

55 P

N ←

ARROYO BURRO PARK

ALSO SEE MAP
ON PAGE 122

54. Elings Park

55. Douglas Family Preserve

Hiking distance: 1.5 miles round trip
Hiking time: 1 hour
Elevation gain: 150 feet
Maps: U.S.G.S. Santa Barbara
　　　　Santa Barbara Front Country and Paradise Road map

Summary of hike: The Douglas Family Preserve is a 70-acre grassy mesa with over 2,200 feet of rare, undeveloped ocean frontage. The dog-friendly preserve is covered with mature coast live oak, eucalyptus trees, and cypress woodlands. Migrating monarch butterflies cluster in the eucaluptus grove. The trail loops around the flat, 150-foot mesa along the edge of the cliffs. From the bluffs are expansive views of the Santa Barbara coast, from Point Mugu to Gaviota. Below the cliffs is the picturesque Arroyo Burro Beach (locally known as Hendry's Beach). There are picnic areas and a paved biking and walking path.

Driving directions: SANTA BARBARA. From Highway 101 in Santa Barbara, exit on Las Positas Road. Head 1.8 miles south (towards the ocean) to Cliff Drive and turn right. Continue 0.2 miles to the Arroyo Burro Beach parking lot on the left and park.

Hiking directions: From the parking lot, walk east on Cliff Drive to Las Positas Road. From here, the Oak Grove Trail, a narrow road, heads south past a chained gate into the forest. The trail curves left through the shady canopy and up the hill to the mesa, where the trail levels out. Continue south along the eastern edge of the open space. Along the way, several paths intersect from the right and several access trails merge from the left. At the bluffs overlooking the ocean, head west along the cliffs. At the west end of the cliffs is an overlook of Arroyo Burro Beach. The trail curves to the right and loops back to a junction at the top of the hill. Head left, retracing your steps down the hill and back to the parking lot. ∎

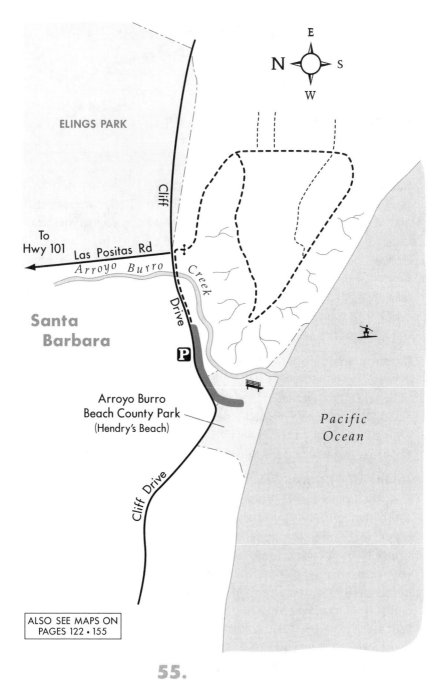

ELINGS PARK

Cliff

To
Hwy 101   Las Positas Rd

Arroyo Burro   Creek

Drive

**Santa
Barbara**

P

Arroyo Burro
Beach County Park
(Hendry's Beach)

Cliff Drive

N · E · S · W

*Pacific
Ocean*

ALSO SEE MAPS ON
PAGES 122 · 155

**55.
Douglas Family Preserve**

56. San Antonio Creek Trail
SAN ANTONIO CANYON PARK

Hiking distance: 3.4 miles round trip
Hiking time: 1.5 hours
Elevation gain: 300 feet
Maps: U.S.G.S. Goleta
Santa Barbara Front Country and Paradise Road map

Summary of hike: San Antonio Canyon Park is a long, narrow park that follows San Antonio Creek through shady woodlands and grassy meadows from Cathedral Oaks Road to San Marcos Pass Road. Access to the dog-friendly park is from Tuckers Grove County Park, a developed park with picnic facilities, ball fields, and a playground. The San Antonio Creek Trail is an easy hike through San Antonio Canyon along the watercourse of the creek. The trail weaves through meadows and a mixed forest of oaks, sycamores, and bay laurel.

Driving directions: SANTA BARBARA. From Santa Barbara, drive northbound on Highway 101, and exit on Turnpike Road in Goleta. Turn right and drive 0.6 miles north to Cathedral Oaks Road. Drive straight—through the intersection—entering Tuckers Grove Park. Bear to the right through the parking lot, and drive 0.3 miles to the last parking area.

Hiking directions: From the parking lot, hike up the road and past the upper picnic ground (Kiwanis Meadow). Cross through the opening in the log fence to the left, heading towards the creek. Take the trail upstream along the east side of San Antonio Creek. Numerous spur trails lead down to the creek. At one mile, rock hop across the creek, and continue to a second crossing located between steep canyon walls. After crossing, the trail ascends a hill to a bench near a concrete flood-control dam. Head left across the top of the dam. The trail proceeds to the right (upstream) and recrosses San Antonio Creek. The forested canyon trail passes alongside a chainlink fence on the east side of the stream. The trail ends at 1.7 miles under a bridge, where the trail intersects with Highway 154. Return along the same trail. ■

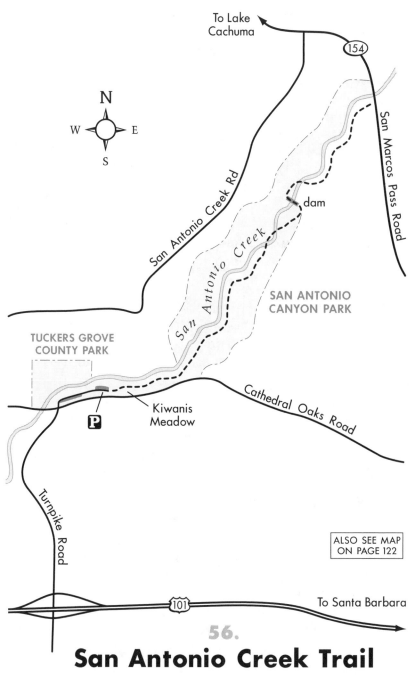

To Lake Cachuma

154

San Marcos Pass Road

San Antonio Creek Rd

dam

San Antonio Creek

SAN ANTONIO
CANYON PARK

TUCKERS GROVE
COUNTY PARK

Cathedral Oaks Road

Kiwanis
Meadow

P

Turnpike Road

ALSO SEE MAP
ON PAGE 122

101

To Santa Barbara

56.

San Antonio Creek Trail
SAN ANTONIO CANYON PARK

57. More Mesa

Hiking distance: 2.6 miles round trip
Hiking time: 1.5 hours
Elevation gain: Near level
Maps: U.S.G.S. Goleta

Summary of hike: More Mesa is an undeveloped 300-acre oceanfront expanse in Goleta. The blufftop mesa includes oak woodlands, riparian habitats, and wetlands that connect to Atascadero Creek. The gently sloping grassland is marbled with hiking, biking, and equestrian trails. The main trail follows the edge of the sandstone bluffs 120 feet above the ocean. The panoramic views extend from the Santa Ynez Mountains to the Channel Islands. The secluded, mile-long beach at the base of the mesa is clothing optional.

Driving directions: SANTA BARBARA. From Santa Barbara, drive northbound on Highway 101, and exit on Turnpike Road in Goleta. Turn left (south) and drive 0.4 miles to Hollister Avenue. Turn left (east) and go 0.3 miles to the first signal at Puente Drive. Turn right and continue 0.7 miles to Mockingbird Lane. (En route, Puente Drive becomes Vieja Drive.) Parking is not allowed on Mockingbird Lane, so park on Vieja Drive by Mockingbird Lane.

To access More Mesa from the west end, take Highway 101 to Patterson Avenue. Drive south 1.6 miles to the trailhead by the Orchid Drive Sign at the right bend in the road.

Hiking directions: From the east trailhead, walk up Mockingbird Lane to the hiking path at the end of the street. Pass the metal trailhead gate, and cross the wide, sloping marine terrace towards the ocean. At 0.6 miles, the path reaches a grove of mature eucalyptus trees lining the edge of the cliffs 120 feet above the ocean. A steep, narrow path descends down the cliffs to the secluded sandy beach. The left fork leads a short distance to a fenced residential area. Take the right fork, following the edge of the bluffs to the west. At 1.3 miles, the trail ends by oceanfront homes. Various interconnecting trails crisscross the open space.

From the west end trailhead (Shoreline Drive), walk through the lush riparian coridor on the south side of Atascadero Creek. Pass under an oak canopy and emerge at a T-junction at 0.3 miles. Both paths gently climb out of the arroyo to the network of informal paths that marble More Mesa. ■

Patterson Ave
To Hwy 101

Maria Ygnacio Cr.

Shoreline Drive

Orchid Drive

P WEST TRAILHEAD

W
S — N
E

Atascadero Creek

OBERN TRAIL

Santa Barbara

Pacific Ocean

CLIFFS

MORE

MESA

58

Hidden Oaks
Golf Course

Vieja Drive

P EAST
TRAILHEAD

Mockingbird Ln

FENCE

Pueta
Drive

To Hwy 101

ALSO SEE MAPS ON
PAGES 122 • 165

57.
More Mesa

58. Obern Trail
(formerly Atascadero Creek Bikeway)

Hiking distance: 6.4 miles round trip
Hiking time: 3 hours
Elevation gain: Level
Maps: U.S.G.S. Goleta
      Santa Barbara Front Country and Paradise Road map

map
page 164

Summary of hike: The Obern Trail (formerly the Atascadero Creek Bikeway) is a seven-mile-long trail that follows the lower end of Atascadero Creek to Goleta Beach County Park, where the creek empties into the Pacific Ocean. The multi-use trail—open to hiking, jogging, biking, and equestrian use—passes through creekside riparian habitat and cultivated fields, with views of the creeks and Santa Ynez Mountains. This section of the level trail parallels Atascadero Creek between Puente Drive and the Goleta Slough. The riparian habitat is home to blue herons, egrets, coots, mallards, kingfishers, and redwing blackbirds.

Information panels along the route describe the stories of early settlers and travelers through the area, including George and Vie Obern, Chumash rancher Jose Maria Ygnacio, and the Juan Bautista de Anza historic expedition in 1775—1776. The de Anza expedition of 240 soldiers and families walked nearly 1,300 miles from Sonora, Mexico, to found the mission and presidio in San Francisco. The Patterson Ave Trailhead was the site of their camp on February 25, 1776. According to de Anza's diary, the group slept along the waterways now called Maria Ygnacio Creek and Atascadero Creek.

Driving directions: The Obern Trail may be accessed from three main points.

THIS HIKE BEGINS FROM THE PUENTE DRIVE TRAILHEAD. From Highway 101 in Goleta, exit on Turnpike Road. Drive 0.4 miles south to Hollister Avenue. Turn left and go 0.3 miles to Puente Drive, the first signal. Turn right and drive 0.35 miles to the signed Obern Trail on the right, directly across from More Mesa Drive. Park in the pullout on the right.

PATTERSON AVENUE TRAILHEAD: From Highway 101 in Goleta, exit on Patterson Avenue. Drive 1.2 miles south to the bridge crossing over Atascadero Creek. Park in the large pullout on the right, just before crossing the creek.

GOLETA BEACH PARK TRAILHEAD. From Highway 101 in Goleta, exit on Ward Memorial Boulevard/Highway 217. Continue 2 miles to the Sandspit Road exit, and turn left at the stop sign. Drive 0.3 miles to the Goleta Beach Park parking lot turnoff. Turn right and cross the lagoon into the parking lot.

Hiking directions: FROM THE PUENTE DRIVE TRAILHEAD. Take the paved biking–hiking path west, parallel to Atascadero Creek on the right. Pass the creek's confluence with a tributary, and skirt the edge of Hidden Oaks Golf Course to a bridge. Cross the bridge over Atascadero Creek to a T-junction. The right fork follows the tributary upstream to Hollister Avenue. Bear left and continue downstream on the north side of the creek amid willow, sycamore, cottonwood, coast live oak, and mudwort trees. Leave the paved route and take the parallel dirt trail on the left. Stroll through the riparian vegetation on the low bluff above the creek. At 1.6 miles is a junction at the confluence of Maria Ygnacio Creek. The right fork follows Ygnacio Creek north to Hollister Avenue.

Cross the bridge over Ygnacio Creek to Patterson Avenue. On the east side of the road is a historic site. From September 1775 through June 1776, Juan Bautista de Anza and more than 240 soldiers and families traveled 1,296 miles on foot and horseback from Sonora, Mexico, to found the mission and presidio at San Francisco. As recorded in his diary, on February 25, 1776, they camped at this sight along Maria Ignacio Creek, just above its confluence with Atascadero Creek.

Cross Patterson Avenue and continue west through the lush corridor. A dirt path parallels the paved bike path along the creek. At 2.3 miles, the creek widens to the size of a river, and the vegetation gives way to agricultural fields. The views open to the Santa Ynez Mountains. The unpaved footpath follows the low bluff. Near Ward Memorial Boulevard, the dirt path merges with the paved Obern Trail. Curve left and cross a bridge spanning San Pedro Creek, just above its confluence with Atascadero Creek. Cross another bridge over Goleta Slough to Goleta Beach County Park, where the trail ends. Return by retracing your steps.

To continue hiking, Hike 59 can be accessed at the west end of Goleta Beach County Park. ■

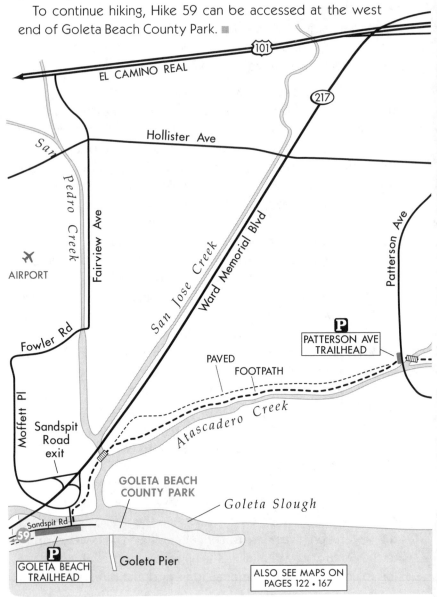

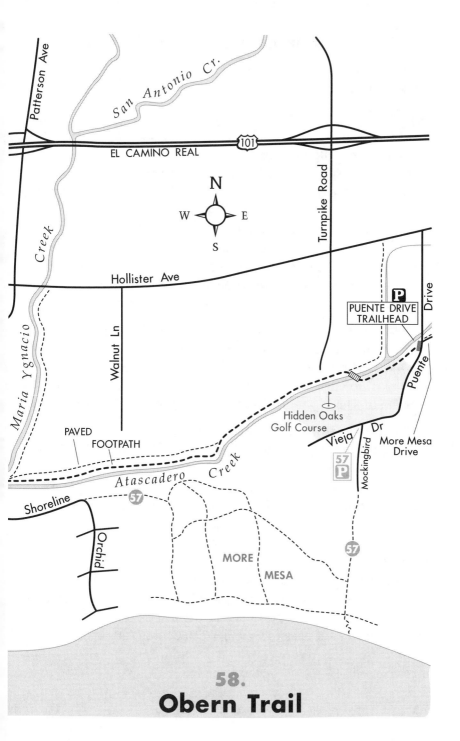

58.
Obern Trail

59. Goleta Beach and the UCSB Lagoon

Hiking distance: 4 miles round trip
Hiking time: 2 hours
Elevation gain: 50 feet
Maps: U.S.G.S. Goleta

Summary of hike: Goleta Beach County Park, sheltered by Goleta Point, is a long, narrow peninsula sandwiched between Goleta Slough and the ocean. This hike begins on the park's grassy lawn backed by the white sand beach, west of Goleta Pier, and follows the coastal cliffs into the University of California—Santa Barbara. The trail circles the brackish waters of the UCSB Lagoon to Goleta Point (also called Campus Point). The ocean surrounds the point on three sides, where there are tidepools and a beautiful coastline.

Driving directions: GOLETA. From Highway 101 in Goleta, exit onto Ward Memorial Boulevard/Highway 217. Continue 2 miles to the Sandspit Road exit, and turn left at the stop sign, heading towards Goleta Beach Park. Drive 0.3 miles to the beach parking lot turnoff. Turn right and cross the lagoon into the parking lot.

Hiking directions: Head west along the park lawn to the bluffs overlooking the ocean. Continue past the natural bridge, and walk parallel to the cliff edge into the university. At the marine laboratory, take the right fork, crossing the road to the UCSB Lagoon on Goleta Point. Take the path to the right around the northeast side of the lagoon. At the north end, the trail joins a walking path in the university. At the west end of the lagoon, the trail heads south on the return section of the loop. Once back at the ocean, climb up the bluff to the left. Continue around the lagoon, and descend the steps between the lagoon and the ocean. Complete the loop back at the marine laboratory and bluffs. Head east, back to Goleta Beach County Park. ■

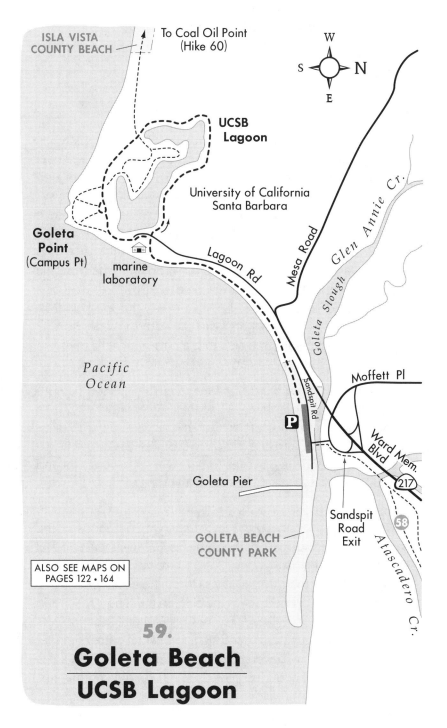

ISLA VISTA
COUNTY BEACH

To Coal Oil Point
(Hike 60)

W N
S E

**UCSB
Lagoon**

University of California
Santa Barbara

**Goleta
Point**
(Campus Pt)

marine
laboratory

Lagoon Rd

Mesa Road

Glen Annie Cr.

Goleta Slough

*Pacific
Ocean*

Moffett Pl

Sandspit Rd

Ward Mem. Blvd

217

P

Goleta Pier

GOLETA BEACH
COUNTY PARK

Sandspit
Road
Exit

58

Atascadero Cr.

ALSO SEE MAPS ON
PAGES 122 • 164

59.

Goleta Beach
UCSB Lagoon

60. Coal Oil Point Reserve

Hiking distance: 3 miles round trip
Hiking time: 1.5 hours
Elevation gain: Near level
Maps: U.S.G.S. Goleta and Dos Pueblos Canyon

Summary of hike: Coal Oil Point, located in the Isla Vista section of Goleta, is named for its numerous natural oil seeps near the coast. At the point is a rocky reef and a great tidepool area. Coal Oil Point Reserve has several coastal wildlife habitats set aside for research, education, and preservation. The 117-acre ecological study enclave, managed by UCSB, has undisturbed coastal dunes, eucalyptus groves, grasslands, a salt marsh, and a 45-acre lagoon. The trail parallels the eroding bluffs from the western edge of Isla Vista to the reserve. Devereaux Lagoon, in the heart of the reserve, is a seasonally flooded tidal lagoon where a mix of freshwater and saltwater provides several coastal lagoon habitats. The slough is a bird-watcher's paradise, home to a wide variety of native and migratory species.

Driving directions: SANTA BARBARA. From Santa Barbara, drive northbound on Highway 101 to the Glen Annie Road/Storke Road exit in Goleta. Turn left on Storke Road, and drive 1.3 miles to El Colegio Road. Turn left and drive 0.2 miles to Camino Corto. Turn right and continue 0.5 miles to Del Playa Drive. Turn right and park in the parking area at the end of the block.

Hiking directions: Take the well-defined path to the ocean bluffs and a T-junction. To the left, a stairway descends to the beach, and the blufftop path continues 0.2 miles east to Del Playa Park and Isla Vista County Beach. Take the right fork, parallel to the edge of the cliffs, and pass through a eucalyptus grove. Several surfing paths lead down the cliffs to the sandy beach and tidepools. The main trail leads to the Coal Oil Point Reserve. Pass through the habitat gate to Sands Beach. Several paths meander across the dunes to Devereaux Lagoon. The Pond Trail circles the lagoon, returning on the paved Slough Road along the east side of the lagoon. You may also follow the beach for another mile northwest to the Ellwood Bluffs and the Coronado Butterfly Preserve (Hikes 61 and 62). ■

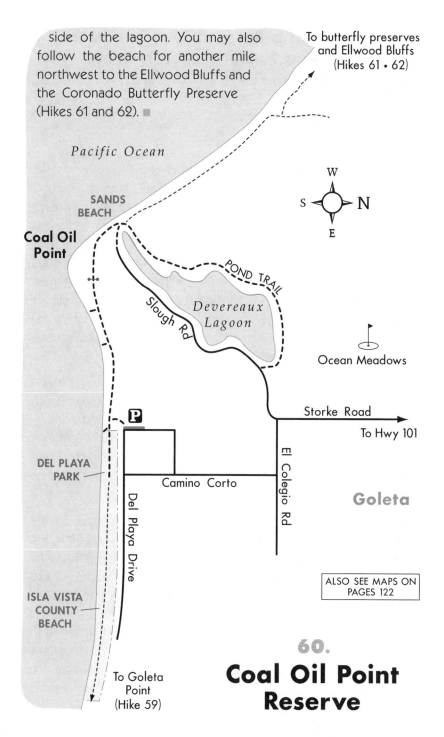

To butterfly preserves and Ellwood Bluffs (Hikes 61 • 62)

Pacific Ocean

SANDS BEACH

Coal Oil Point

POND TRAIL

Devereaux Lagoon

Slough Rd

Ocean Meadows

Storke Road

To Hwy 101

P

DEL PLAYA PARK

Camino Corto

El Colegio Rd

Goleta

Del Playa Drive

ALSO SEE MAPS ON PAGES 122

ISLA VISTA COUNTY BEACH

To Goleta Point (Hike 59)

60.
Coal Oil Point Reserve

61. Coronado Butterfly Preserve and Ellwood Main Monarch Grove

Hiking distance: 1 mile round trip
Hiking time: 30 minutes
Elevation gain: 40 feet
Maps: U.S.G.S. Dos Pueblos Canyon

Summary of hike: The Coronado Butterfly Preserve was established as a nature preserve by the Land Trust for Santa Barbara in 1998. The 9.3-acre preserve and the Ellwood Main Monarch Grove are among the largest monarch butterfly wintering sites in southern California. Thousands of monarch butterflies hang from the eucalyptus trees in thick clusters and fly wildly around. The peak season for the migrating butterfly runs from December through February. Within the small preserve are woodlands, native coastal sage scrub, meadows, and a creek. Interconnecting trails link the preserves with the Ellwood Bluffs and beach to the west (Hike 62) and Coal Oil Point to the east (Hike 60).

Driving directions: SANTA BARBARA. From Santa Barbara, drive northbound on Highway 101 to the Glen Annie Road/Storke Road exit in Goleta. Turn left on Storke Road, and drive a quarter mile to Hollister Avenue, the first intersection. Turn right on Hollister Avenue, and continue 1.1 mile to Coronado Drive. Turn left and go 0.3 miles to the posted butterfly preserve on the right. Park alongside the street.

Hiking directions: Follow the wide path up the hill to the monarch butterfly information station. Gently descend into the large eucalyptus grove in the heart of the Coronado Butterfly Preserve. Cross a footbridge over seasonal Devereaux Creek to a T-junction. The right fork meanders through the grove to the west, connecting with the trails along Ellwood Bluffs (Hike 62). Bear left and head deeper into the grove to another junction. The left fork returns to the south end of Coronado Drive. Take the right fork, meandering through the Ellwood Main Monarch Grove. Climb up the hill through the towering eucalyptus trees to an expansive open meadow. A network of interconnecting trails weaves across the bluffs. At the south edge of the 80-foot ocean bluffs, the left fork leads to Devereaux Lagoon and Coal Oil Point (Hike 60). The right fork heads west, connecting with Ellwood Bluffs. ▪

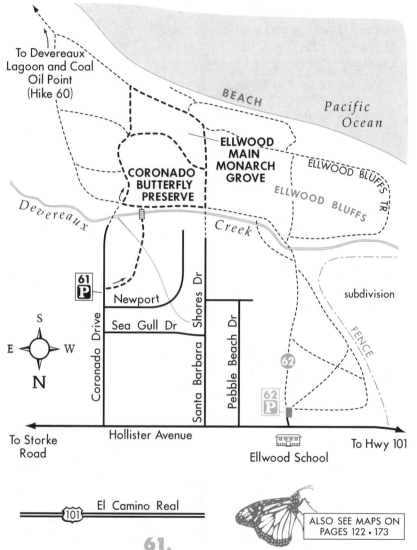

ALSO SEE MAPS ON PAGES 122 • 173

61.

Coronado Butterfly Preserve
Ellwood Main Monarch Grove

62. Ellwood Bluffs

SANTA BARBARA SHORES COUNTY PARK
and SPERLING PRESERVE at ELLWOOD MESA

Hiking distance: 3.5 miles round trip
Hiking time: 1.5 hours
Elevation gain: Level
Maps: U.S.G.S. Dos Pueblos Canyon
       Santa Barbara County Recreational Map Series #8

Summary of hike: Santa Barbara Shores County Park has a network of interconnecting trails across 200 acres of flat grasslands with eucalyptus groves, vernal pools, and spectacular ocean views. The Ellwood Bluffs Trail parallels 80-foot cliffs along the ocean's edge. The eucalyptus groves in the area are home to monarch butterflies during the winter months.

Driving directions: SANTA BARBARA. From Santa Barbara, drive northbound on Highway 101 to the Glen Annie Road/ Storke Road exit in Goleta. Turn left on Storke Road, and drive a quarter mile to Hollister Avenue, the first intersection. Turn right on Hollister Avenue, and continue 1.5 miles to the Santa Barbara County Park parking lot on the left, directly across from Ellwood School.

Hiking directions: The right fork follows the west edge of the parkland, skirting a walled subdivision. Take the trail straight ahead. Walk south along the edge of the eucalyptus grove to seasonal Devereaux Creek. Cross the creek to the open grasslands and veer to the right. Follow the path as it curves left and heads south to the bluffs, overlooking the ocean. Follow the trail to the left along the cliff's edge. Several trails cut across the open space to the left, returning to the trailhead for a shorter hike. At 0.5 miles is a junction with a beach access trail heading down to the mile-long beach. Farther along the bluffs, take the trail inland, heading north along a row of eucalyptus trees. As you approach the eucalyptus groves, return along the prominent footpath to the left. The trail returns to the trailhead on the edge of the open meadows next to the groves.

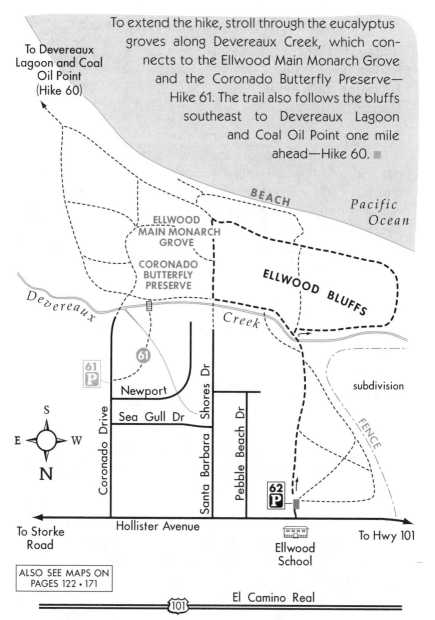

To extend the hike, stroll through the eucalyptus groves along Devereaux Creek, which connects to the Ellwood Main Monarch Grove and the Coronado Butterfly Preserve—Hike 61. The trail also follows the bluffs southeast to Devereaux Lagoon and Coal Oil Point one mile ahead—Hike 60. ■

To Devereaux Lagoon and Coal Oil Point (Hike 60)

BEACH

Pacific Ocean

ELLWOOD MAIN MONARCH GROVE

CORONADO BUTTERFLY PRESERVE

ELLWOOD BLUFFS

Devereaux

Creek

61 P

Newport

Sea Gull Dr

Coronado Drive

Santa Barbara Shores Dr

Pebble Beach Dr

subdivision

FENCE

S

E ← → W

N

62 P

To Storke Road

Hollister Avenue

Ellwood School

To Hwy 101

ALSO SEE MAPS ON PAGES 122 • 171

101 El Camino Real

62. **Ellwood Bluffs**
SANTA BARBARA SHORES COUNTY PARK
SPERLING PRESERVE at ELLWOOD MESA

63. Los Carneros County Park

Hiking distance: 1.5-mile loop
Hiking time: 1 hour
Elevation gain: Level
Maps: U.S.G.S. Goleta

Summary of hike: Los Carneros County Park in Goleta is a nature preserve and bird habitat with a large 25-acre lake. A network of trails meanders across the park through rolling meadows and a forest of eucalyptus, oak, and pine trees. A wooden bridge crosses the northern end of the lake among tule and willows. At the trailhead is the Stow House, a Victorian home built in 1872, and the South Coast Railroad Museum, the original Goleta Train Station built in 1901. Both sites offer tours and exhibits.

Driving directions: SANTA BARBARA. From Santa Barbara, drive northbound on Highway 101 to Los Carneros Road in Goleta. Turn right and drive 0.3 miles north to the Stow House and Railroad Museum parking lot on the right. Turn right and park.

Hiking directions: From the parking lot, follow the rail fence past the Stow House. Continue straight ahead, following the sign to Los Carneros Lake and a junction. Take the paved path to the right, overlooking the lake. At the south end of the lake, a trail leads to the left and down to the lakeshore. Follow the shoreline around the southern end of the lake before heading up along the lake's east side. As you head north, the Santa Ynez Mountains are in full view. Several trails loop around the park, intersecting with each other. At the north end of the lake, cross a wooden bridge over the willow and reed wetland. After crossing, the trail leads to the paved road near the trailhead, completing the loop. ∎

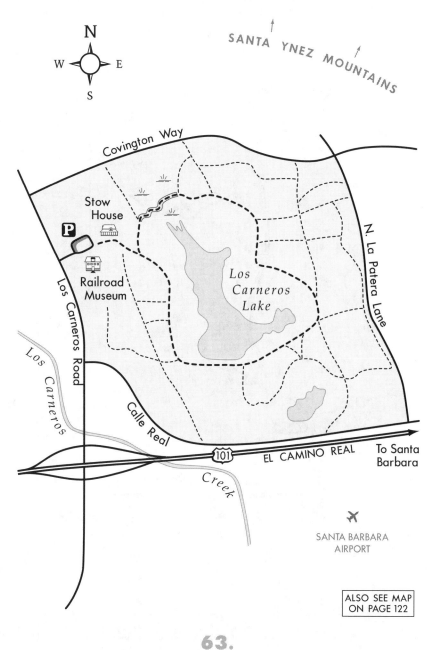

N
W — E
S

SANTA YNEZ MOUNTAINS

Covington Way

Stow House

P

Railroad Museum

Los Carneros Road

Los Carneros

Calle Real

Los Carneros Lake

N. La Patera Lane

101 EL CAMINO REAL To Santa Barbara

Creek

✈
SANTA BARBARA
AIRPORT

ALSO SEE MAP
ON PAGE 122

63.
Los Carneros County Park

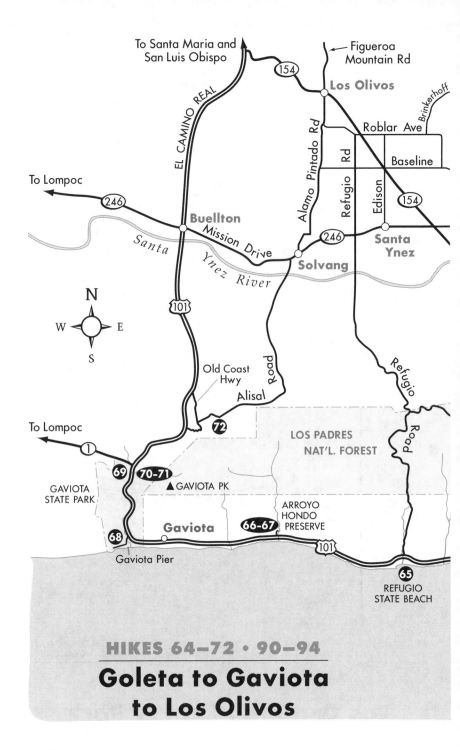

To Santa Maria and
San Luis Obispo

Figueroa
Mountain Rd

154

Los Olivos

EL CAMINO REAL

Roblar Ave

Brinkerhoff

Alamo Pintado Rd

Refugio Rd

Baseline

Edison

154

To Lompoc

246

Buellton

Mission Drive

Santa

Ynez River

246

Solvang

Santa
Ynez

N
W E
S

101

Old Coast
Hwy

Alisal

Road

Refugio

Road

72

LOS PADRES
NAT'L. FOREST

To Lompoc

1

69

70-71

GAVIOTA
STATE PARK

▲ GAVIOTA PK

ARROYO
HONDO
PRESERVE

Gaviota

66-67

68

101

Gaviota Pier

65

REFUGIO
STATE BEACH

HIKES 64–72 • 90–94

Goleta to Gaviota
to Los Olivos

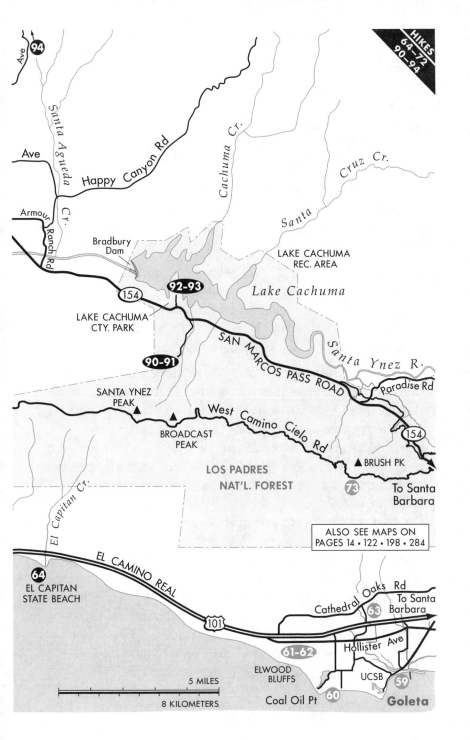

94

Ave

Santa Agueda Cr.

Cachuma Cr.

Santa Cruz Cr.

Ave

Happy Canyon Rd

Armour Ranch Rd

Bradbury Dam

Santa

LAKE CACHUMA
REC. AREA

Lake Cachuma

154

92-93

LAKE CACHUMA
CTY. PARK

90-91

SAN MARCOS PASS ROAD

Santa Ynez R.

Paradise Rd

SANTA YNEZ
PEAK ▲

▲
BROADCAST
PEAK

West Camino Cielo Rd

154

▲ BRUSH PK

LOS PADRES
NAT'L. FOREST

73

To Santa
Barbara

El Capitan Cr.

ALSO SEE MAPS ON
PAGES 14 • 122 • 198 • 284

EL CAMINO REAL

64

EL CAPITAN
STATE BEACH

101

Cathedral Oaks Rd

63

To Santa
Barbara

61-62

Hollister Ave

ELWOOD
BLUFFS

60

UCSB

59

Coal Oil Pt

Goleta

5 MILES

8 KILOMETERS

64. El Capitan State Beach

Hiking distance: 1.5 miles round trip
Hiking time: 1 hour
Elevation gain: Level
Maps: U.S.G.S. Tajiguas
       El Capitan and Refugio State Beach—Park Service Map

Summary of hike: El Capitan State Beach, located along the coastline west of Santa Barbara, has a beautiful sandy beach with rocky tidepools. El Capitan Creek flows through a forested canyon to the tidepools at El Capitan Point. Nature trails weave through stands of sycamore and oak trees alongside the creek.

Driving directions: SANTA BARBARA. From Santa Barbara, drive 20 miles northbound on Highway 101 to the El Capitan State Beach exit. It is located 0.8 miles past the El Capitan Ranch Road exit. Turn left (south) and drive 0.3 miles to the state park entrance. Park in the day-use lot straight ahead.

Hiking directions: For a short walk, take the paved path down the hillside from the general store to the oceanfront. The quarter-mile paved trail follows the sandy shoreline a short distance to the east before looping back to the parking lot.

For a longer hike, continue along the shore on the unpaved path past a picnic area to El Capitan Creek at the point. Near the mouth of the creek are the tidepools. Take the nature trail footpath, heading inland through the woods while following El Capitan Creek upstream. Pass several intersecting trails that loop back to the park entrance station and parking lot. Near the entrance station, pick up the trail on the west side of the road. Parallel the western edge of El Capitan Creek through the forested canyon. The trail ends at a railroad bridge where the trail meets the road. Return by reversing your route or by exploring one of the intersecting nature trails.

For a longer walk, the Aniso Trail (Hike 65) continues along the shoreline to Refugio State Beach, 2.5 miles west. ■

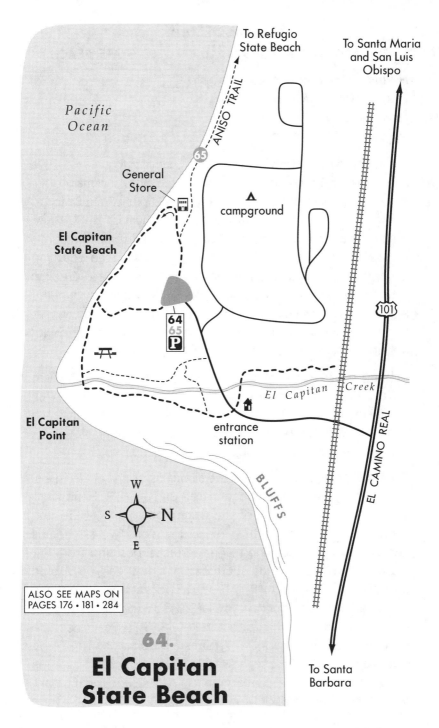

To Refugio
State Beach

To Santa Maria
and San Luis
Obispo

*Pacific
Ocean*

ANISO TRAIL

65

General
Store

campground

**El Capitan
State Beach**

64
65
P

El Capitan Creek

**El Capitan
Point**

entrance
station

101

EL CAMINO REAL

BLUFFS

W
S — N
E

ALSO SEE MAPS ON
PAGES 176 • 181 • 284

64.
El Capitan
State Beach

To Santa
Barbara

65. Aniso Trail
EL CAPITAN STATE BEACH to REFUGIO STATE BEACH

Hiking distance: 5 miles round trip
Hiking time: 2.5 hours
Elevation gain: Near level
Maps: U.S.G.S. Tajiguas

Summary of hike: The Aniso Trail (Chumash for *seagull*) is a paved hiking and biking trail along the sea cliffs and marine terraces on the Gaviota coast, connecting El Capitan State Beach to Refugio State Beach. The trail, an ancient Chumash trade route, follows the sandstone bluffs past weathered rock formations and secluded coves, offering constant views of the coastline. El Capitan State Beach sits at the mouth of El Capitan Creek in a extensive riparian woodland of coastal oaks and sycamores. Refugio State Beach lies at the mouth of Refugio Canyon, where there is a palm-lined sandy beach cove and rocky shoreline with tidepools. Refugio Creek meanders through the park.

Driving directions: SANTA BARBARA. From Santa Barbara, drive 20 miles northbound on Highway 101 to the El Capitan State Beach exit. It is located 0.8 miles past the El Capitan Ranch Road exit. Turn left (south) and drive 0.3 miles to the state park entrance. Park in the day-use lot straight ahead.

Hiking directions: The paved trail begins on the north (right) side of the general store. (See the map on page 179.) Head west, skirting around the edge of the campground, and follow the contours of the cliffs past a lifeguard station. Two side paths descend to the beach and marine terraces. Descend from the bluffs to the beach at the south end of Corral Canyon. A side path curves left to Corral Beach, a small pocket beach. Continue straight ahead, returning to the bluffs past weathered rock formations. At 2.5 miles, the trail enters Refugio State Beach near the palm-lined bay. Refugio Creek forms a tropical-looking freshwater lagoon near the ocean. Refugio Point, a low bluff, extends seaward at the west end of the beach. After exploring the park, return along the same route. ■

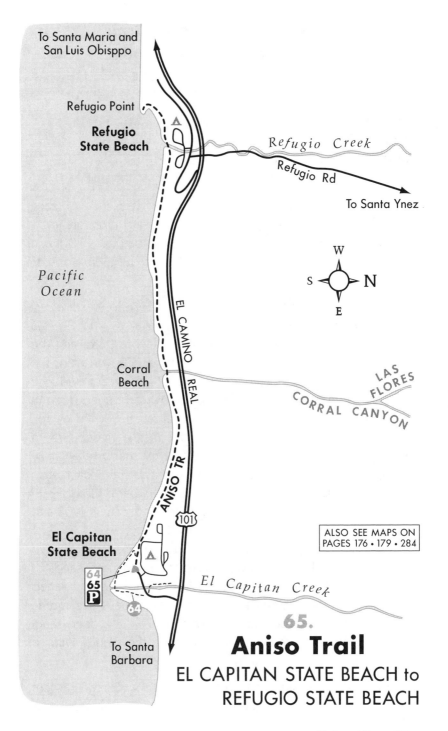

To Santa Maria and
San Luis Obisppo

Refugio Point

**Refugio
State Beach**

Refugio Creek

Refugio Rd

To Santa Ynez

W
S — N
E

*Pacific
Ocean*

EL CAMINO REAL

Corral
Beach

LAS FLORES

CORRAL CANYON

ANISO TR

101

ALSO SEE MAPS ON
PAGES 176 • 179 • 284

**El Capitan
State Beach**

64
65
P

64

El Capitan Creek

To Santa
Barbara

65.
Aniso Trail
EL CAPITAN STATE BEACH to
REFUGIO STATE BEACH

66. Brandy's West Creek Trail and Upper Creek Trail

ARROYO HONDO PRESERVE

Hiking distance: 3 miles round trip
Hiking time: 1.5 hours
Elevation gain: 200 feet
Maps: U.S.G.S. Gaviota
   Arroyo Hondo Preserve Trail Guide (at the trailhead)

The preserve is open the first and third weekends of each month from 10:00 a.m.–4:00 p.m. Docent-led hikes are available on the first Saturday and third Sunday at 10:00 a.m. Advanced reservations are required. Please call (805) 567-1115 or www.sblandtrust.org.

Summary of hike: The 782-acre Arroyo Hondo Preserve envelopes a magnificent stream-fed canyon along the Gaviota Coast between Refugio State Beach and Gaviota State Park. The earliest known inhabitants of Arroyo Hondo Canyon were the Barbareno–Chumash Indians, dating back 5,000 years. Evidence of their permanent camp has been discovered buried deep in the lower canyon. In the 1800s, it was a ranch, owned by former Santa Barbara Presidio Commandant Jose Francisco Ortega. The historic Ortega adobe, built in 1842 by the Ortega family, is located near the trailhead. It was used as a stagecoach stop on the route between Lompoc and Santa Barbara. The Hollister family purchased the ranch from the Ortega family in 1908 and J.J. Hollister sold it to the Land Trust in 2001.

This hike follows the cool canyon floor along shaded Arroyo Hondo Creek. The pristine watershed is home to thousands of plants and animals, including several endangered and threatened species. The stream-side paths meander under bays, sycamores, and ancient oak woodlands to fern grottos in the deep sandstone gorge. Interpretive panels describe the plants, wildlife, and geology.

Driving directions: SANTA BARBARA. From Santa Barbara, drive 27 miles northbound on Highway 101 to the preserve. It is located 4.6 miles past the Refugio State Beach exit and is adjacent to the CalTrans Call Box #101-412. Slow down when you see the call box approaching, and signal your turn. Turn right off the highway, immediately after the call box, and follow the driveway a quarter mile downhill. Cross the bridge over Arroyo Hondo Creek, and park by the barn.

BUELLTON/LOMPOC. From Buellton/Lompoc, drive 5.8 miles past Gaviota State Park to the Tajiguas Landfill turnoff on the left. The turnoff is located a quarter mile after the Vista Point Rest Area. Make a U-turn into the northbound lanes of Highway 101. Drive 0.7 miles northbound to the preserve entrance, adjacent to the CalTrans Call Box #101-412. Slow down when you see the call box approaching, and signal your turn. Turn

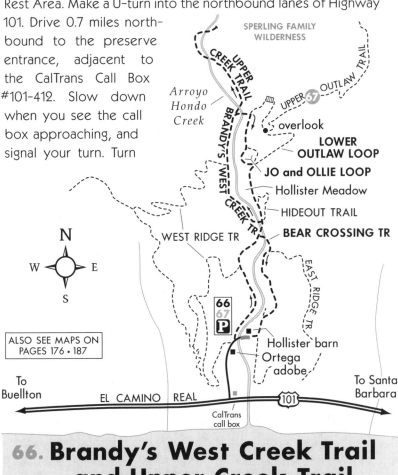

ALSO SEE MAPS ON
PAGES 176 • 187

66. Brandy's West Creek Trail and Upper Creek Trail
ARROYO HONDO PRESERVE

right and follow the directions above.

TO RETURN TO SANTA BARBARA. From the top of the driveway at Highway 101, turn right (northbound) and go 1.8 miles to a turn-around with a left hand turning lane. If it feels safer, drive 3.2 miles (1.4 miles past the turn-around) to the Mariposa Reina exit 128. Go over the bridge and take the on-ramp, heading southbound to Santa Barbara.

Hiking directions: From the historic Hollister Barn, walk back over Arroyo Hondo Creek, and bear right on the dirt road. Follow the west side of the creek into a meadow, with a view of the peaks at the head of the Arroyo Hondo Canyon. Gently gain elevation among the sycamores and bay laurels as the canyon narrows. Pass the Bear Crossing Trail on the right. Cross wood planks over the creek to the Hideout Trail on the right and Brandy's West Creek Trail on the left. Bear left and begin the loop, crossing planks over Arroyo Hondo Creek. Stroll under a riparian forest canopy that includes black cottonwood, big leaf maple, white alder, California bay, and western sycamore. Pass a junction with the West Ridge Trail, which climbs and follows the 800-foot west canyon ridge and has spectacular coastal vistas. Continue to the creek and a posted Y-fork. The Outlaw Trail to the right is our return route.

For now, detour on the Upper Creek Trail to the left. Cross the creek on planks, and traverse the shaded hillside. Rock-hop over the creek among giant boulders and outcroppings. Climb the slope, passing small waterfalls and pools. Cross the creek again to the trail's end in a rock grotto with caves and a pool.

Return to the Outlaw Trail. Bear left (east) and cross planks over the creek to a junction with the Lower Outlaw Loop Trail. Hike 67 goes left and climbs to the Upper Outlaw Loop. For this hike go to the right and descend into Hollister Meadow, a grassy park with a picnic area. Continue down-canyon to Brandy's West Creek Trail, completing the loop. At the signed Bear Crossing Trail, bear left, crossing the creek again, and head south to a T-junction with a grassy road. The East Ridge Trail goes left. Bear right and stroll through the open gardens to a gravel road. Go left, returning to the trailhead. ■

67. Lower Outlaw Trail and Upper Outlaw Trail

ARROYO HONDO PRESERVE

Hiking distance: 3-miles round trip
Hiking time: 2 hours
Elevation gain: 900 feet
Maps: U.S.G.S. Gaviota
      Arroyo Hondo Preserve Trail Guide (at the trailhead)

**map
page 187**

The preserve is open the first and third weekends of each month from 10:00 a.m.–4:00 p.m. Docent-led hikes are available on the first Saturday and third Sunday at 10:00 a.m. Advanced reservations are required. Please call (805) 567-1115 or www.sblandtrust.org.

Summary of hike: Arroyo Hondo Preserve encompasses 782 acres in the Santa Ynez Mountains on the Gaviota Coast. The preserve has a wide diversity of trails that range from easy creekside strolls to rigorous ridgeline trails. The arboreous drainage with steep canyon walls was used as a refuge for well-known outlaws in the late 1800s and early 1900s.

This hike begins in the bucolic canyon and climbs the east canyon wall on the Outlaw Trails, forming two loops. The trails weave through aromatic coastal sage scrub and chaparral habitats to towering sandstone formations on the ridges, with sweeping vistas of the Gaviota coastline, the Channel Islands, and the Santa Ynez Mountains.

Driving directions: SANTA BARBARA. From Santa Barbara, drive 27 miles northbound on Highway 101 to the preserve. It is located 4.6 miles past the Refugio State Beach exit and is adjacent to the CalTrans Call Box #101-412. Slow down when you see the call box approaching, and signal your turn. Turn right off the highway, immediately after the call box, and follow the driveway a quarter mile downhill. Cross the bridge over Arroyo Hondo Creek, and park by the barn.

BUELLTON/LOMPOC. From Buellton/Lompoc, drive 5.8 miles

past Gaviota State Park to the Tajiguas Landfill turnoff on the left. The turnoff is located a quarter mile after the Vista Point Rest Area. Make a U-turn into the northbound lanes of Highway 101. Drive 0.7 miles northbound to the preserve entrance, adjacent to the CalTrans Call Box #101-412. Slow down when you see the call box approaching, and signal your turn. Turn right and follow the directions above.

TO RETURN TO SANTA BARBARA. From the top of the driveway at Highway 101, turn right (northbound) and go 1.8 miles to a turn-around with a left hand turning lane. If it feels safer, drive 3.2 miles (1.4 miles past the turn-around) to the Mariposa Reina exit 128. Go over the bridge and take the on-ramp, heading southbound to Santa Barbara.

Hiking directions: From the historic Hollister Barn, walk back over Arroyo Hondo Creek and bear right on the dirt road. Follow the west side of the creek into a meadow, with a view of the peaks at the head of the Arroyo Hondo Canyon. Gently gain elevation among the sycamores and bay laurels as the canyon narrows. Pass the Bear Crossing Trail on the right. Cross wood planks over the creek to the Hideout Trail on the right and Brandy's West Creek Trail on the left. Pass the remains of the historic grist mill, dating back to the 1840s. It was used by the Jose Ortega family when the land was part of Ortega Rancho Refugio. Continue straight through Hollister Meadow, a grassy park with a picnic area, to the signed Jo & Ollie Loop Trail.

Begin the first loop on the left fork, staying near the canyon floor to another junction. The left fork crosses Arroyo Hondo Creek, connecting with Brandy's West Creek Trail and the Upper Creek Trail (Hike 66). Instead, go to the right on the Lower Outlaw Loop Trail, and head up the side canyon. Cross a wooden footbridge over the drainage and climb up the east wall of Arroyo Hondo Canyon to an overlook with a bench and a trail split. At the overlook are vistas from the rocky peaks at the head of the canyon to the Pacific Ocean.

At the trail split, the right fork is our return route. For now, take the Upper Outlaw Trail to the left. Steadily climb the ridge between two steep canyons to the preserve's eastern boundary.

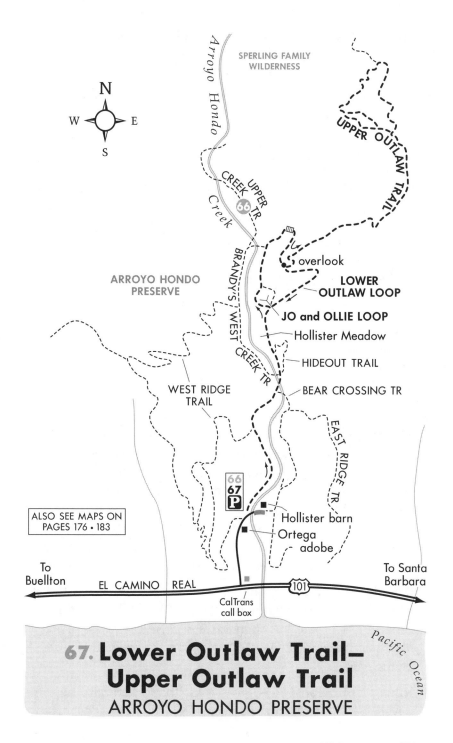

SPERLING FAMILY
WILDERNESS

Arroyo Hondo

N
W   E
S

UPPER OUTLAW TRAIL

UPPER CREEK TR

66

Creek

BRANDY'S WEST CREEK TR

ARROYO HONDO
PRESERVE

overlook

**LOWER
OUTLAW LOOP**

JO and OLLIE LOOP

Hollister Meadow

HIDEOUT TRAIL

BEAR CROSSING TR

WEST RIDGE
TRAIL

EAST RIDGE TR

66
67
P

ALSO SEE MAPS ON
PAGES 176 • 183

Hollister barn

Ortega
adobe

To
Buellton

EL CAMINO REAL

101

To Santa
Barbara

CalTrans
call box

Pacific Ocean

**67. Lower Outlaw Trail–
Upper Outlaw Trail**
ARROYO HONDO PRESERVE

Curve left and cross the head of the side canyon overlooking the scenic Tajiguas Landfill and the Santa Ynez Range towards Santa Barbara. At a Y-fork, begin the second loop, hiking clockwise. Pass under a majestic oak and weave through weather-sculpted sandstone formations. Stroll among the garden of rocks while enjoying the awesome coastal views. Loop around the gently rolling summit, completing the loop. Bear left back to the junction with the Lower Outlaw Loop Trail. Bear left again and descend on an old ranch road. Reenter an oak and bay forest, completing the second loop at Hollister Meadow. Return back to the trailhead on the same trail, or take the Bear Crossing Trail on the east side of the creek. ■

68. Beach to Backcountry Trail
GAVIOTA STATE PARK

Hiking distance: 3 miles round trip
Hiking time: 1.5 hours
Elevation gain: 750 feet
Maps: U.S.G.S. Gaviota
　　　　 Gaviota State Park map

Summary of hike: In the mountainous backcountry of Gaviota State Park, a network of trails leads to scenic overlooks, sandstone outcroppings, intriguing caves, and oak-studded rolling hills. This hike begins on the bluffs overlooking Gaviota Pier and the undeveloped coastline. The trail crosses the rolling terrain in the Santa Ynez Mountains to a vista point high above Gaviota Pass. There are great views of Gaviota Peak, the Gaviota tunnel, the Pacific Ocean, and the Channel Islands.

Driving directions: SANTA BARBARA. From Santa Barbara, drive 33 miles northbound on Highway 101 to the Gaviota State Park turnoff on the left. Turn left and drive 0.4 miles, bearing right near the entrance kiosk. Drive to the trailhead parking area on the right.

Hiking directions: Head north past the locked gate on the paved road. The half-mile road leads through dense scrub brush.

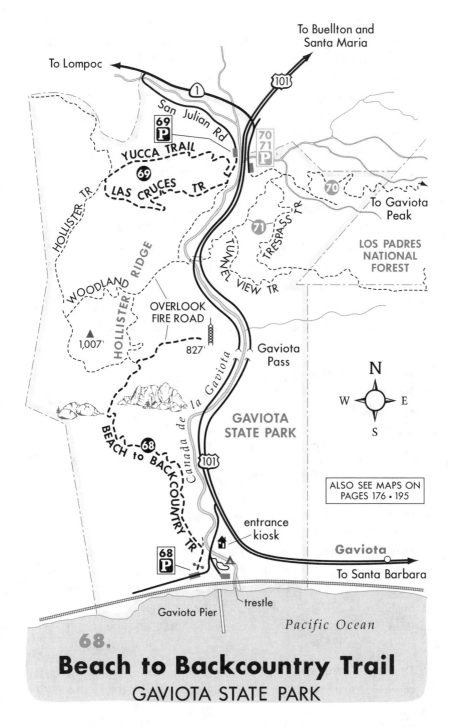

To Buellton and
Santa Maria

To Lompoc

1

101

San Julian Rd

69
P

YUCCA TRAIL

70
71
P

69

LAS CRUCES TR

HOLLISTER TR

70

To Gaviota
Peak

71

TRESPASS TR

LOS PADRES
NATIONAL
FOREST

WOODLAND RIDGE

HOLLISTER RIDGE

TUNNEL VIEW TR

OVERLOOK
FIRE ROAD

▲
1,007'

827'

Gaviota
Pass

N

W   E

S

Canada de la Gaviota

GAVIOTA
STATE PARK

BEACH to BACKCOUNTRY TR

68

ALSO SEE MAPS ON
PAGES 176 • 195

68
P

entrance
kiosk

Gaviota

101

To Santa Barbara

trestle

Gaviota Pier

Pacific Ocean

68.

Beach to Backcountry Trail
GAVIOTA STATE PARK

A hundred yards before the end of the road is a signed multi-purpose trail on the left—the Beach to Backcountry Trail. Take this footpath up the south-facing hillside of the canyon. Views open to the Pacific Ocean and Gaviota Peak during the ascent. The trail steadily zigzags up to a ridge. At one mile the trail levels out near large, sculpted sandstone outcroppings and caves. Begin a second ascent to the largest formation, and curve around to the backside of the outcropping. Cross a ravine and continue uphill to the top and a junction with the Overlook Fire Road. The left fork heads north along Hollister Ridge into the mountainous interior of Gaviota State Park. Take the right fork for a half mile, contouring up and down the rolling ridge. The panoramic overlook is located by the radio tower at the edge of the ridge, where it drops off sharply on all three sides. After enjoying the views, return by retracing your steps. ■

69. Yucca—Las Cruces Loop Trail
GAVIOTA STATE PARK

Hiking distance: 2-mile loop
Hiking time: 1 hour
Elevation gain: 600 feet
Maps: U.S.G.S. Solvang and Gaviota
      Gaviota State Park map

map
pages 189 • 191

Summary of hike: This loop hike is part of a network of trails in the mountainous backcountry of Gaviota State Park. The 2,775-acre state park extends from the Pacific coast to the crest of the Santa Ynez Mountains, adjacent to the Los Padres National Forest. The Las Cruces Trail is located in the rugged uplands of the park on an old ranch road. The road crosses coastal grasslands and chaparral to Hollister Ridge, overlooking rolling hills and canyons. The Yucca Trail has phenomenal views of Gaviota Peak, the Pacific Ocean, the Channel Islands, and the folded hills of the inland valley.

Driving directions: SANTA BARBARA. From Santa Barbara, drive 35 miles northbound on Highway 101 to the Highway 1/

Lompoc exit. Turn left and drive 0.7 miles west to San Julian Road. Turn left and continue 0.8 miles to the gated trailhead at the end of the road. Park along the side of the road.

Hiking directions: Walk past the trailhead gate on the unpaved road along the west side of Highway 101. Pass large oak trees to a signed trail on the right at 0.2 miles. Begin the loop to the right on the Yucca Trail, winding up the hillside. Soon the gradient steepens and parallels the ridge leading up to the mountain top. Along the way, the Las Cruces Trail, the return route, can be seen to the south in the drainage below. Descend a short distance down the back side of the mountain to a T-junction with the Las Cruces Trail, an unpaved road on Hollister Ridge. Bear left and descend down the oak-studded canyon. Complete the loop and return to the trailhead. ■

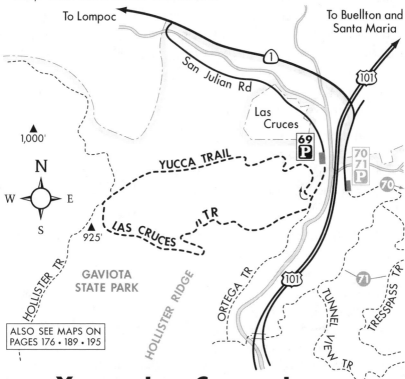

69. Yucca–Las Cruces Loop
GAVIOTA STATE PARK

70. Gaviota Peak
with a side trip to Gaviota Hot Springs
GAVIOTA STATE PARK

Hiking distance: 6 miles round trip
Hiking time: 4 hours
Elevation gain: 1,900 feet
Maps: U.S.G.S. Solvang and Gaviota
      Gaviota State Park map

map
page 195

Summary of hike: Gaviota Peak towers over the Santa Barbara Coastline in the southern branch of the Santa Ynez Mountains. The isolated peak, located in the Los Padres National Forest, is accessed from Gaviota State Park on the inland side of Highway 101. The hike to Gaviota Peak is a substantial workout. Atop the 2,458-foot summit are magnificent 360-degree vistas of the Santa Ynez Mountains, Las Cruces Hills, Lompoc Valley, the Gaviota coast, and the Channel Islands. The trail weaves through sycamore and oak woodlands, grasslands, and chaparral. En route, a spur trail leads to Gaviota Hot Springs, a series of lukewarm primitive pools fed by sulphurous springs.

Driving directions: SANTA BARBARA. From Santa Barbara, drive 35 miles northbound on Highway 101 to the Highway 1/ Lompoc exit. Turn sharply to the right onto the frontage road, and continue 0.3 miles to the Gaviota State Park parking lot at road's end.

Hiking directions: Hike east past the trailhead on the wide, unpaved road under the shade of oak and sycamore trees. Stay on the main trail past a junction with the Trespass Trail (Hike 71). Cross a stream to a junction at 0.4 miles. The right fork is a short side trip to Gaviota Hot Springs.

After enjoying the springs, return to the junction and continue on the main trail, following the old road as it curves around the grassy hillside. The views include the rolling hills and ranches of the Lompoc Valley. Long, gradual switchbacks lead up to the national forest boundary at 1.5 miles. At two miles, the trail reaches a saddle with more great views. The grade of the trail is never steep, but it rarely levels out. Near the top, pass a metal gate to a junction. The left fork follows the ridge east. The path straight ahead descends into San Onofre Canyon. Take the right fork for the final ascent to Gaviota Peak and the spectacular views. Return along the same trail. ■

71. Tunnel View—Trespass Trail Loop
GAVIOTA STATE PARK

Hiking distance: 2.5-mile loop
Hiking time: 1.5 hours
Elevation gain: 600 feet
Maps: U.S.G.S. Solvang and Gaviota
     Gaviota State Park map

map
page 195

Summary of hike: The Tunnel View and Trespass Trails sit at the western base of Gaviota Peak on the inland side of Gaviota State Park. The hike follows the forested paths on the east side of Highway 101, which bisects the 2,776-acre park. The trail winds through shaded groves of gnarled oaks, sycamores, open grasslands, and native chaparral. Throughout the loop hike are panoramic views of the tunnels along Highway 101, the Pacific Ocean, the Gaviota coastline, the Channel Islands, and the rolling hills of the inland valley.

Driving directions: SANTA BARBARA. From Santa Barbara, drive 35 miles northbound on Highway 101 to the Highway 1/ Lompoc exit. Turn sharply to the right onto the frontage road, and continue 0.3 miles to the Gaviota State Park parking lot at road's end.

Hiking directions: Head east past the trailhead sign on the wide, unpaved road under the shade of oak and sycamore trees. At 0.2 miles is a signed junction. The left fork leads to Gaviota Peak (Hike 70). Bear right on the Trespass Trail past large oak trees to a signed junction. Leave the old road and begin the loop to the right on the Tunnel View Trail. Cross over two seasonal drainages, and traverse the lower grassy foothills of Gaviota

Peak. Cross Corral Springs on a lush, stream-fed knoll. Curve east, heading up the hillside through a grove of stately oaks. At 0.7 miles, the path reaches an overlook on the ridge descending from Gaviota Peak. From the ridge are views of the Highway 101 tunnels and the Pacific Ocean. Bear left around the hillside up the stream-fed side canyon. Pass sedimentary rock outcroppings to a ridge at a T-junction with the Trespass Trail, the old ranch road. The right fork climbs steeply to Gaviota Peak (Hike 70). Instead, bear left and descend on the wide path through chaparral and grass meadows, completing the loop. Take the right fork and return along the same trail. ■

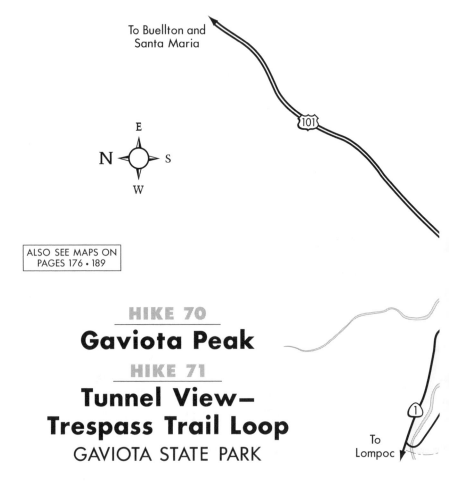

To Buellton and
Santa Maria

101

E

N ✦ S

W

ALSO SEE MAPS ON
PAGES 176 • 189

HIKE 70

Gaviota Peak

HIKE 71

Tunnel View–
Trespass Trail Loop
GAVIOTA STATE PARK

To
Lompoc

1

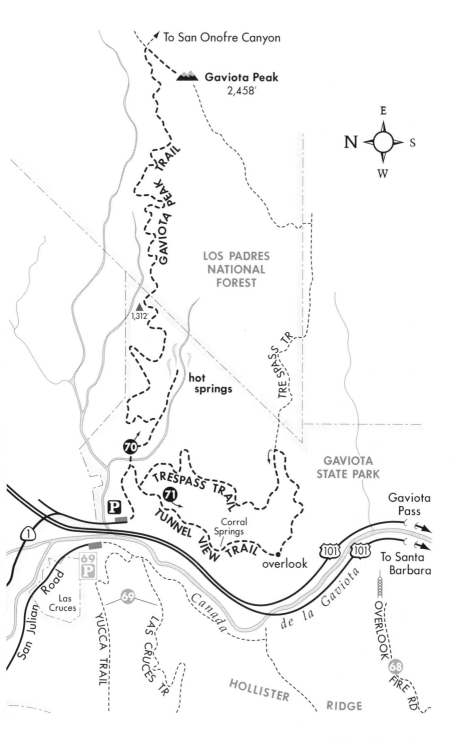

To San Onofre Canyon

Gaviota Peak
2,458'

N E S W

GAVIOTA PEAK TRAIL

LOS PADRES
NATIONAL
FOREST

1,312'

hot
springs

TRESPASS TR

70

GAVIOTA
STATE PARK

TRESPASS TRAIL

71

Gaviota
Pass

TUNNEL VIEW TRAIL

Corral
Springs

overlook

101 101 To Santa
Barbara

1

San Julian Road

69
P

Las
Cruces

69

YUCCA TRAIL

LAS CRUCES TR

Canada de la Gaviota

OVERLOOK FIRE RD

68

HOLLISTER RIDGE

72. Nojoqui Falls

Hiking distance: 0.6 miles round trip
Hiking time: 30 minutes
Elevation gain: 50 feet
Maps: U.S.G.S. Solvang

Summary of hike: Nojoqui Falls County Park is a picturesque park tucked into the Santa Ynez Mountains south of Solvang. It has a large grassy area, picnic sites, and Nojoqui (pronounced *NAH-ho-wee*) Creek flowing through the park. A short wooded trail leads to 66-foot Nojoqui Falls in a cool, north-facing box canyon. The falls cascades during the winter rains (and trickles in the summer) off a vertical sandstone wall into a pool and grotto. The canyon walls are green with moss and clusters of maiden-hair ferns. The well-maintained trail winds up the narrow canyon through a shady glen under oaks, bay laurels, and sycamores, crossing three bridges over the creek.

Driving directions: SANTA BARBARA. From Santa Barbara, drive 38 miles northbound on Highway 101. Turn right at the Nojoqui Falls Park sign on the Old Coast Highway, 3.6 miles past the Highway 1 exit. Drive one mile to Alisal Road. Turn left and continue 0.8 miles to the Nojoqui Falls Park entrance on the right. Turn right and drive straight ahead to the last parking lot. If full, park in the first parking area.

If heading south on Highway 101, the Nojoqui Falls Park turnoff is 4.1 miles south of the Santa Rosa Road exit, the southernmost exit of Buellton.

Hiking directions: Hike to the trailhead at the south end of the second parking area. The wide path parallels Nojoqui Creek as it cascades down the narrow canyon. A series of three bridge crossings lead to the base of the falls below the sandstone cliffs. Relax on the large rock slabs and benches at the trail's end while viewing the falls. ■

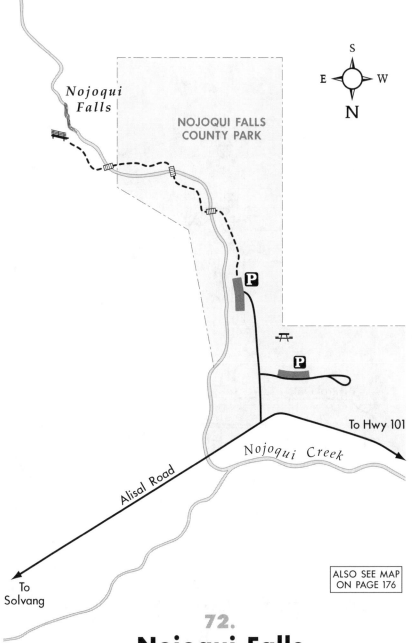

Nojoqui
Falls

NOJOQUI FALLS
COUNTY PARK

S

E — W

N

P

P

To Hwy 101

Nojoqui Creek

Alisal Road

To
Solvang

ALSO SEE MAP
ON PAGE 176

72.
Nojoqui Falls
NOJOQUI FALLS COUNTY PARK

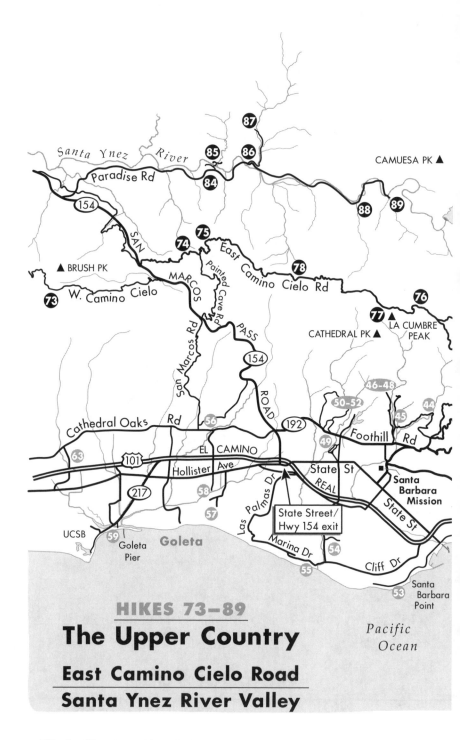

HIKES 73–89
The Upper Country
East Camino Cielo Road
Santa Ynez River Valley

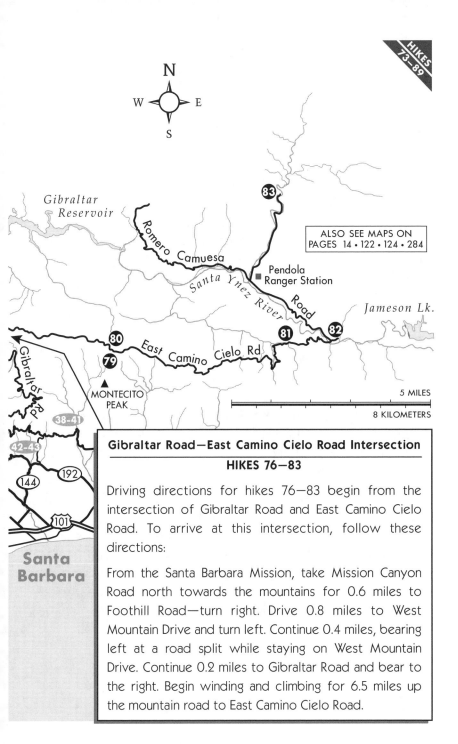

N

W ⊕ E

S

Gibraltar Reservoir

83

ALSO SEE MAPS ON
PAGES 14 • 122 • 124 • 284

Romero Camuesa

Santa Ynez River Road

■ Pendola
Ranger Station

Jameson Lk.

80

81

82

East Camino Cielo Rd

79

Gibraltar Rd

▲ MONTECITO
PEAK

38-41

42-43

192

144

101

5 MILES

8 KILOMETERS

Santa Barbara

Gibraltar Road—East Camino Cielo Road Intersection

HIKES 76—83

Driving directions for hikes 76—83 begin from the intersection of Gibraltar Road and East Camino Cielo Road. To arrive at this intersection, follow these directions:

From the Santa Barbara Mission, take Mission Canyon Road north towards the mountains for 0.6 miles to Foothill Road—turn right. Drive 0.8 miles to West Mountain Drive and turn left. Continue 0.4 miles, bearing left at a road split while staying on West Mountain Drive. Continue 0.2 miles to Gibraltar Road and bear to the right. Begin winding and climbing for 6.5 miles up the mountain road to East Camino Cielo Road.

73. Lizard's Mouth

(West Camino Cielo Road)

Hiking distance: 0.5 to 1 mile round trip
Hiking time: 30 minutes
Elevation gain: 100 feet
Maps: U.S.G.S. Tajiguas

Summary of hike: Lizard's Mouth is named for a specific weatherworn formation jutting skyward that appears like a lizard with its mouth open. The landscape around the area is filled with huge slab rocks, sculpted sandstone outcroppings, jumbles of boulders, and a variety of caves and crevices. The dramatic rock garden is perched on the south-facing, chaparral-covered slopes of the Santa Ynez Mountains, overlooking Santa Barbara, Goleta, the Pacific Ocean, and the Channel Islands.

Driving directions: SANTA BARBARA. From Highway 101 in Santa Barbara, take the State Street/Highway 154 exit. Turn northwest on Highway 154 (San Marcos Pass Road), and drive 7 miles to West Camino Cielo Road on the left. Turn left and continue 3.8 miles to pullouts along both sides of the road. The unmarked trail is to the left (south). If you reach the Winchester Gun Club entrance on the left, you have gone about 100 yards past the trailhead.

Hiking directions: From the parking pullout, hike south through the chaparral for a short 200 feet to a clearing at the unique rock formations. Several other unmarked paths also lead south through the brush to these formations. Once at the outcroppings, pick your own trail to the numerous overlooks, caves, and crevices. The trails meander across the giant slabs of rock among the primeval-looking sandstone boulders. ■

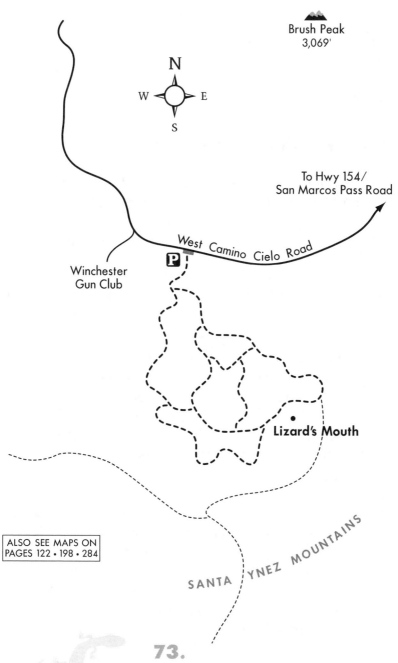

Brush Peak
3,069'

N
W · E
S

To Hwy 154/
San Marcos Pass Road

West Camino Cielo Road

P

Winchester
Gun Club

Lizard's Mouth

ALSO SEE MAPS ON
PAGES 122 · 198 · 284

SANTA YNEZ MOUNTAINS

**73.
Lizard's Mouth**

74. Fremont Ridge Trail

Hiking distance: 4 miles round trip
Hiking time: 2 hours
Elevation gain: 800 feet

map
page 204

Maps: U.S.G.S. San Marcos Pass
Santa Barbara Front Country and Paradise Road map

Summary of hike: The Fremont Ridge Trail begins atop the crest of the Santa Ynez Mountains at East Camino Cielo Road and descends into Paradise Canyon. The trail is named for John C. Fremont, who led an American Army battalion from Monterey over the Santa Ynez Mountains in 1846. The trail, an old Chumash Indian route, is now a vehicle-restricted road that winds down a ridge that divides two canyons, passing sandstone formations and a series of knolls. There are great vistas of the Santa Ynez River Valley, Lake Cachuma, Figueroa Mountain, the San Rafael Mountains, the Sierra Madre Mountains, the Pacific Ocean, and the Channel Islands.

Driving directions: SANTA BARBARA. From Highway 101 in Santa Barbara, take the State Street/Highway 154 exit. Turn northwest on Highway 154 (San Marcos Pass Road), and drive 7.8 miles to East Camino Cielo Road on the right. Turn right and continue 1.6 miles to a Forest Service gate on the left. Parking pullouts are on the left (north) past the trailhead gate.

Hiking directions: Walk past the Forest Service gate and head downhill. Follow the ridge, overlooking Los Laureles Canyon and Lake Cachuma to the west, the Santa Ynez River Valley below, and the Los Padres National Forest beyond. After the initial half-mile descent, the trail levels out. At one mile, begin a second descent and curve to the west. The trail passes under utility poles at two miles. This is a good turn-around point before the trail drops steeply to the Santa Ynez River Valley at Paradise Road. Return along the same trail. ■

75. Knapp's Castle
from EAST CAMINO CIELO ROAD

Hiking distance: 0.8 miles round trip
Hiking time: 30 minutes
Elevation gain: 100 feet
Maps: U.S.G.S. San Marcos Pass
    Santa Barbara Front Country and Paradise Road map

map
page 206

Summary of hike: Knapp's Castle is a stone ruin that sits on a rocky point with stunning vistas. The views span across the Santa Ynez River Valley, from Gibraltar Reservoir to Lake Cachuma, and across the valley to the San Rafael Mountains and the Sierra Madre Range.

The towering sandstone mansion was built by George Owen Knapp, founder of Union Carbide, between 1916 and 1920. The private mountain lodge included seven buildings carved from sandstone blocks. Knapp was instrumental in opening up the mountains behind Santa Barbara and helped build East Camino Cielo Road along the ridgeline. The structures were consumed in the 1940 Paradise Canyon Fire. The remains include the massive sandstone foundations, rock arches, fireplace pillars, rock stairways, and walls of the seven structures.

Knapp's Castle is an easy half-mile hike from East Camino Cielo Road. Although the castle sits on private property, the current owner graciously allows access. Knapp's Castle can also be reached from Paradise Road via the Snyder Trail—Hike 84.

Driving directions: SANTA BARBARA. From Highway 101 in Santa Barbara, take the State Street/Highway 154 exit. Turn northwest on Highway 154 (San Marcos Pass Road), and drive 7.8 miles to East Camino Cielo Road on the right. Turn right and continue 3 miles to a Forest Service gate on the left, 0.9 miles past Painted Cave Road. Pullouts are on the right (south) side of the road.

Hiking directions: Cross East Camino Cielo Road and hike north past the Forest Service "private property" gate. The trail, an unpaved road, crosses the hillside through chaparral to a trail split at 0.4 miles. The left fork is Knapp Road, part of the Snyder

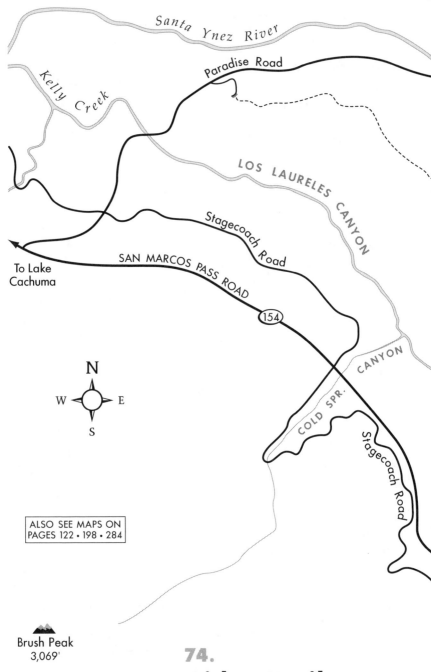

Santa Ynez River

Kelly Creek

Paradise Road

LOS LAURELES CANYON

Stagecoach Road

SAN MARCOS PASS ROAD

To Lake
Cachuma

154

N

W ← → E

S

CANYON

COLD SPR.

Stagecoach Road

ALSO SEE MAPS ON
PAGES 122 • 198 • 284

Brush Peak
3,069'

74.

Fremont Ridge Trail

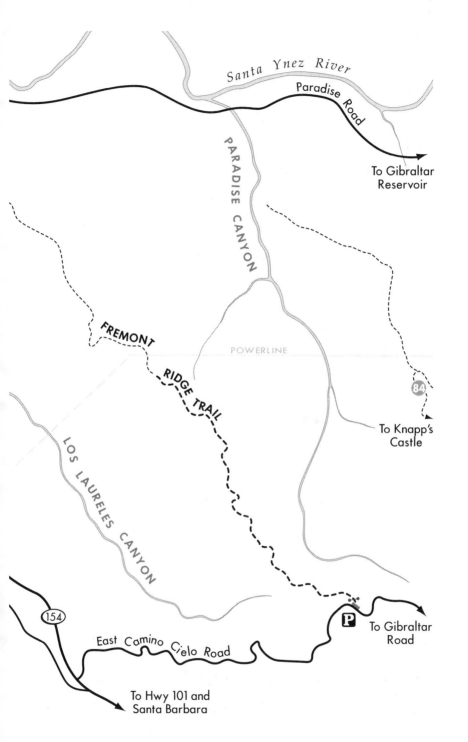

Santa Ynez River

Paradise Road

To Gibraltar
Reservoir

PARADISE CANYON

FREMONT

RIDGE TRAIL

POWERLINE

84

To Knapp's
Castle

LOS LAURELES CANYON

154

East Camino Cielo Road

P

To Gibraltar
Road

To Hwy 101 and
Santa Barbara

Trail, leading three miles down to Paradise Road in the Santa Ynez River Valley (Hike 84). Bear to the right past a second private property gate. In less than a half mile, the castle ruins come into view on a point overlooking the river valley and the San Rafael Mountains. After walking through the ruins and marveling at the views, return along the same path. ■

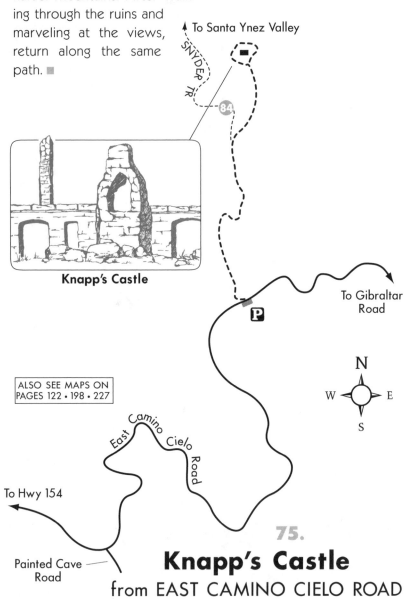

Knapp's Castle

ALSO SEE MAPS ON
PAGES 122 • 198 • 227

75.

Knapp's Castle
from EAST CAMINO CIELO ROAD

76. Angostura Pass Road

Hiking distance: 3 to 14 miles round trip
Hiking time: 1.5 to 7 hours
Elevation gain: 1,000 to 2,000 feet
Maps: U.S.G.S. Santa Barbara and Little Pine Mountain
  Santa Barbara Front Country and Paradise Road map

**map
page 208**

Summary of hike: The Angostura Pass Road is a service road that leads seven miles down the north face of the Santa Ynez Mountains to Gibraltar Dam. The hike down the road overlooks Gibraltar Reservoir and the dam. There are great views across the Santa Ynez River Valley of Little Pine and Big Pine Mountains. En route, the Matias Potrero Trail connects the Angostura Pass Road with the Arroyo Burro Road (Hike 78). You may walk as long as you prefer, returning back along the same road. The Matias Potrero Trail and the Devil's Canyon Trail form an optional return loop for this hike.

Driving directions: SANTA BARBARA. From the Santa Barbara Mission, take Mission Canyon Road north towards the mountains for 0.6 miles to Foothill Road—turn left. Drive 0.8 miles to West Mountain Drive and turn left. Continue 0.4 miles, bearing left at a road split while staying on West Mountain Drive. Continue 0.2 miles to Gibraltar Road and bear to the right. Begin winding and climbing for 6.5 miles up the mountain road to East Camino Cielo Road. From the intersection of Gibraltar Road and East Camino Cielo Road, go left (west) on East Camino Cielo Road. Drive 0.7 miles to an unpaved road and parking pullout on the right.

FROM HIGHWAY 154 (San Marcos Pass Road), drive 10.4 miles east on East Camino Cielo Road to the parking pullout on the left (north).

Hiking directions: Take the graded road 100 yards north to the locked gate. Continue past the gate for about a mile to a signed junction with the steep Matias Potrero Trail, a footpath heading down to the left. The trail leads 2.2 miles to Matias Potrero Camp (Hike 88). Stay on the road as it heads east across the contours of the mountain. At two miles, the trail begins heading around

Devil's Canyon. As you look across the mountainside, the road can be seen winding its way down to Gibraltar Dam. Choose your own turn-around spot anywhere along the road. The entire length of the road is 7 miles. (Returning via the Devil's Canyon/Matias Potrero Trails forms an 11-mile loop hike.)

The trail can also be started from the Santa Ynez River Valley at Gibraltar Dam. Follow the driving and hiking directions for Hike 89, hiking on the High Road for 2.6 miles to Angostura Pass Road. ■

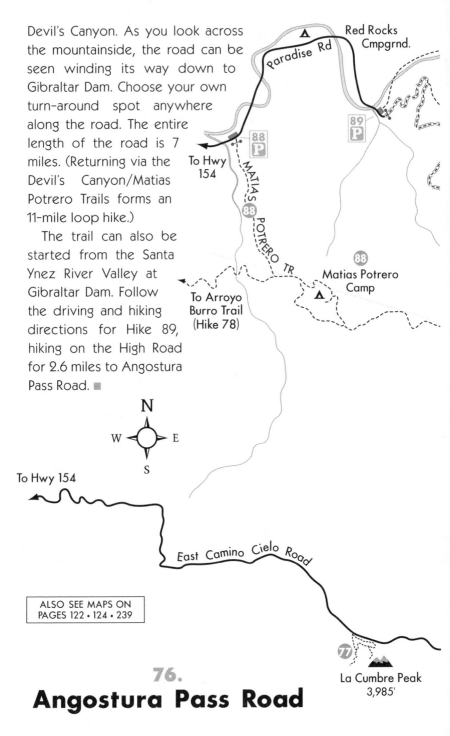

ALSO SEE MAPS ON
PAGES 122 • 124 • 239

76.
Angostura Pass Road

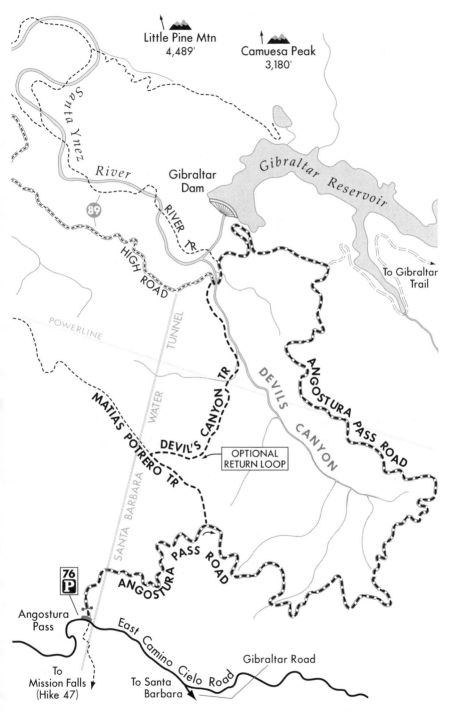

Little Pine Mtn
4,489'

Camuesa Peak
3,180'

Santa Ynez

River

89

Gibraltar Dam

Gibraltar Reservoir

RIVER TR

To Gibraltar
Trail

HIGH ROAD

POWERLINE

TUNNEL

WATER

MATÍAS POTRERO TR

DEVIL'S CANYON TR

DEVIL'S CANYON

DEVILS CANYON

ANGOSTURA PASS ROAD

OPTIONAL
RETURN LOOP

SANTA BARBARA

ANGOSTURA PASS ROAD

76
P

Angostura
Pass

East Camino Cielo Road

Gibraltar Road

To
Mission Falls
(Hike 47)

To Santa
Barbara

77. La Cumbre Vista Point

Hiking distance: 0.3 to 0.8 miles round trip
Hiking time: 30 minutes
Elevation gain: 100 feet
Maps: U.S.G.S. Santa Barbara

Summary of hike: Although this is a short hike, it is a magical location and well worth the stop. The loop trail leads to La Cumbre Peak, the highest peak in the Santa Ynez Mountains. From the 3,985-foot summit are panoramic views of the rugged backcountry. The coastal vistas span from Point Mugu in the Santa Monica Mountains to Point Conception. Cathedral Peak can be seen a short half mile to the south and 650 feet lower in elevation. The unobstructed views of Santa Barbara and the coastline are superb. A paved path loops around the old fire lookout tower, passing picnic tables and benches under digger and Coulter pines. The abandoned tower is fenced off and currently a satellite station.

Driving directions: SANTA BARBARA. From the Santa Barbara Mission, take Mission Canyon Road north towards the mountains for 0.6 miles to Foothill Road—turn left. Drive 0.8 miles to West Mountain Drive and turn left. Continue 0.4 miles, bearing left at a road split while staying on West Mountain Drive. Continue 0.2 miles to Gibraltar Road and bear to the right. Begin winding and climbing for 6.5 miles up the mountain road to East Camino Cielo Road. From the intersection of Gibraltar Road and East Camino Cielo Road, go left (west) on East Camino Cielo Road. Drive 1.9 miles to the signed trailhead and parking pullouts on the left (south).

FROM HIGHWAY 154 (San Marcos Pass Road), drive 9.2 miles east on East Camino Cielo Road to the trailhead and parking pullouts on the right (south).

Hiking directions: From the parking pullout, hike up the gated asphalt road past the pine trees to a junction. Take the right fork and return on the left fork. At the first overlook is a bench. Footpaths lead down to large, sculpted sandstone boulders and additional overlooks. Continue on the winding road, heading east to a second overlook with benches. Again, footpaths lead downhill to more overlooks. The main trail makes a loop, passing the fenced satellite station back to the trailhead. ■

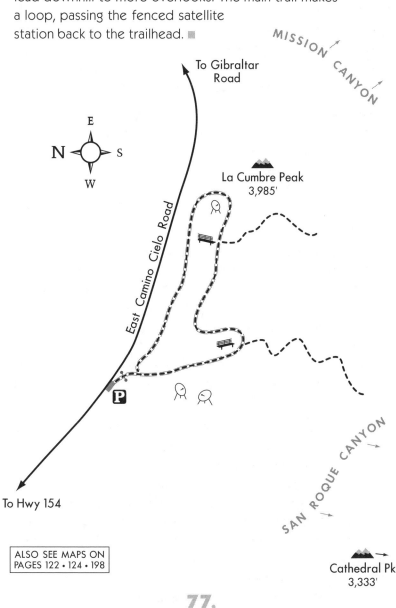

To Gibraltar
Road

MISSION CANYON

La Cumbre Peak
3,985'

East Camino Cielo Road

To Hwy 154

SAN ROQUE CANYON

ALSO SEE MAPS ON
PAGES 122 • 124 • 198

Cathedral Pk
3,333'

77.
La Cumbre Vista Point

78. Arroyo Burro Loop
from EAST CAMINO CIELO ROAD

Hiking distance: 6.5-mile loop
Hiking time: 3.5 hours
Elevation gain: 1,700 feet
Maps: U.S.G.S. San Marcos Pass and Little Pine Mountain
Santa Barbara Front Country and Paradise Road map

Summary of hike: The Arroyo Burro Trail, originally a Chumash Indian passageway and a supply route for miners, leads down the narrow, rocky Arroyo Burro Canyon along its perennial stream. This hike begins on the north side of East Camino Cielo Road. The trail connects with the Arroyo Burro Road just south of White Oak Camp to make a loop. The return hike winds steadily uphill along Arroyo Burro Road, an unpaved, vehicle-restricted road.

Driving directions: SANTA BARBARA. From the intersection of Gibraltar Road and East Camino Cielo Road—northeast of downtown Santa Barbara (see page 199)—turn left and drive 4.9 miles west on East Camino Cielo Road to an unpaved road on the right (north). Turn right and head north 0.1 mile to a locked gate and parking pullouts.

FROM HIGHWAY 154 (San Marcos Pass Road), drive 6.2 miles east on East Camino Cielo Road to the turnoff on the left (north).

Hiking directions: Hike north past the locked gate on the graded Arroyo Burro Road. A hundred yards past the gate is a signed junction on the left for the Arroyo Burro Trail. Leave the road and head downhill to the left on the footpath. This is the beginning of the loop, as you will return on the graded road. Quickly descend into the narrow Arroyo Burro Canyon, and cross the stream several times. At three miles, the trail rejoins the Arroyo Burro Road just above White Oak Camp, less than a mile from the Santa Ynez River.

For the return, take the winding dirt road along the east canyon wall. At 4.5 miles is a connector trail that leads 2.6 miles to Matias Potrero Campsite (Hike 88). The Arroyo Burro Road steadily climbs for 3.5 miles back to the trailhead on East Camino Cielo Road. ■

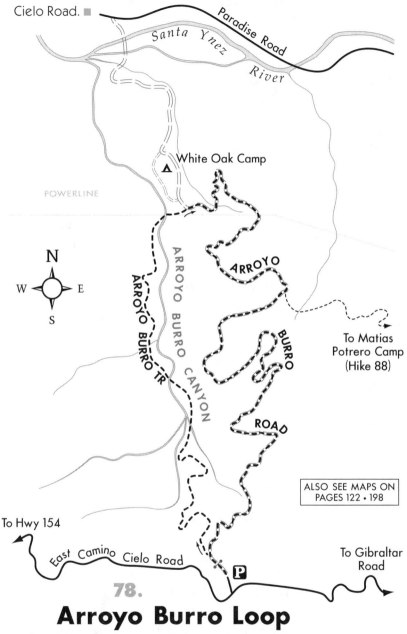

ALSO SEE MAPS ON
PAGES 122 • 198

To Matias
Potrero Camp
(Hike 88)

To Hwy 154

To Gibraltar
Road

78.
Arroyo Burro Loop
from EAST CAMINO CIELO ROAD

79. Montecito Peak
COLD SPRING TRAIL from EAST CAMINO CIELO ROAD

Hiking distance: 3 miles round trip
Hiking time: 1.5 hours
Elevation gain: 700 feet
Maps: U.S.G.S. Santa Barbara
Santa Barbara Front Country and Paradise Road map

Summary of hike: This hike leads 1.4 miles to Montecito Peak, a bald, dome-shaped mountain with a 3,214-foot summit and a diameter of about 50 feet. There are magnificent 360-degree views of the coastal communities and the ocean. The hike begins at the top of the Santa Ynez Mountains on East Camino Cielo Road and descends 700 feet down the south face of the mountains. Hike 39 accesses Montecito Peak from the south via the East Fork of Cold Spring Canyon.

Driving directions: SANTA BARBARA. From the intersection of Gibraltar Road and East Camino Cielo Road—northeast of downtown Santa Barbara (see page 199)—turn right and drive 3.6 miles east on East Camino Cielo Road. The trailhead parking area is on the right (south) side of the road by a large cement water tank.

Hiking directions: From the parking area, take the Cold Spring Trail heading south on the right side of the water tank. The well-defined path overlooks Santa Barbara, the ocean, and the Channel Islands as it heads downhill. At the head of the East Fork of Cold Spring Canyon, the trail curves around the mountainside towards the prominent Montecito Peak. At 1.2 miles, the trail approaches the northwest side of the dome, then skirts around the western edge of the mountain, heading down to the East Fork Cold Spring Canyon and the trailhead for Hikes 38—41. As you near the dome, watch for a steep and narrow unmarked path on the left. Take this path to a ridge. From here, it is a short, but steep, 200-foot rocky scramble to the summit. Careful footing is a must! Return on the same trail to the road and parking lot. ■

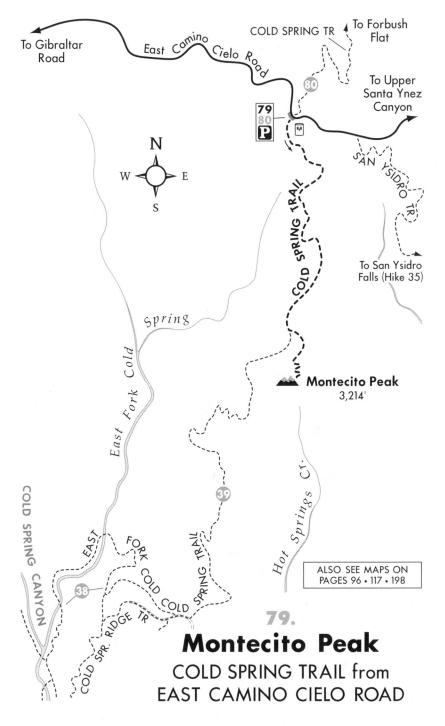

To Gibraltar Road

East Camino Cielo Road

COLD SPRING TR

To Forbush Flat

To Upper Santa Ynez Canyon

80

79
80
P

COLD SPRING TRAIL

SAN YSIDRO TR

To San Ysidro Falls (Hike 35)

N
W · E
S

Spring

East Fork Cold

▲ **Montecito Peak**
3,214'

39

Hot Springs Cr.

COLD SPRING CANYON

EAST

FORK COLD

COLD SPRING TRAIL

38

COLD SPR. RIDGE TR

ALSO SEE MAPS ON
PAGES 96 • 117 • 198

79.

Montecito Peak
COLD SPRING TRAIL from
EAST CAMINO CIELO ROAD

80. Forbush Flat
COLD SPRING TRAIL

Hiking distance: 4 miles round trip
Hiking time: 2.5 hours
Elevation gain: 1,000 feet
Maps: U.S.G.S. Santa Barbara
      Santa Barbara Front Country and Paradise Road map
      Montecito Trails Foundation map

Summary of hike: This hike descends a thousand feet down the north slope of the Santa Ynez Mountains to Forbush Flat, a beautiful meadow located by Gidney Creek. Forbush Flat was the location of Fred Forbush's homestead from the early 1900s. The only remnant of the old homestead is an aging apple orchard. From the flat, the trail continues west down Forbush Canyon to the Blue Canyon Trail and Hike 81. The Cold Spring Trail continues north to the Santa Ynez River.

Driving directions: SANTA BARBARA. From the intersection of Gibraltar Road and East Camino Cielo Road—northeast of downtown Santa Barbara (see page 199)—turn right and drive 3.6 miles east on East Camino Cielo Road. The trailhead parking area is on the right (south) side of the road by a large cement water tank.

Hiking directions: Cross East Camino Cielo Road to the Cold Spring Trail. Head steeply downhill on the west side of the canyon. At 0.5 miles, after a few switchbacks, the trail crosses a seasonal stream to a bench. Continue downhill along the chaparral-covered canyon wall. At one mile, the trail opens up to beautiful vistas of Blue Canyon on the right, the Santa Ynez Valley, and the San Rafael Mountains beyond. From here, look back up the canyon. When the creek is flowing, a 25-foot waterfall cascades off the rock wall. At two miles, the trail reaches Forbush Flat. The orchard, meadow, and campsites are on the left. The main trail continues a short distance down a series of switchbacks to Gidney Creek and a junction, the turn-around spot.

    The right fork leads two miles to Cottam Camp, where

Forbush Canyon and Blue Canyon merge, and 5.5 miles to Upper Blue Canyon Camp (Hike 81). Straight ahead, the Cold Spring Trail continues another two miles to the Santa Ynez River. To return, take the same trail back. ■

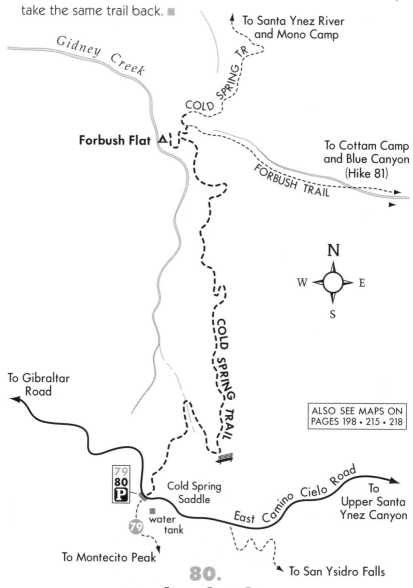

Forbush Flat:
COLD SPRING TRAIL to FORBUSH CANYON

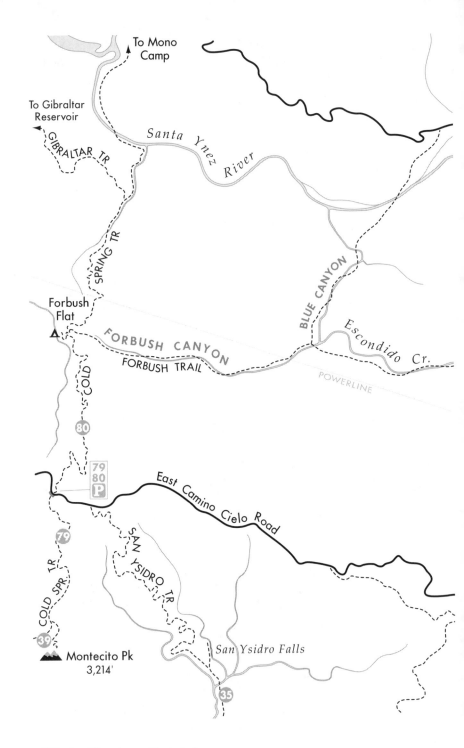

To Mono Camp

To Gibraltar Reservoir

GIBRALTAR TR

Santa Ynez River

SPRING TR

Forbush Flat

FORBUSH CANYON

FORBUSH TRAIL

BLUE CANYON

Escondido Cr.

POWERLINE

COLD

80

79
80
P

East Camino Cielo Road

79

COLD SPR. TR

SAN YSIDRO TR

San Ysidro Falls

39

Montecito Pk
3,214'

35

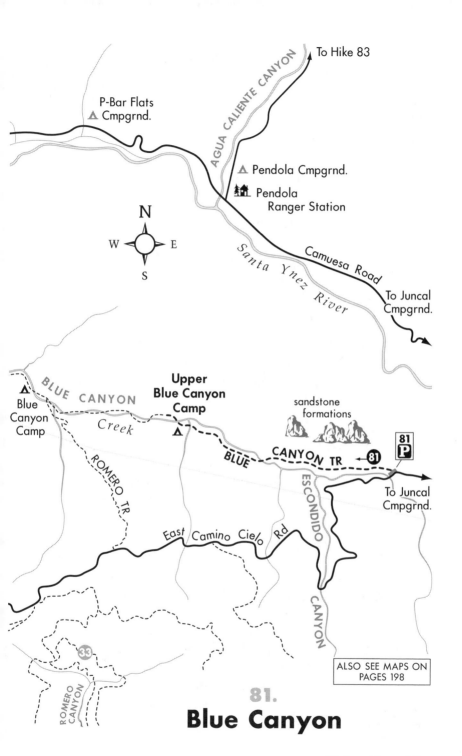

To Hike 83

AGUA CALIENTE CANYON

P-Bar Flats
△ Cmpgrnd.

△ Pendola Cmpgrnd.

Pendola
Ranger Station

N
W — E
S

Santa Ynez River

Camuesa Road

To Juncal
Cmpgrnd.

BLUE CANYON

Upper
Blue Canyon
Camp

sandstone
formations

Blue
Canyon
Camp

Creek

△

BLUE CANYON TR
81

81
P

ROMERO TR

ESCONDIDO CANYON

To Juncal
Cmpgrnd.

East Camino Cielo Rd

33

ROMERO CANYON

ALSO SEE MAPS ON
PAGES 198

81.
Blue Canyon

81. Blue Canyon

Hiking distance: 3.2 miles round trip
Hiking time: 1.5 hours
Elevation gain: 200 feet
Maps: U.S.G.S. Carpinteria
Santa Barbara Front Country and Paradise Road map
Montecito Trails Foundation map

map
page 219

Summary of hike: The Blue Canyon Trail follows Escondido Creek through a narrow canyon past weathered sandstone out-croppings and blue-green serpentine rock. The small, lush canyon has stands of oak, sycamore, and alder trees. This near-level hike leads to Upper Blue Canyon Camp, a primitive camp along the banks of a stream near pools and cascades. For extended hiking, the trail continues for several miles along the creek.

Driving directions: SANTA BARBARA. From the intersection of Gibraltar Road and East Camino Cielo Road—northeast of downtown Santa Barbara (see page 199)—turn right and drive 10.4 miles east on East Camino Cielo Road to the trailhead and parking pullout on the left (north).

Hiking directions: Hike west along the north canyon wall, immediately dropping into Blue Canyon. At 0.3 miles and again at 0.6 miles, the trail passes a series of beautifully eroded sandstone formations. The trail gradually descends to Escondido Creek and the forested canyon floor at one mile. Cross the creek and continue downstream to a small stream crossing at 1.5 miles. Cross the stream to Upper Blue Canyon Camp on a small flat above the water. A short distance beyond the camp is another crossing of Escondido Creek. This is the turn-around point for a 3.2-mile round-trip hike.

The Blue Canyon Trail continues along the creek. Blue Canyon Camp is 2 miles from Upper Blue Canyon Camp. Cottam Camp is located in a large, oak-dotted streamside meadow, 3.5 miles from Upper Blue Canyon Camp. At Cottam Camp, the Blue Canyon Trail heads north to the Santa Ynez River. Forbush Flat—Hike 80— is 2 miles west of Cottam Camp. ■

82. Jameson Lake

Hiking distance: 7 miles round trip
Hiking time: 3.5 hours
Elevation gain: 500 feet
Maps: U.S.G.S. Carpinteria and White Ledge Peak

map
page 222

Summary of hike: Jameson Lake lies near the headwaters of the Santa Ynez River on the upper east end of the Santa Ynez Valley. The lake was created in 1930 with the creation of the Juncal Dam. The 138-acre reservoir supplies water to the Montecito water district via a tunnel under the Santa Ynez Mountains.

The hike to picturesque Jameson Lake begins at Juncal Campground along the banks of the Santa Ynez River. The trail heads up Juncal Canyon along an unpaved road, following the river to the upper end of the Santa Ynez drainage. The dirt trail then parallels the south shore of the reservoir. Throughout the hike are great views down the Santa Ynez Valley to the west and to the upper valley in the east.

Driving directions: SANTA BARBARA. From the Santa Barbara Mission, take Mission Canyon Road north towards the mountains for 0.6 miles to Foothill Road—turn left. Drive 0.8 miles to West Mountain Drive and turn left. Continue 0.4 miles, bearing left at a road split while staying on West Mountain Drive. Continue 0.2 miles to Gibraltar Road and bear to the right. Begin winding and climbing for 6.5 miles up the mountain road to East Camino Cielo Road. From the intersection of Gibraltar Road and East Camino Cielo Road, go right on East Camino Cielo Road. Drive 12 miles east to the Juncal Campground on the valley floor. Turn right, entering the campground, and continue straight ahead. Park at the far east end.

Hiking directions: At the far east end of the Juncal Campground, head east past the gate on the unpaved Juncal Road. Cross the tributary stream and follow the near-level road through meadows dotted with oak trees. Head to the upper end of the canyon, parallel to the Santa Ynez River. The side trails lead down to the river. At 1.5 miles, cross the Santa Ynez River.

After crossing, the trail begins a 300-foot ascent, curving up and around the west side of the mountain. Views open up to the east and west, including the first look at Jameson Lake. As you round the mountain towards the south, the trail continues above Alder Creek, parallel to the south shore of Jameson Lake. At 3.5 miles is a junction on the right with the Alder Creek Trail. This is the turn-around spot.

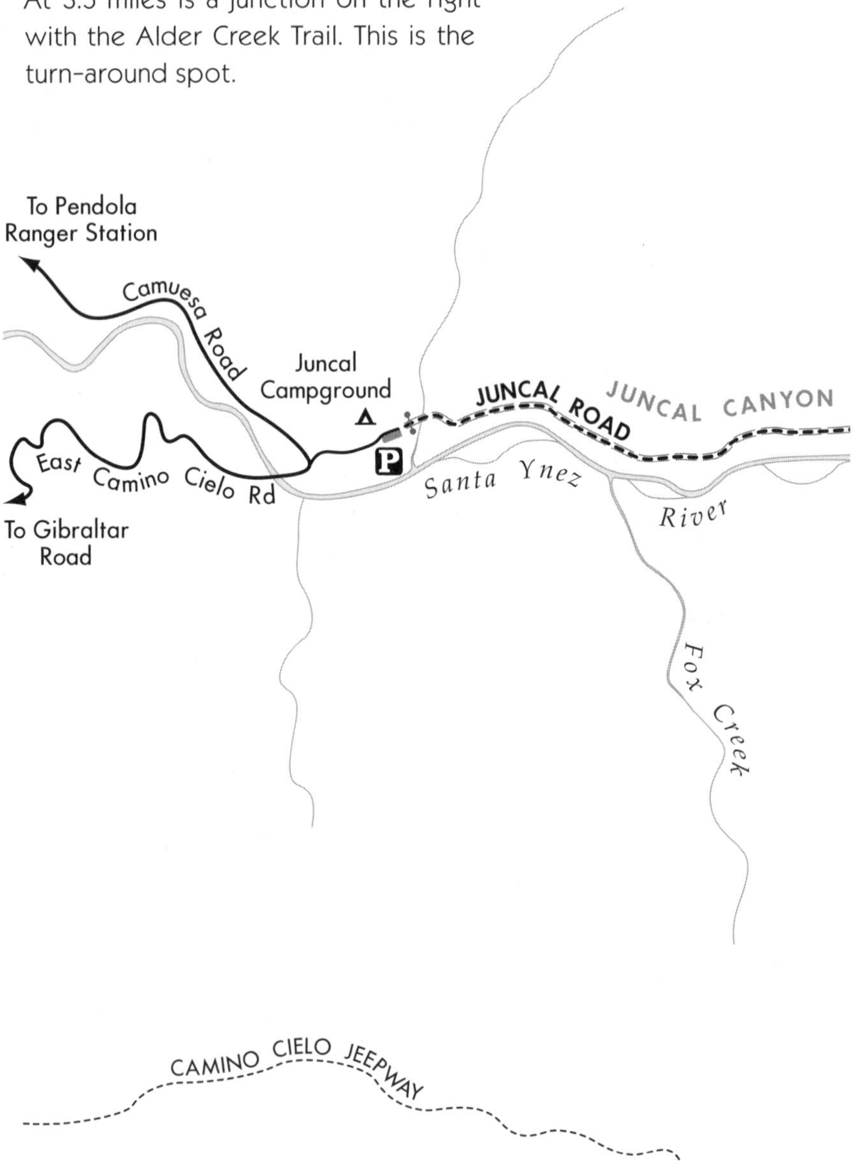

To Pendola
Ranger Station

Camuesa Road

Juncal
Campground

JUNCAL ROAD

JUNCAL CANYON

East Camino Cielo Rd

To Gibraltar
Road

Santa Ynez

River

Fox Creek

CAMINO CIELO JEEPWAY

To hike farther, the Alder Creek Trail leads down to the creek, following the creek past pools and small waterfalls to Alder Camp, one mile ahead. The main trail continues east from Jameson Lake to Murietta Divide, then on to Matilija Creek at Ojai (Hike 9). ■

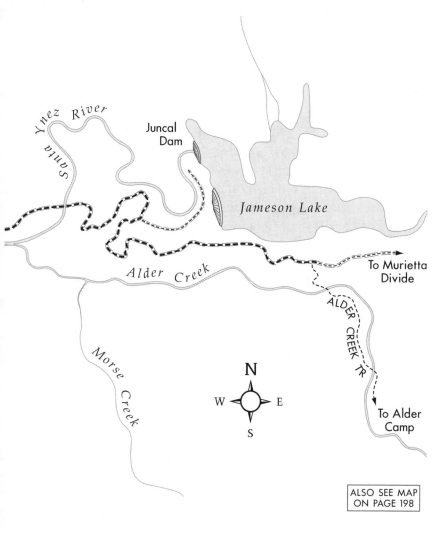

Santa Ynez River

Juncal Dam

Jameson Lake

To Murietta Divide

Alder Creek

ALDER CREEK TR

To Alder Camp

Morse Creek

N
W ✦ E
S

ALSO SEE MAP
ON PAGE 198

82.
Jameson Lake

83. Agua Caliente Canyon and Hot Springs

Hiking distance: 4 miles round trip
Hiking time: 2 hours
Elevation gain: 200 feet
Maps: U.S.G.S. Hildreth Peak
Santa Barbara Front Country and Paradise Road map
Dick Smith Wilderness map

Summary of hike: Agua Caliente, which means *hot water*, is home to Big Caliente Hot Springs, a bathing pool on the upper end of the Santa Ynez Valley. George Owen Knapp, of Knapp's Castle fame (Hikes 75 and 84), discovered the spring and built a small pool for himself and his friends to bathe. The bathing pool is near the trailhead and is perfect for soaking after the hike.

This hike follows Agua Caliente Creek up Agua Caliente Canyon on an old pack trail, passing sandstone formations and the Big Caliente Debris Dam. The dam was built in the 1930s to help keep sediment from flowing into Gibraltar Dam. At the debris dam is an overlook of its 70-foot tall spillway and a pool at the base of the dam. En route, the trail passes steep chaparral slopes, dense oak woodlands, expansive grasslands, and riparian vegetation along the boulder-strewn creek.

Driving directions: SANTA BARBARA. From the intersection of Gibraltar Road and East Camino Cielo Road—northeast of downtown Santa Barbara (see page 199)—turn right and drive 12 miles east on East Camino Cielo Road to the Juncal Campground on the valley floor. Bear left and continue 3 miles to the Pendola Ranger Station at Big Caliente Road on the right (north). Turn right and drive 2.4 miles to Caliente Hot Springs. Park off the road.

Hiking directions: Follow the unpaved road up canyon past the cement hot springs pool. A short distance ahead, the road narrows to a footpath by a trail sign. The path parallels Agua Caliente Creek past a series of pools. At 0.5 miles, cross the creek and head gently uphill to the Big Caliente Dam and the spillway overlook. Past the dam, the trail levels out through a lush, forested flat, staying close to the watercourse. The trail recrosses the creek at 1.6 miles near the mouth of Diablo Canyon on the right. Bear to the left (north), continuing deeper into Agua Caliente Canyon. At two miles, cross the main creek as the canyon narrows. This is a good turn-around spot. To hike farther, the Agua Caliente Trail continues for several miles up the canyon. ▪

To La Carpa Spring

Hildreth Peak
5,065'

AGUA CALIENTE CANYON

N
W ✦ E
S

DIABLO CANYON

Big Caliente Dam

Big Caliente Hot Springs

P

ALSO SEE MAPS ON PAGES 198

Big Caliente Road

To Pendola Ranger Station

83.
Agua Caliente Canyon and Hot Springs

84. Knapp's Castle
from PARADISE ROAD and SNYDER TRAIL

Hiking distance: 6.6 miles round trip
Hiking time: 3.5 hours
Elevation gain: 2,000 feet
Maps: U.S.G.S. San Marcos Pass
Santa Barbara Front Country and Paradise Road map

Summary of hike: Knapp's Castle is the former hilltop sanctuary and hunting lodge of George Owen Knapp. The ruins are perched on a ridge with incredible views of the entire Santa Ynez Valley and the San Rafael Mountains. (A description of Knapp's Castle is on page 203.) In 1920, after the sandstone mansion was built, Knapp discovered cascades in Lewis Canyon, southeast of the lodge. He installed lighting to highlight the waterfall and built a bathhouse.

The Snyder Trail is a longer and steeper trail to Knapp's Castle than the easy stroll from East Camino Cielo Road (Hike 75). The trail begins from Paradise Road in the Santa Ynez River Valley and heads up the ridge alongside Lewis Canyon. (En route to Knapp's Castle, an unsigned fork leads to seasonal Wellhouse Falls, the cascades that Knapp discovered along Lewis Creek.) The hike utilizes service roads and footpaths as it steadily climbs up the ridge to ever-improving views.

Driving directions: SANTA BARBARA. From Highway 101 in Santa Barbara, take the State Street/Highway 154 exit. Turn northwest on Highway 154 (San Marcos Pass Road), and drive 10.6 miles to Paradise Road on the right. Turn right and continue 4.2 miles to the turnout on the right (south) by a "No Vehicle" gate. Park in the turnout. If you reach the Los Prietos Ranger Station, you have gone a little too far.

Hiking directions: From the turnout, hike past the gate on the unpaved road. Fifty yards ahead is the Snyder Trail sign. Stay on the service road past a water tank to a trail split at 0.3 miles. Bear to the right. At 0.7 miles is another water tank on the left and a trail split. Go left on the footpath. The trail gains elevation up

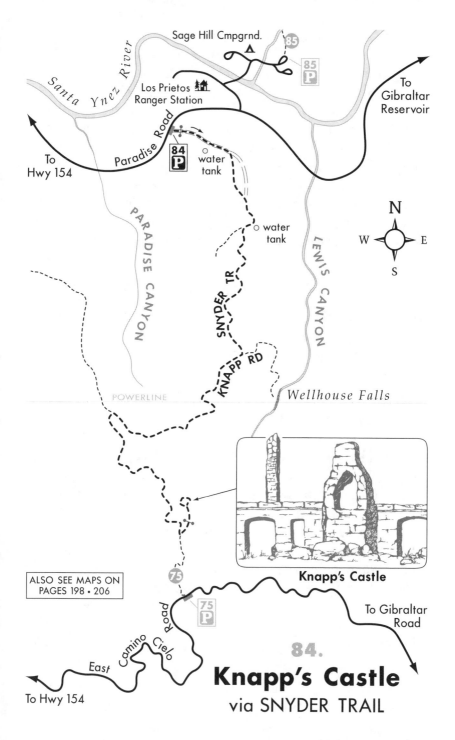

Santa Ynez River

Sage Hill Cmpgrnd.

85

85 P

Los Prietos
Ranger Station

To
Gibraltar
Reservoir

Paradise Road

84 P

water
tank

To
Hwy 154

water
tank

N

W · E

S

PARADISE CANYON

SNYDER TR

LEWIS CANYON

KNAPP RD

POWERLINE

Wellhouse Falls

Knapp's Castle

ALSO SEE MAPS ON
PAGES 198 · 206

75

75 P

To Gibraltar
Road

84.

Knapp's Castle
via SNYDER TRAIL

Camino Cielo Road

East

To Hwy 154

several switchbacks through a forested area, then heads across grassy slopes and knolls. Along the way, the knolls offer stop-over points to enjoy the views.

At 1.8 miles, the Snyder Trail joins Knapp Road at a faint, un-signed junction. To the left, an eroded path overgrown with chaparral leads 0.3 miles into Lewis Canyon to ephemeral Wellhouse Falls. From the junction, head west as the dirt road curves around the contours of the hillside through a forest of oaks and bays and under towering power lines. At 3.1 miles the trail joins an unpaved road that leads to East Camino Cielo Road. Take the unpaved road to the left, and pass the "private prop-erty" gate to Knapp's Castle. Return along the same route. ∎

85. Aliso Canyon Loop Trail

Hiking distance: 3.5-mile loop
Hiking time: 2 hours
Elevation gain: 800 feet
Maps: U.S.G.S. San Marcos Pass
      Santa Barbara Front Country and Paradise Road map

Summary of hike: Aliso Canyon sits on the northern slopes of Paradise Valley on the north side of the Santa Ynez River. Aliso Creek merges with the Santa Ynez River near Sage Hill Campground, where this hike begins. The Aliso Canyon Loop Trail starts on an interpretive trail along Aliso Creek on the eastern foot of 2,124-foot Sage Hill. Panels describe Native American life in the local area, told through the eyes of two Chumash children. The trail heads up Aliso Canyon through shady riparian vegeta-tion and continuously crosses the creek. At one mile, the trail climbs to a grassy plateau on the ridge dividing Aliso Canyon and Oso Canyon. The return hike along the ridge includes views that overlook the Santa Ynez River, the valley, and the surround-ing mountains.

Driving directions: SANTA BARBARA. From Highway 101 in Santa Barbara, take the State Street/Highway 154 exit. Turn northwest on Highway 154 (San Marcos Pass Road), and drive

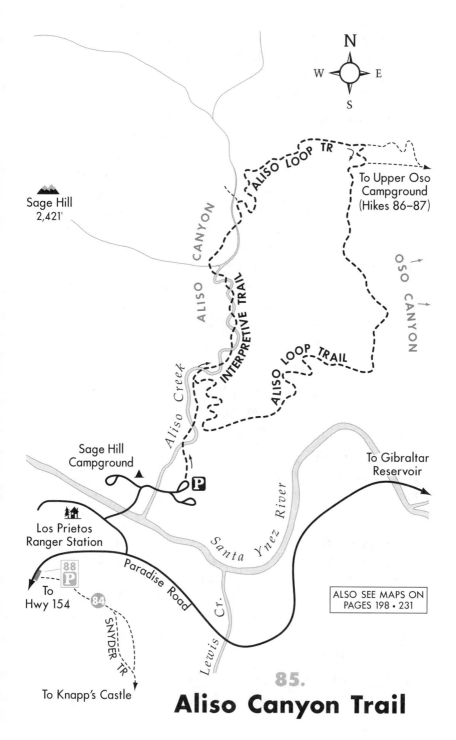

N
W   E
S

ALISO LOOP TR

To Upper Oso
Campground
(Hikes 86–87)

Sage Hill
2,421'

ALISO CANYON

OSO CANYON

INTERPRETIVE TRAIL

Aliso Creek

ALISO LOOP TRAIL

Sage Hill
Campground

P

To Gibraltar
Reservoir

Santa Ynez River

Los Prietos
Ranger Station

88 P

To
Hwy 154

84

Paradise Road

Lewis Cr.

SNYDER TR

ALSO SEE MAPS ON
PAGES 198 • 231

To Knapp's Castle

85.
Aliso Canyon Trail

10.6 miles to Paradise Road on the right. Turn right and continue 4.5 miles to the Los Prietos Ranger Station on the left (north). Turn left and follow the park road to the Sage Hill Campground. Park in the upper east end of the campground.

Hiking directions: Hike north into the forested canyon. At a quarter mile, after a few creek crossings, there is a junction with the Aliso Loop Trail, the return route. Continue straight ahead, crossing the creek numerous times and winding up the canyon. Just past sign post #15, the trail heads over a small sage-covered hill before dropping back down to the creek. Cross the creek to a junction with the Aliso Loop Trail at one mile. Ascend the eastern hillside of the canyon to the right, away from the creek. Climb steadily for a half mile to a grassy meadow and a junction with a trail heading left (east) to Upper Oso Campground (Hikes 86 and 87). Take the right fork, traversing the ridge that divides the canyons. Switchbacks descend back into Aliso Canyon. Rejoin the interpretive trail and return to the trailhead. ■

86. Lower Oso Trail
OSO CANYON

Hiking distance: 2 miles round trip
Hiking time: 1 hour
Elevation gain: 200 feet
Maps: U.S.G.S. San Marcos Pass
      Santa Barbara Front Country and Paradise Road map

Summary of hike: Oso Creek, a tributary of the Santa Ynez River, forms on the southern slopes of Little Pine Mountain and Alexander Peak. The perennial creek flows down Oso Canyon, merging with the Santa Ynez by Lower Oso Campground. This hike is a short meander that winds through a beautiful meadow along the banks of Oso Creek, connecting the Lower and Upper Oso Campgrounds.

Driving directions: SANTA BARBARA. From Highway 101 in Santa Barbara, take the State Street/Highway 154 exit. Turn

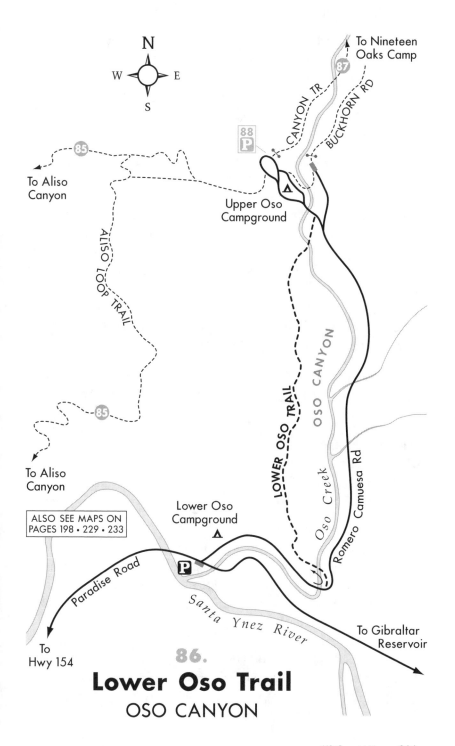

N
W   E
S

To Nineteen
Oaks Camp

87

CANYON TR

BUCKHORN RD

88 P

To Aliso
Canyon

85

Upper Oso
Campground

ALISO LOOP TRAIL

OSO CANYON

85

LOWER OSO TRAIL

Oso Creek

To Aliso
Canyon

Lower Oso
Campground

Romero Camuesa Rd

ALSO SEE MAPS ON
PAGES 198 • 229 • 233

P

Paradise Road

Santa Ynez River

To Gibraltar
Reservoir

To
Hwy 154

86.

Lower Oso Trail
OSO CANYON

northwest on Highway 154 (San Marcos Pass Road), and drive 10.6 miles to Paradise Road on the right. Turn right and continue 5.8 miles to the Lower Oso Campground on the left (north). The campground is just beyond the first crossing of the Santa Ynez River. Park in the lot on the right, across from the junction with Romero Camuesa Road.

Hiking directions: From the parking area near Lower Oso Campground, hike up the paved Romero Camuesa Road. Parallel Oso Creek towards Upper Oso Campground. At 0.3 miles, the road crosses a bridge over the creek. After crossing, leave the road on a footpath to the left. Cross Oso Creek and follow the path through the forested meadow along the west side of the creek. At 1.2 miles, cross the creek again and head into the lower end of Upper Oso Campground. This is the turn-around spot.

For extended hiking, continue with Hike 87, which begins in Upper Oso Campground and heads up to Nineteen Oaks Camp at the base of Little Pine Mountain. ■

87. Oso Canyon to Nineteen Oaks Camp
OSO CANYON

Hiking distance: 4 miles round trip
Hiking time: 2 hours
Elevation gain: 700 feet
Maps: U.S.G.S. San Marcos Pass

Summary of hike: The hike to Nineteen Oaks Camp follows Oso Canyon through the steep sandstone cliffs of Oso Narrows. The trail parallels Oso Creek up the canyon, passing pools along the creek. Nineteen Oaks Camp is located at the southwest base of Little Pine Mountain. The camp sits on a shady knoll in an oak grove with picnic tables, fire pits, and beautiful views down Oso Canyon.

The hike to the camp begins from Upper Oso Campground in the lower Santa Ynez Recreation Area of the Los Padres National Forest. The campground, which is rich with oak trees,

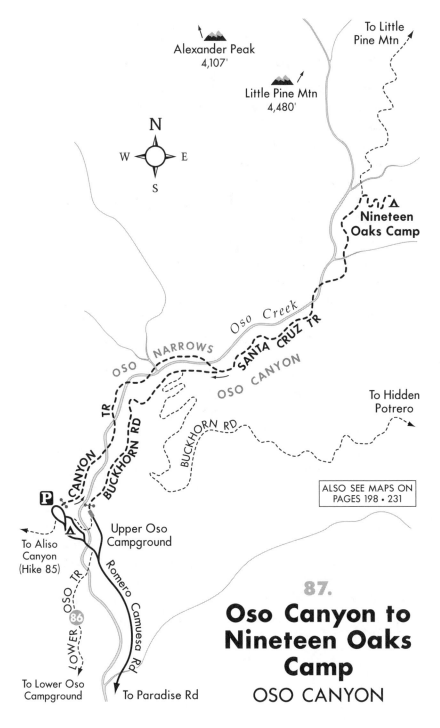

To Little
Pine Mtn

Alexander Peak
4,107'

Little Pine Mtn
4,480'

N
W · E
S

Nineteen
Oaks Camp

Oso Creek

NARROWS

SANTA CRUZ TR

OSO

OSO CANYON

CANYON TR

BUCKHORN RD

BUCKHORN RD

To Hidden
Potrero

ALSO SEE MAPS ON
PAGES 198 · 231

P

To Aliso
Canyon
(Hike 85)

Upper Oso
Campground

LOWER OSO TR

86

Romero Camuesa Rd

To Lower Oso
Campground

To Paradise Rd

87.
Oso Canyon to
Nineteen Oaks
Camp
OSO CANYON

lies in Oso Canyon on the banks of Oso Creek. From Upper Oso Campground, a short connector trail leads west up to the ridge separating Oso Canyon from Aliso Canyon (Hike 85).

Driving directions: SANTA BARBARA. From Highway 101 in Santa Barbara, take the State Street/Highway 154 exit. Turn northwest on Highway 154 (San Marcos Pass Road), and drive 10.6 miles to Paradise Road on the right. Turn right and continue 5.8 miles to the Lower Oso Campground on the left (north). The campground is just beyond the first crossing of the Santa Ynez River. Turn left into Lower Oso Campground on Romero Camuesa Road, and drive one mile to the Upper Oso Campground. Head to the far end of the campground, past the horse corrals.

Hiking directions: Take the Canyon Trail past the gate, and enter the steep-walled canyon. At one mile, after several creek crossings, the lush trail intersects with the Santa Cruz Trail veering off to the left. Continue on the Santa Cruz Trail parallel to Oso Creek, crossing the creek a few more times past pools and cascades. Various side paths lead downhill to the pools. At 1.8 miles is a signed junction to Nineteen Oaks Camp. (The main trail begins its ascent to the summit of Little Pine Mountain.) Take the right fork a quarter mile uphill to Nineteen Oaks Camp, located on a knoll overlooking the canyon.

On the return, stay on the Santa Cruz Trail until arriving at the Buckhorn Road junction, a short distance past the junction with the Canyon Trail. Take the unpaved Buckhorn Road to the right along the creek, returning to the lower end of the Upper Oso Campground. Return through the campground to the trailhead.

To extend the hike from Nineteen Oaks Camp, the trail continues climbing 3.5 miles up the south flank of 4,506-foot Little Pine Mountain. The steep path—with awe-inspiring views—winds through chaparral to Happy Hollow Camp near the summit, which sits in a grove of oaks and Jeffrey pines. ▪

88. Matias Potrero Trail

Hiking distance: 3 miles round trip
Hiking time: 1.5 hours
Elevation gain: 600 feet

map
page 236

Maps: U.S.G.S. Little Pine Mountain
Santa Ynez Recreation Area map
Santa Barbara Front Country and Paradise Road map

Summary of hike: The Matias Potrero Trail is a connector trail between Arroyo Burro Trail and Angostura Pass Road (Hikes 76 and 78). The picturesque trail follows the Santa Ynez Fault along the grassy north slopes of the Santa Ynez Mountains, passing meadows, rolling hills, canyons, rock formations, and chaparral. The trail leads to Matias Potrero Camp, a primitive campsite in an oak grove with a picnic table and a rock cookstove. From the camp, trails lead east and west to Angostura Pass Road and Arroyo Burro Canyon.

Driving directions: SANTA BARBARA. From Highway 101 in Santa Barbara, take the State Street/Highway 154 exit. Turn northwest on Highway 154 (San Marcos Pass Road), and drive 10.6 miles to Paradise Road on the right. Turn right and continue 9 miles to the parking area on the left (north), across the road from the signed trailhead.

Hiking directions: Cross the road and head south past the trail sign and metal gate. Ascend a steep hill for the first 100 yards. Continue south along the ridge between two ravines. A stream flows through the drainage on the right. At 1.2 miles, cross under power poles to a signed junction. The right fork heads west to the Arroyo Burro Trail (Hike 78). Go east on the left fork (towards Gibraltar Road and Matias Potrero Camp) to a second junction in another 0.2 miles. The right fork (the main trail) continues to Angostura Pass Road and Gibraltar Road (Hike 76). Take the left fork downhill to Matias Potrero Camp. The trail continues beyond the camp and rejoins the main trail. To return, take the same path back.

From the camp, the trail continues 2.2 miles to Angostura Pass Road, connecting to Devil's Canyon and Gibraltar Reservoir. Heading west from the camp, the trail leads 2.6 miles to Arroyo Burro Road. ■

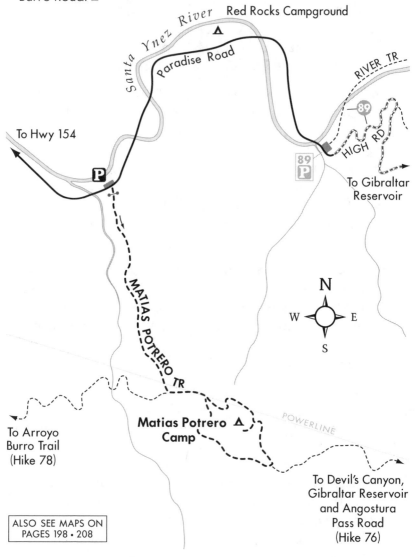

88.
Matias Potrero Trail

89. Red Rocks Pool • Gibraltar Dam
High Road — River Trail Loop

Hiking distance: 6.5 miles round trip
Hiking time: 3 hours
Elevation gain: 500 feet
Maps: U.S.G.S. Little Pine Mountain
    Santa Barbara Front Country and Paradise Road map

map
page 238

Summary of hike: Red Rocks is the name of a small, gorgeous canyon with swimming holes along the Santa Ynez River downstream from Gibraltar Reservoir. This hike, known as the Red Rocks Loop, follows the Santa Ynez River up the twisting canyon to Gibraltar Dam and the reservoir. Along the way are numerous swimming holes and beautiful rock formations. Two routes lead to the dam, creating a loop hike. The Upper Road, known locally as the High Road, is a vehicle-restricted road that traverses the mountains while overlooking the Santa Ynez River, the swimming holes, and the surrounding hills. The River Trail, once a mining road, winds along the canyon floor, crossing the river several times. The River Trail can be challenging, especially during high water. At that time, stay on the High Road.

Driving directions: SANTA BARBARA. From Highway 101 in Santa Barbara, take the State Street/Highway 154 exit. Turn northwest on Highway 154 (San Marcos Pass Road), and drive 10.6 miles to Paradise Road on the right. Turn right and continue 10.4 miles to the trailhead parking area on the left. It is located near the end of the road.

Hiking directions: The High Road begins at the end of Paradise Road at the locked gate. The road skirts along the contours of the mountain, gaining a quick 200 feet up switchbacks before leveling off on a plateau. At 2 miles are the first views of Gibraltar Reservoir. Descend a half mile, passing the Devil's Canyon Trail, to the junction with the River Trail. The right fork leads uphill to the top of the dam and Angostura Pass Road (Hike 76). The left fork leads to a swimming hole at the river and begins the return trip on the River Trail. The trail meanders down the canyon, frequently crossing the Santa Ynez River back to the trailhead.

If you are here to just cool off in a pool, take the River Trail (at the east end of the parking area) 0.3 miles to the popular Red Rocks pool. Just before the pool is a trail split. The left fork is the main trail to Gibraltar Dam. The right fork leads down to the shoreline. Red rock cliffs tower over the pool. ■

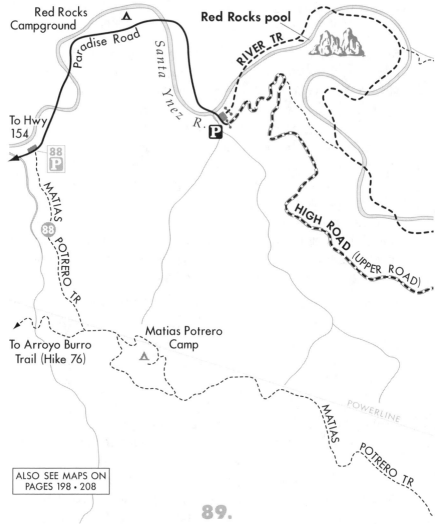

ALSO SEE MAPS ON
PAGES 198 • 208

89.
Red Rocks Pool • Gibraltar Dam
High Road—River Trail Loop

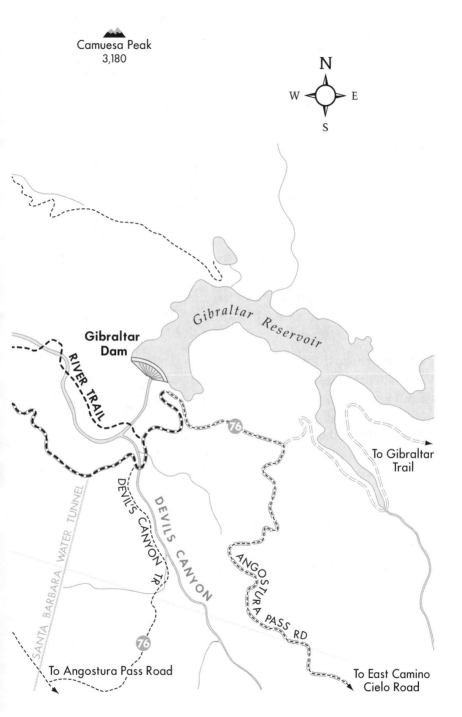

Camuesa Peak
3,180

N
W E
S

Gibraltar Reservoir

Gibraltar
Dam

RIVER TRAIL

To Gibraltar
Trail

DEVIL'S CANYON TR

DEVILS CANYON

SANTA BARBARA WATER TUNNEL

ANGOSTURA PASS RD

To Angostura Pass Road

To East Camino
Cielo Road

90. Tequepis Canyon

Hiking distance: 2 miles round trip
Hiking time: 1 hour
Elevation gain: 500 feet
Maps: U.S.G.S. Lake Cachuma
    The Cachuma Lake Recreation Area map

map
page 243

Summary of hike: Tequepis Canyon sits on the north slope of the Santa Ynez Mountains across from Lake Cachuma. Tequepis Creek, a feeder stream of the lake, forms on the upper canyon slope between Santa Ynez Peak and Broadcast Peak. The Tequepis Trail follows the creek up-canyon, then climbs to West Camino Cielo Road atop the 3,500-foot ridge. This hike follows the lower portion of the canyon, parallel to Tequepis Creek. The well-defined trail leads one mile through a shaded coastal oak and sycamore forest, crossing the creek three times. Hike 91 continues on the Tequepis Trail up to the ridge for a longer and more strenuous hike.

Driving directions: SANTA BARBARA. From Highway 101 in Santa Barbara, take the State Street/Highway 154 exit. Turn northwest on Highway 154 (San Marcos Pass Road), and drive 16.9 miles to the signed turnoff for Circle V Ranch Camp, Ranch Alegre, and Camp Whittier on the left/south. (The turnoff is located 0.6 miles before the entrance to Lake Cachuma.) Turn left and continue 1.3 miles, passing private ranch camps, to the road's end at the designated parking area on the right.

BUELLTON. From Highway 101 and Highway 246 at Buellton, take the Highway 246 exit. Drive 8.4 miles east on Highway 246 (Mission Drive), passing through Solvang to Highway 154. Turn right and continue 7.2 miles to the signed turnoff for Circle V Ranch Camp, Ranch Alegre, and Camp Whittier on the right/south. (The turnoff is located 0.6 miles past the entrance to Lake Cachuma.) Turn right and drive 1.3 miles, passing private camps, to the road's end at the designated parking area on the right.

Hiking directions: Cross the road and enter St. Vincent de Paul Ranch Camp. Walk up the camp road, passing the pool.

Follow the trail signs 150 yards through the camp. Cross over Tequepis Creek, leaving the camp, and enter the Los Padres National Forest. Follow the east side of Tequepis Creek under majestic oaks and sycamores. Cross the creek two more times, and head up the east canyon wall in the shade of the forest. Emerge from the oaks to views of the San Rafael Mountain Range, Lake Cachuma, and Broadcast Peak at the crest of West Cielo Ridge. At one mile is a trail sign, where the trail narrows and turns left. The trail leaves the creek and begins the ascent out of the canyon—the turn-around spot for this hike.

To extend the hike up to West Camino Cielo Road, continue on the Tequepis Trail—Hike 91. It is an additional 3 miles to the ridgetop. ∎

91. Tequepis Trail to West Cielo Ridge
TEQUEPIS CANYON

Hiking distance: 8 miles round trip
Hiking time: 4.5 hours
Elevation gain: 2,300 feet
Maps: U.S.G.S. Lake Cachuma
San Rafael Wilderness Map Guide

map
page 243

Summary of hike: The Tequepis (Chumash for *seed gatherer*) Trail is located in the Los Padres National Forest near Lake Cachuma. The trail climbs the north slope of the Santa Ynez Mountains through Tequepis Canyon to West Cielo Ridge, cresting at 3,500 feet. The lightly used trail weaves up the mountain with gradual, long switchbacks, from the forested canyon bottom to madrone and tanbark oak trees at the summit. Throughout the hike are views of Lake Cachuma, the Santa Ynez Valley, and the San Raphael Mountain Range. From the crest are unobstructed panoramic vistas of Santa Barbara, Goleta, the Pacific Ocean, and the Channel Islands.

Driving directions: SANTA BARBARA. From Highway 101 in Santa Barbara, take the State Street/Highway 154 exit. Turn northwest on Highway 154 (San Marcos Pass Road), and drive

16.9 miles to the signed turnoff for Circle V Ranch Camp, Ranch Alegre, and Camp Whittier on the left/south. (The turnoff is located 0.6 miles before the entrance to Lake Cachuma.) Turn left and continue 1.3 miles, passing private ranch camps, to the road's end at the designated parking area on the right.

BUELLTON. From Highway 101 and Highway 246 at Buellton, take the Highway 246 exit. Drive 8.4 miles east on Highway 246 (Mission Drive), passing through Solvang to Highway 154. Turn right and continue 7.2 miles to the signed turnoff for Circle V Ranch Camp, Ranch Alegre, and Camp Whittier on the right/south. (The turnoff is located 0.6 miles past the entrance to Lake Cachuma.) Turn right and drive 1.3 miles, passing private camps, to the road's end at the designated parking area on the right.

Hiking directions: Cross the road and enter St. Vincent de Paul Ranch Camp. Walk up the camp road, passing the pool. Follow the trail signs 150 yards through the camp. Cross over Tequepis Creek, leaving the camp, and enter the Los Padres National Forest. Follow the east side of Tequepis Creek under majestic oaks and sycamores. Cross the creek two more times, and head up the east canyon wall in the shade of the forest. Emerge from the oaks to views of the San Rafael Mountain Range, Lake Cachuma, and Broadcast Peak at the crest of West Cielo Ridge. At one mile is a trail sign, where the trail narrows and turns left. This is the turn-around point for Hike 90.

Leave the creek and begin ascending the north slope of the Santa Ynez Mountains. The trail steadily climbs upward with the aid of eight switchbacks, but rarely at a steep grade. During the ascent, the vistas increasingly expand to include Lake Cachuma and the stunning mountain range across the lake. After the last switchback, traverse the mountain under the shade of bay laurel, madrone, and tanbark oak trees, with a rich understory of ferns. At 4 miles, the trail reaches the narrow dirt road atop West Cielo Ridge on the east flank of Broadcast Peak. The views now stretch to the south as well, overlooking Santa Barbara, Goleta, the Channel Islands, and the Pacific Ocean. This is the turn-around point.

To extend the hike another 1.5 miles, bear right and climb an additional 500 feet in elevation to the top of Broadcast Peak. Return along the same trail. ■

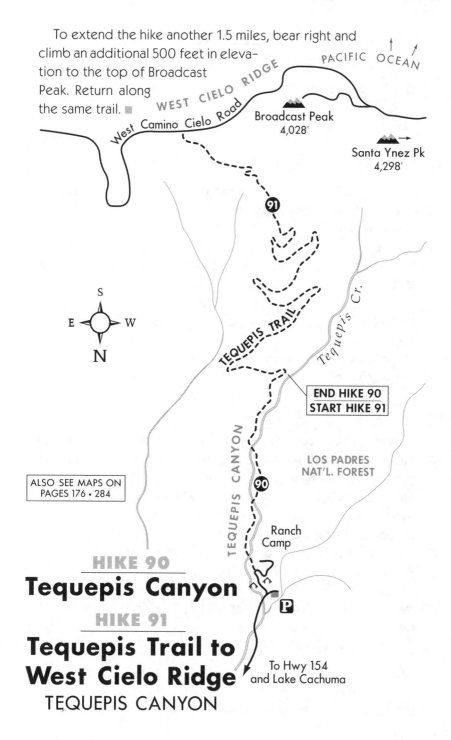

PACIFIC OCEAN

WEST CIELO RIDGE

West Camino Cielo Road

Broadcast Peak
4,028'

Santa Ynez Pk
4,298'

91

TEQUEPIS TRAIL

Tequepis Cr.

**END HIKE 90
START HIKE 91**

S
E — W
N

TEQUEPIS CANYON

LOS PADRES
NAT'L. FOREST

ALSO SEE MAPS ON
PAGES 176 • 284

90

Ranch
Camp

HIKE 90
Tequepis Canyon
HIKE 91
Tequepis Trail to
West Cielo Ridge
TEQUEPIS CANYON

P

To Hwy 154
and Lake Cachuma

92. Mohawk Mesa Trail
LAKE CACHUMA · LAKE CACHUMA COUNTY PARK

Hiking distance: 0.6-mile loop
Hiking time: 15 minutes
Elevation gain: Level
Maps: U.S.G.S. Lake Cachuma
The Cachuma Lake Recreation Area map

Summary of hike: Lake Cachuma is the largest of three reservoirs on the Santa Ynez River, covering 3,200 acres. It measures five miles in length and has 42 miles of shoreline. The water is diverted south under the Santa Ynez Mountains, supplying agricultural irrigation and drinking water to the cities of Santa Barbara, Goleta, Montecito, and Carpinteria. The lake, a designated recreation area, is also fed by several tributaries, including Cachuma Creek, Santa Cruz Creek, Sweetwater Creek, and Tequepis Creek.

Mohawk Mesa is a peninsula jutting into Lake Cachuma from the south shore. The Mohawk Mesa Trail is a short, scenic loop around the perimeter of the promontory. At the northern tip is a fishing pier at Mohawk Point.

Driving directions: SANTA BARBARA. From Highway 101 in Santa Barbara, take the State Street/Highway 154 exit. Turn northwest on Highway 154 (San Marcos Pass Road), and drive 17.5 miles to the Lake Cachuma County Park entrance on the right (north). Turn right and continue past the entrance kiosk, straight ahead for 0.1 mile. Turn right, following the signs to the overflow area. Continue 0.5 miles to the signed Mohawk Mesa Trail on the left. Park in the pullout by the trailhead.

BUELLTON. From Highway 101 and Highway 246 at Buellton, take the Highway 246 exit. Drive 8.4 miles east on Highway 246 (Mission Drive), passing through Solvang to Highway 154. Turn right and continue 6.6 miles to the Lake Cachuma County Park entrance on the left (north).

Hiking directions: From the parking pullout, hike beside the northeast edge of Mohawk Mesa along Martini Cove. The forested path leads to Mohawk Point, overlooking Lake Cachuma on three sides. Near the northern point is a fishing pier. Along the way, several side paths lead down to the water's edge. The trail returns beside Drake Cove, a small, quiet inlet. At the park road, head back to the trailhead to the left. ▪

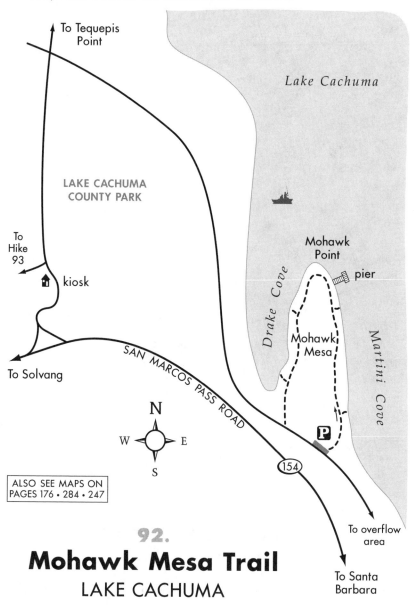

92.
Mohawk Mesa Trail
LAKE CACHUMA

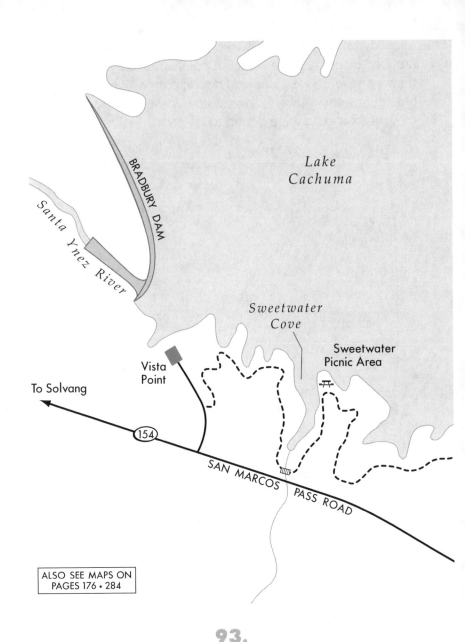

Lake
Cachuma

BRADBURY DAM

Santa Ynez River

Sweetwater
Cove

Sweetwater
Picnic Area

Vista
Point

To Solvang

154

SAN MARCOS PASS ROAD

ALSO SEE MAPS ON
PAGES 176 • 284

93.
Sweetwater Trail
to Vista Point
LAKE CACHUMA • LAKE CACHUMA CTY. PARK

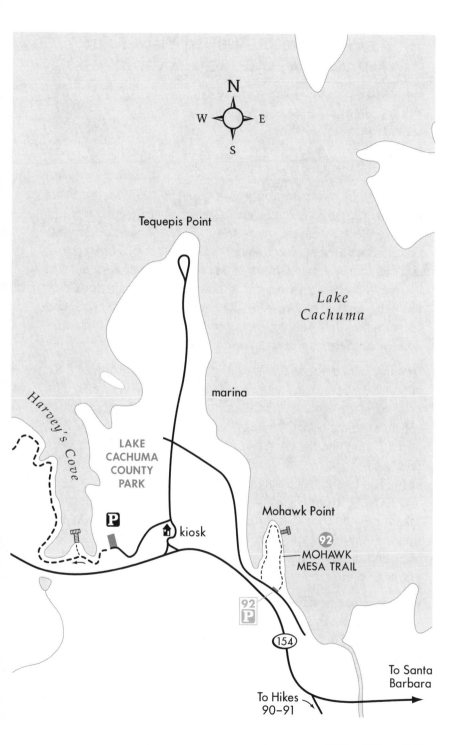

N
W E
S

Tequepis Point

Lake Cachuma

marina

Harvey's Cove

LAKE CACHUMA COUNTY PARK

P

kiosk

Mohawk Point

92

MOHAWK MESA TRAIL

92 P

154

To Santa Barbara

To Hikes 90-91

93. Sweetwater Trail to Vista Point
LAKE CACHUMA • LAKE CACHUMA COUNTY PARK

Hiking distance: 5 miles round trip
Hiking time: 2.5 hours
Elevation gain: 160 feet
Maps: U.S.G.S. Lake Cachuma
      The Cachuma Lake Recreation Area map

map
page 246

Summary of hike: Bradbury Dam, built in 1953 on the Santa Ynez River, created Lake Cachuma. The 2.5-mile Sweetwater Trail follows the south shore of the lake. The hike begins at Harvey's Cove, a beautiful inlet with a handicap-accessible fishing dock and picnic area under a grove of oak trees. The trail ends at Vista Point and Bradbury Dam, where there is a scenic overlook near the west end of the lake. Along the way, the trail hugs the shoreline around inlets and coves, passing additional lake overlooks while meandering through an oak and sycamore forest.

Driving directions: SANTA BARBARA. From Highway 101 in Santa Barbara, take the State Street/Highway 154 exit. Turn northwest on Highway 154 (San Marcos Pass Road), and drive 17.5 miles to the Lake Cachuma County Park entrance on the right (north). Turn into the park, and continue past the entrance kiosk. Take the road to the left for 0.3 miles to the trailhead parking lot at the road's end, following the signs to Harvey's Cove.

BUELLTON. From Highway 101 and Highway 246 at Buellton, take the Highway 246 exit. Drive 8.4 miles east on Highway 246 (Mission Drive), passing through Solvang to Highway 154. Turn right and continue 6.6 miles to the Lake Cachuma County Park entrance on the left (north).

Hiking directions: From the parking lot, take the paved path around the south shoreline of Harvey's Cove. As you near the pier, take the hiking trail veering off to the left. Stay close to the water's edge, curving around each inlet. Once past Harvey's Cove, the trail curves inland and gains elevation, soon arriving at the Sweetwater Picnic Area. From the picnic area, follow the trail past the Vista Point sign, curving completely around Sweetwater

Cove. At the south end of the cove, the trail joins an unpaved road for a short distance before picking up the trail again on the right and crossing a bridge. At 2.5 miles, the trail ends at the Vista Point parking lot and an overlook of the Bradbury Dam. Return along the same route. ■

94. Sedgwick Reserve

3566 Brinkerhoff Avenue · Santa Ynez

3 docent-led hikes at 9:00 a.m. · 2nd Saturday/every month
Call for info at (805) 686-1941 · sedgwick@lifesci.ucsb.edu

Hiking distance: 8-mile loop
Hiking time: 4 hours
Elevation gain: 600 feet
Maps: U.S.G.S. Los Olivos
      Sedgwick Reserve map

**map
page 251**

Summary of hike: The Sedgwick Reserve is a 5,896-acre protected natural area in the Santa Ynez Valley on the southern slopes of the San Rafael Mountains. The ranch, purchased by Francis "Duke" Sedgwick in 1952, was donated to UC Santa Barbara in 1967. Perched on the flanks of Figueroa Mountain, the reserve is home to canyons, woodlands, expansive fields, rocky outcroppings, wetland habitats, vernal pools, and two watersheds. The diverse vegetation includes coastal live oak, valley oak savannah, blue oak woodland, chaparral, sage scrub, riparian willow and sycamore habitats, grasslands, and a gray pine forest that extends into the Los Padres National Forest.

The reserve, administered by UC Santa Barbara, is a teaching and research facility. Research on the former cattle ranch includes oak regeneration, valley oak genetics, interactions between native and introduced grasses, and identification of plant species. Once a month, the reserve offers three interpretive hikes: an easy hike with an emphasis on interpretation, a moderate 3—5 mile hike, and a strenuous 6—8 mile hike. This hike—the strenuous one—begins in the Figueroa Creek drainage and forms a loop through the heart of the reserve.

Driving directions: SANTA BARBARA. From Highway 101 in Santa Barbara, take the State Street/Highway 154 exit. Turn northwest on Highway 154 (San Marcos Pass Road), and drive 16.9 miles to Edison Street. (The turnoff is located 8.7 miles past the entrance to Lake Cachuma.) Turn right and continue 1.1 mile on Edison Street to Roblar Avenue. Turn right and go 0.8 miles to Brinkerhoff Avenue. Turn left and drive 2.5 miles to the Sedgwick Reserve entrance. Wind 1.1 miles up and over the hill to the staging area on the right at the end of the road.

BUELLTON. From Highway 101 and Highway 246 at Buellton, take the Highway 246 exit. Drive 8.4 miles east on Highway 246 (Mission Drive), passing through Solvang and Santa Ynez, to Highway 154. Turn left and continue 2.2 miles to Edison Street. Turn right and follow the directions above.

BUELLTON (NORTH). From Highway 101 and Highway 154, located 6 miles north of Buellton, take the Highway 154 exit. Turn southwest on Highway 154 (San Marcos Pass Road) and drive 5 miles to Roblar Avenue. Turn left and continue 2 miles east to Brinkerhoff Avenue. Turn left and follow the directions above.

Hiking directions: From the north end of the road, walk up Figueroa Creek Road, a dirt road. Follow the west edge of Figueroa Creek, a tributary of the Santa Ynez River, and stroll through the oak-dotted valley. Pass a pond on the right while enjoying the views of the San Rafael Mountains to the north (including Zaca Peak, Figueroa Mountain, and Ranger Peak) and the Santa Ynez Mountains to the south. At one mile, veer left, leaving the road, and gently climb through groves of oaks draped with lace-lichen to a Y-fork.

Begin the loop to the right, leaving the forest to the open chaparral. Make a long, easy descent to the east, passing gray pines. At 2.6 miles, curve left and steadily gain elevation through the forest. As the path levels out, curve left and continue through oak-covered grassland to a trail split. Meander through the meadow among the blue oaks in the Lisque Creek drainage. Bear left and climb to the ridge. Follow the ridge and make a short but steep descent, completing the loop. Retrace your steps to the right. ■

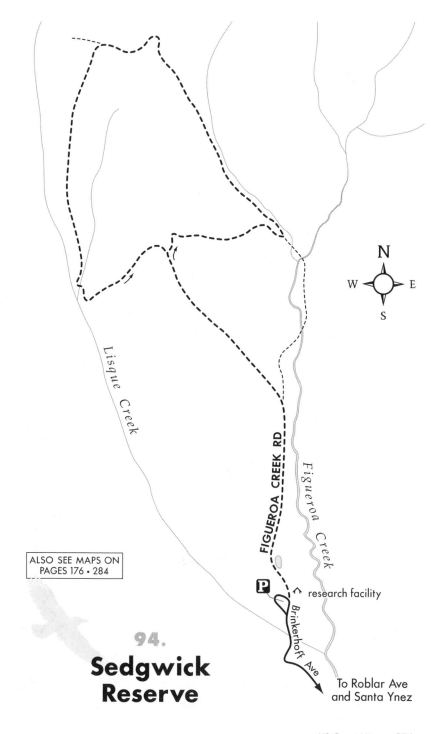

ALSO SEE MAPS ON
PAGES 176 · 284

N
W · E
S

Lisque Creek

FIGUEROA CREEK RD

Figueroa Creek

Brinkerhoff Ave

research facility

P

94.
Sedgwick
Reserve

To Roblar Ave
and Santa Ynez

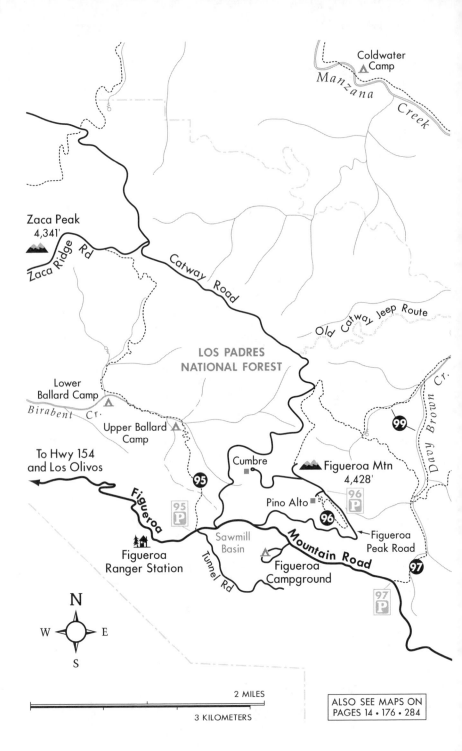

Coldwater Camp

Manzana Creek

Zaca Peak
4,341'

Zaca Ridge Rd

Catway Road

Old Catway Jeep Route

LOS PADRES
NATIONAL FOREST

Lower
Ballard Camp

Birabent Cr.

Upper Ballard
Camp

Davy Brown Cr.

99

To Hwy 154
and Los Olivos

Cumbre

Figueroa Mtn
4,428'

95

Figueroa

95
P

Pino Alto

96
P

96

Figueroa
Peak Road

97

Sawmill
Basin

Mountain Road

Figueroa
Ranger Station

Tunnel Rd

Figueroa
Campground

97
P

N
W   E
S

2 MILES

3 KILOMETERS

ALSO SEE MAPS ON
PAGES 14 • 176 • 284

Figueroa Mountain Recreation Area

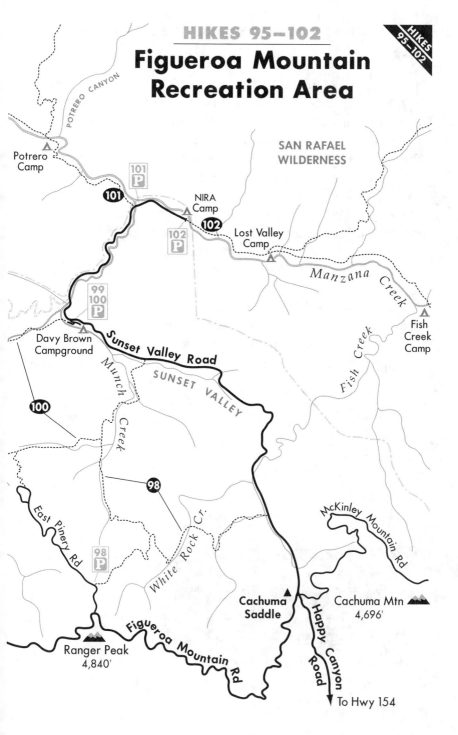

SAN RAFAEL
WILDERNESS

POTRERO CANYON

Potrero
Camp

101
101 P

NIRA
Camp

102

102 P

Lost Valley
Camp

Manzana Creek

99
100 P

Davy Brown
Campground

Sunset Valley Road

SUNSET VALLEY

Munch Creek

Fish Creek

Fish
Creek
Camp

100

98

White Rock Cr.

McKinley Mountain Rd

East Pinery Rd

98 P

Cachuma
Saddle

Cachuma Mtn
4,696'

Figueroa Mountain Rd

Ranger Peak
4,840'

Happy Canyon Road

To Hwy 154

Figueroa Mountain Recreation Area

HIKES 95–102

The Figueroa Mountain Recreation Area offers natural solitude in a largely undeveloped tract of land along the San Rafael Mountains. The area is 12 miles northeast of Los Olivos and is one of three recreational areas in the Los Padres National Forest. The San Rafael Wilderness runs through the forest land. The rolling landscape has chapparal-covered slopes and cool, wooded canyons with several year-round creeks. There are over 30 miles of hiking and biking trails as well as picnic areas and primitive to modern camping facilities. Remains of homesteads and old mine sites can be spotted along several trails.

Hikes 95–102 are located along the slopes of Figueroa Mountain. The peak rises over 4,500 feet to the northeast of the Santa Ynez Valley. The mountain is well-known for its beautiful displays of wildflowers in the spring. A lookout at the summit offers picnic facilities and an expansive panorama that stretches from the mountains to the Pacific Ocean and the Channel Islands.

The recreational area is accessed from either Figueroa Mountain Road or Happy Canyon Road. Driving directions are provided for both roads.

Manzana Schoolhouse · Hike 101

95. La Jolla Trail
Figueroa Mountain Road to Upper Ballard Camp
FIGUEROA MOUNTAIN RECREATION AREA

Hiking distance: 4 miles round trip
Hiking time: 2.5 hours
Elevation gain: 1,100 feet

map
page 257

Maps: U.S.G.S. Figueroa Mountain, Los Olivos, and Zaca Lake
    Backcountry Guide: San Rafael Wilderness

Summary of hike: The La Jolla Trail begins from the exposed upper slopes of Figueroa Mountain on a saddle off of Figueroa Mountain Road (front cover photo). The trail descends along the west flank of the mountain into Birabent Canyon, leading to the banks of Birabent Creek and Upper Ballard Camp. The camp is named for William Ballard, who used the site as a hunting camp in the 1880s. The primitive camp is tucked into a steep and cool canyon bottom between Zaca Peak and Figueroa Mountain. En route, the trail weaves through a mixed forest with pockets of Coulter pine, yellow pine, big cone spruce, big leaf maple, blue oaks, coastal valley oaks, and California bay laurel.

Driving directions: FROM SANTA BARBARA VIA HAPPY CANYON ROAD: From Highway 101 in Santa Barbara, take the State Street/Highway 154 exit. Turn northwest on Highway 154 (San Marcos Pass Road), and drive 22 miles to Armour Ranch Road. (The turn-off is located 4.6 miles past the entrance to Lake Cachuma.) Turn right and continue 1.3 miles to Happy Canyon Road. Turn right and drive 13.7 miles to the posted Cachuma Saddle and a road junction. Turn left on Figueroa Mountain Road, and go 7.5 miles to the signed trailhead on the right. The trailhead is directly across from Tunnel Road at mile marker 12.45. Park in the wide dirt pull-out on the left.

    FROM SANTA BARBARA VIA FIGUEROA MOUNTAIN ROAD: From Highway 101 in Santa Barbara, take the State Street/Highway 154 exit. Turn northwest on Highway 154 (San Marcos Pass Road), and drive 29.4 miles on Highway 154 to Figueroa Mountain Road at Los Olivos. Turn right and continue 12.5 miles to the posted trailhead on the left, directly across from the signed Tunnel Road at mile marker 12.45. (The trailhead is a half mile past the Figueroa Ranger Station.) Park in the wide dirt pullout on the right.

FROM BUELLTON VIA FIGUEROA MOUNTAIN ROAD: From Highway 101 at Buellton, take the Highway 246 exit. Drive 8.4 miles east on Highway 246 (Mission Drive), passing through Solvang and Santa Ynez, to Highway 154. Turn left and continue 5.3 miles to Figueroa Mountain Road at Los Olivos. Turn right and continue 12.5 miles to the posted trailhead on the left, directly across from the signed Tunnel Road at mile marker 12.45. (The trailhead is a half mile past the Figueroa Ranger Station.) Park in the wide dirt pullout on the right.

Hiking directions: Cross Figueroa Mountain Road to the signed trailhead on the saddle. Walk through the open grassland while views of Zaca Peak and Birabent Canyon stretch to the north. Descend along the oak-dotted hillside on the west flank of Figueroa Mountain. Cross a seasonal tributary of Birabent Creek and veer left, passing pockets of oaks, pines, and manzanita. Traverse the slope above Birabent Canyon, with far-reaching vistas to the ocean. Steadily descend, zigzagging down the mountain to Upper Ballard Camp on the banks of Birabent Creek at two miles. The camp sits at the bottom of the canyon in a shaded oak and sycamore grove with a couple of primitive campsites. This is the turn-around spot.

To extend the hike, cross the creek and head downstream, passing another campsite on the right. The abandoned path crosses the creek and passes a small pool and rock waterslide. The old washed-out path crosses the creek seven more times, which entails some bushwacking, to Lower Ballard Camp by a stream-fed side canyon. A washed-out, overgrown, and difficult-to-follow trail heads 0.4 miles up the canyon to La Jolla Spring (a tributary of Birabent Creek) and continues 2 miles to Zaca Ridge Road at Zaca Peak. ▪

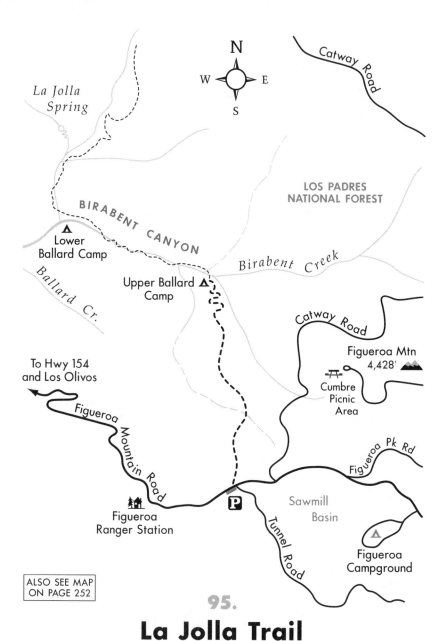

ALSO SEE MAP
ON PAGE 252

95.

La Jolla Trail
Figueroa Mountain Road to Upper Ballard Camp
FIGUEROA MOUNTAIN RECREATION AREA

96. Pino Alto Nature Trail
FIGUEROA MOUNTAIN RECREATION AREA

Hiking distance: 0.5-mile loop
　　　　　　　　(3.7 miles round trip if road is gated)
Hiking time: 30 minutes to 2.5 hours
Elevation gain: 120 feet to 900 feet
Maps: U.S.G.S. Figueroa Mountain
　　　　Backcountry Guide: San Rafael Wilderness

Summary of hike: The Pino Alto (meaning *high pine*) Nature Trail is a paved, handicapped-accessible interpretive trail near the summit of Figueroa Mountain. The self-guided trail begins under Douglas and ponderosa pines at a pristine picnic area. Numbered posts correspond with an interpretive guide describing the forest environment, including the surrounding trees; the effects of weather, soil, and fire; and Native American life. If the interpretive guides are not available at the trailhead, check at the ranger station.

Heavy rains can cause a closure of the unpaved Figueroa Peak Road to vehicles. In this event, it is a great 1.6-mile walk up the winding, forested road to the nature trail. The views from the road span across the San Rafael Mountains, overlooking Hurricane Deck, Fir Canyon, and Sunset Valley.

Driving directions: FROM SANTA BARBARA VIA HAPPY CANYON ROAD: From Highway 101 in Santa Barbara, take the State Street/Highway 154 exit. Turn northwest on Highway 154 (San Marcos Pass Road), and drive 22 miles to Armour Ranch Road. (The turnoff is located 4.6 miles past the entrance to Lake Cachuma.) Turn right and continue 1.3 miles to Happy Canyon Road. Turn right and drive 13.7 miles to the posted Cachuma Saddle and a road junction. Turn left on Figueroa Mountain Road, and go 6.9 miles to Figueroa Peak Road on the right. It is located 0.4 miles past the Figueroa Campground. Turn right on Figueroa Peak Road, and drive 1.6 miles on the narrow, winding, unpaved road to the signed Pino Alto Picnic Area on the left. Turn left and park on the left by the signed trailhead kiosk. If Figueroa Peak Road is gated,

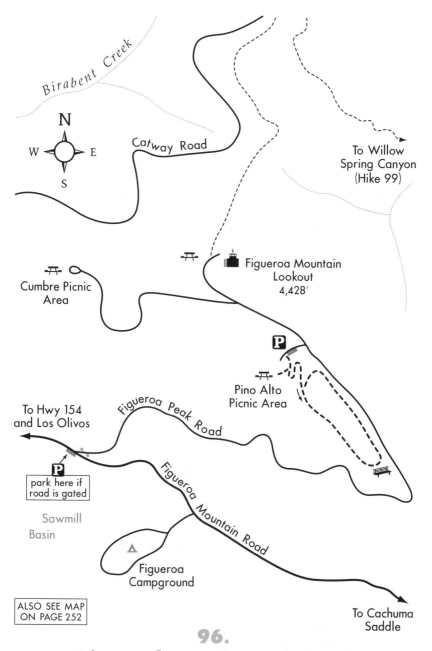

Birabent Creek

N
W   E
S

Catway Road

To Willow
Spring Canyon
(Hike 99)

Figueroa Mountain
Lookout
4,428'

Cumbre Picnic
Area

Pino Alto
Picnic Area

To Hwy 154
and Los Olivos

Figueroa Peak Road

P
park here if
road is gated

Sawmill
Basin

Figueroa
Mountain Road

Figueroa
Campground

ALSO SEE MAP
ON PAGE 252

To Cachuma
Saddle

96.

Pino Alto Nature Trail
FIGUEROA MOUNTAIN RECREATION AREA

park in the pullout on the right. Walk up the forested road for 1.6 miles while enjoying the spectacular views of the mountains.

FROM SANTA BARBARA VIA FIGUEROA MOUNTAIN ROAD: From Highway 101 in Santa Barbara, take the State Street/Highway 154 exit. Turn northwest on Highway 154 (San Marcos Pass Road), and drive 29.4 miles on Highway 154 to Figueroa Mountain Road at Los Olivos. Turn right and continue 13.1 miles to Figueroa Peak Road at the posted trailhead. The turnoff is located on the left, 1.1 miles past the Figueroa Ranger Station. Turn left on Figueroa Peak Road, and drive 1.6 miles on the narrow, winding, unpaved road to the signed Pino Alto Picnic Area on the left. Turn left and park on the left by the signed trailhead kiosk. If Figueroa Peak Road is gated, park in the pullout on the right, and walk up the forested road for 1.6 miles.

FROM BUELLTON VIA FIGUEROA MOUNTAIN ROAD: From Highway 101 at Buellton, take the Highway 246 exit. Drive 8.4 miles east on Highway 246 (Mission Drive), passing through Solvang and Santa Ynez, to Highway 154. Turn left and continue 5.3 miles to Figueroa Mountain Road at Los Olivos. Turn right and continue 13.1 miles to Figueroa Peak Road at the posted trailhead. The turnoff is located on the left, 1.1 miles past the Figueroa Ranger Station. Turn left on Figueroa Peak Road, and drive 1.6 miles on the narrow, winding, unpaved road to the signed Pino Alto Picnic Area on the left. Turn left and park on the left by the signed trailhead kiosk. If Figueroa Peak Road is gated, park in the pullout on the right, and walk up the forested road for 1.6 miles.

Hiking directions: From the kiosk, head south to a trail split, 30 yards straight ahead. The right fork leads to the picnic area. Veer left on the paved path, weaving through ponderosa pine and Douglas fir. The views span across the mountains to Hurricane Deck, the dramatic white rock mountain to the northeast. Continue to a trail split and begin the loop on the right branch. At the south end of the loop are benches and an overlook of the Santa Ynez Valley, the Santa Ynez Mountains, and Lake Cachuma. Return north, completing the nature loop.

To extend the hike to the Figueroa Mountain summit, walk 0.15 miles up Figueroa Peak Road to a Y-fork. The left fork descends a half mile to the Cumbre Picnic Area on a knoll in an oak grove at the end of the road. The right fork leads 0.35 miles to the Figueroa Mountain Lookout atop the 4,528-foot peak. At the summit, there is a picnic area on the open grasslands to the left, with an overlook of the San Rafael Mountains and the Sierra Madre Mountains. To the right is the Fire Lookout Tower, with views across the Santa Ynez Mountains to the Pacific Ocean and Channel Islands. ■

97. Davy Brown Trail: Upper Trailhead
Figueroa Mountain Road to Davy Brown Campground
FIGUEROA MOUNTAIN RECREATION AREA

Hiking distance: 6.2 miles round trip
Hiking time: 4 hours
Elevation gain: 1,750 feet

map page 263

Maps: U.S.G.S. Bald Mountain and Figueroa Mountain
Backcountry Guide: San Rafael Wilderness

Summary of hike: The Davy Brown Trail is located in the San Rafael Mountains above the Santa Ynez Valley near the wilderness boundary. The trail has two trailheads. The lower trailhead—the start for Hikes 99 and 100—begins from Sunset Valley Road. This hike begins from the upper trailhead along Figueroa Mountain Road (back cover photo). The trail follows Davy Brown Creek downstream through lush Fir Canyon under a shady canopy of sycamores, big cone spruce, and a variety of pines. En route, the hike passes an old chrome mine and the remains of miner Harry Robert's cabin from the 1920s, which burned in the 1993 Marre Fire. The Davy Brown Trail connects with Munch Canyon (Hike 98) and Willow Spring Canyon (Hike 99) for extended hiking.

Driving directions: FROM SANTA BARBARA VIA HAPPY CANYON ROAD: From Highway 101 in Santa Barbara, take the State Street/ Highway 154 exit. Turn northwest on Highway 154 (San Marcos Pass Road), and drive 22 miles to Armour Ranch Road. (The turn-off is located 4.6 miles past the entrance to Lake Cachuma.) Turn right and continue 1.3 miles to Happy Canyon Road. Turn right and drive 13.7 miles to the posted Cachuma Saddle and a road junction. Turn left on Figueroa Mountain Road, and go 5.5 miles to the signed trailhead on the right. Park in the dirt pullout on the right.

FROM SANTA BARBARA VIA FIGUEROA MOUNTAIN ROAD: From Highway 101 in Santa Barbara, take the State Street/Highway 154 exit. Turn northwest on Highway 154 (San Marcos Pass Road), and drive 29.4 miles on Highway 154 to Figueroa Mountain Road at Los Olivos. Turn right and continue 14.5 miles to the signed trailhead on the left. (The trailhead is 2.5 miles past the Figueroa Ranger Station.) Park in the dirt pullout on the left.

FROM BUELLTON VIA FIGUEROA MOUNTAIN ROAD: From Highway 101 at Buellton, take the Highway 246 exit. Drive 8.4 miles east on Highway 246 (Mission Drive), passing through Solvang and Santa Ynez, to Highway 154. Turn left and continue 5.3 miles to Figueroa Mountain Road at Los Olivos. Turn right and continue 14.5 miles to the signed trailhead on the left. (The trailhead is 2.5 miles past the Figueroa Ranger Station.) Park in the dirt pullout on the left.

Hiking directions: From the signed trailhead, cross over a small saddle with views back into the Santa Ynez Valley. Traverse the oak-dotted hillside, and drop into the canyon under tall firs, pines, and bay laurel. Walk through an old wooden gate, and follow the narrow canyon downhill through white Monterey shale along the west canyon wall. Pass a series of pools in the bedrock on a branch of Davy Brown Creek. Cross the creek and continue on the east canyon wall among towering fir trees. At the confluence with the main fork of Davy Brown Creek, cross the tributary stream and head left down Fir Canyon. Parallel the creek amid maple trees. At the canyon floor, follow the waterway to a posted junction at one mile. At the junction, a plaque embedded in a boulder honors Edgar Davidson, a forest ranger who patrolled the Zaca Lake Forest Reserve and built the Davy Brown Trail in 1898—1899.

To the right, across Davy Brown Creek, is the Munch Canyon Spur Trail. It leads 1.4 miles to Munch Canyon (Hike 100). Instead, continue straight ahead 80 yards to another trail split. The

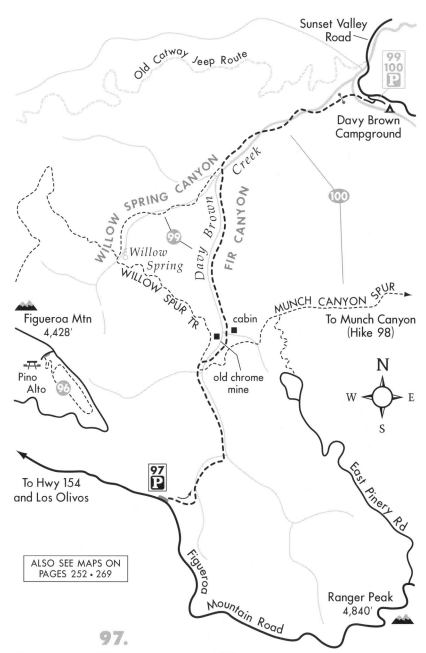

Sunset Valley
Road

Old Catway Jeep Route

99
100
P

Davy Brown
Campground

WILLOW SPRING CANYON

Davy Brown Creek

FIR CANYON

99

Willow Spring

WILLOW SPUR TR

MUNCH CANYON SPUR

100

To Munch Canyon
(Hike 98)

cabin

old chrome
mine

Figueroa Mtn
4,428'

Pino
Alto

96

N

W   E

S

To Hwy 154
and Los Olivos

97
P

East Pinery Rd

ALSO SEE MAPS ON
PAGES 252 • 269

Figueroa Mountain Road

Ranger Peak
4,840'

97.

Davy Brown Trail: Upper Trailhead
FIGUEROA MOUNTAIN RECREATION AREA

Willow Spring Connector Trail veers left and leads one mile to Willow Spring (Hike 99). For this hike, cross Davy Brown Creek and follow the east side of the creek downstream. Watch for an old chrome mine tunnel in the hillside across the creek to the west. One hundred yards ahead, by a side drainage on the right, are the rock foundation ruins of miner Harry Robert's cabin. Continue downhill on the east canyon wall, passing cascades and small pools as northern views open up across the San Rafael Mountains. Weave past huge moss-covered sandstone boulders while passing several more small waterfalls. Rock-hop over the creek to a junction on the left with the Willow Spring Trail (Hike 99). Stroll through the oak-studded meadows, passing swimming holes and crossing the creek three more times. Leave Fir Canyon and pass through a metal gate. Cross a concrete channel over Munch Creek into the Davy Brown Campground at Sunset Valley Road. Return by retracing your steps. ∎

98. White Rock—Munch Canyon Loop
FIGUEROA MOUNTAIN RECREATION AREA

Hiking distance: 9-mile loop
Hiking time: 6 hours
Elevation gain: 2,000 feet

map
page 267

Maps: U.S.G.S. Figueroa Mountain and Bald Mountain
      Backcountry Guide: San Rafael Wilderness

Summary of hike: White Rock Canyon and Munch Canyon are steep stream-fed canyons in the San Rafael Range near Figueroa Mountain. Trails weave through the length of the canyons, connecting Figueroa Mountain Road by Ranger Peak with Sunset Valley Road below. White Rock Canyon is named for the white sandstone outcroppings located about a mile down canyon. The trails, originally chrome ore mining roads, follow the streams and pass open meadows to the old mines with scattered remnants.

This loop hike begins on the north flank of Ranger Peak and descends through White Rock Canyon to Sunset Valley Road. It then follows the forested river-bottom road to Munch Canyon. It is a steep hike up Munch Canyon on the return loop. Throughout the hike are spectacular backcountry vistas of the San Rafael Wilderness, including the distinct ridge of banded white rock called Hurricane Deck.

Driving directions: FROM SANTA BARBARA VIA HAPPY CANYON ROAD: From Highway 101 in Santa Barbara, take the State Street/ Highway 154 exit. Turn northwest on Highway 154 (San Marcos Pass Road), and drive 22 miles to Armour Ranch Road. (The turn-off is located 4.6 miles past the entrance to Lake Cachuma.) Turn right and continue 1.3 miles to Happy Canyon Road. Turn right and drive 13.7 miles to the posted Cachuma Saddle and a road junction. Turn left on Figueroa Mountain Road, and go 3.4 miles to East Pinery Road, a dirt road with a large pullout area on the right. Turn right and drive 0.25 miles to the posted trailhead on the right. Park on the side of the road. If East Pinery Road is gated, park in the large dirt pullout.

FROM SANTA BARBARA VIA FIGUEROA MOUNTAIN ROAD: From Highway 101 in Santa Barbara, take the State Street/Highway 154 exit. Turn northwest on Highway 154 (San Marcos Pass Road), and drive 29.4 miles on Highway 154 to Figueroa Mountain Road at Los Olivos. Turn right and continue 16.6 miles to East Pinery Road on the left, located on a horseshoe right bend. Turn left on the dirt road, and go 0.25 miles to the posted trailhead on the right. Park on the side of the road. If East Pinery Road is gated, park in the large pullout area near the gate.

FROM BUELLTON VIA FIGUEROA MOUNTAIN ROAD: From Highway 101 at Buellton, take the Highway 246 exit. Drive 8.4 miles east on Highway 246 (Mission Drive), passing through Solvang and Santa Ynez, to Highway 154. Turn left and continue 5.3 miles to Figueroa Mountain Road at Los Olivos. Turn right and continue 16.6 miles to East Pinery Road on the left, located on a horseshoe right bend. Turn left on the dirt road, and go 0.25 miles to the posted trailhead on the right. Park on the side of the road. If East Pinery Road is gated, park in the large pullout near the gate.

Hiking directions: If East Pinery Road is gated, walk a quarter mile from Figueroa Mountain Road to the signed trailhead on the right. From the trailhead, bear right and head down the mountain slope on the White Rock Trail. There are spectacular vistas across the interior of the San Rafael Mountains and the Sierra Madre Mountains. Steadily descend, skirting a pine-covered knoll to outcroppings by an old chrome mine with mine tailings and the scattered remains of cabins and equipment. Weave through the rusted metal remnants to a minor saddle and a junction with the Munch Canyon Trail on the left, the return route.

Begin the loop to the right, staying on the White Rock Trail, and drop into White Rock Canyon. Follow a tributary of White Rock Creek downhill and cross the stream, winding down to White Rock Creek. Parallel and cross the creek. Head over a small saddle and steadily drop down into a narrow, stream-fed canyon. Cross a tributary of Fish Creek, and pass another old mining site. Cross the stream six times to the canyon bottom. Rock-hop across Fish Creek to Sunset Valley Road at 3 miles.

For an easier return, bear right on Sunset Valley Road, and walk 0.7 miles to Cachuma Saddle. Bear right again on Figueroa Mountain Road, and weave 3.6 miles up to East Pinery Road to complete the loop.

For this hike, bear left on the narrow, paved Sunset Valley Road. Gently meander for 2.3 miles, overlooking oak-filled Sunset Valley, to a posted trail at a metal rail fence in an oak grove. Pass through the gate at the trailhead and a second gate to the mouth of Munch Canyon. Skirt the east side of Munch Creek, and cross a couple of feeder streams. Cross Munch Creek and follow the west side of the creek upstream. Curve right, leaving the waterway, and climb the west wall of Munch Canyon. A posted junction is located 1.2 miles up Munch Canyon, where two canyons merge.

For an optional return loop, the Munch Canyon Spur veers right and climbs over the ridge to Fir Canyon. At the ridge, a trail zigzags up the hill to a loop at the north end of East Pinery Road.

For this hike continue straight on the Munch Canyon Trail and traverse the hillside. Cross Munch Creek and steadily climb, completing the loop at the White Rock Trail junction. Go to the right, returning 0.9 miles to East Pinery Road. ■

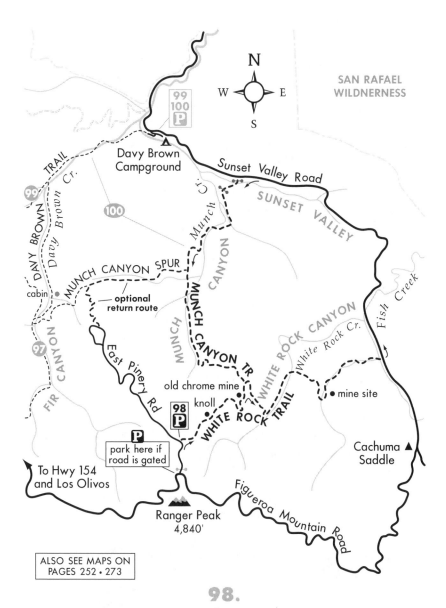

N
W ● E
S

SAN RAFAEL
WILDNERNESS

Davy Brown
Campground

Sunset Valley Road

99 100 P

DAVY BROWN TRAIL

Davy Brown Cr.

99

100

SUNSET VALLEY

Munch Cr.

cabin ●

MUNCH CANYON SPUR

optional
return route

MUNCH CANYON

MUNCH CANYON TR

WHITE ROCK CANYON

White Rock Cr.

Fish Creek

97

FIR CANYON

MUNCH CANYON

East Pinery Rd

old chrome mine ●

knoll ●

WHITE ROCK TRAIL

● mine site

98 P

P

park here if
road is gated

To Hwy 154
and Los Olivos

Figueroa Mountain Road

Ranger Peak
4,840'

Cachuma ▲
Saddle

ALSO SEE MAPS ON
PAGES 252 · 273

98.

White Rock Canyon–
Munch Canyon Loop
FIGUEROA MOUNTAIN RECREATION AREA

99. Davy Brown Trail: Lower Trailhead
Willow Spring Loop from Davy Brown Campground
FIGUEROA MOUNTAIN RECREATION AREA

Hiking distance: 5-mile loop
Hiking time: 3 hours
Elevation gain: 1,500 feet
Maps: U.S.G.S. Bald Mountain and Figueroa Mountain
Backcountry Guide: San Rafael Wilderness

Summary of hike: The Davy Brown Trail can be accessed from two trailheads. Hike 97 begins from the upper trailhead on Figueroa Mountain Road. This hike begins at the other end of the trail from the Davy Brown Campground in Sunset Valley. The campground, originally an old homestead from the late 1800s, sits at an elevation of 2,100 feet under the shade of pines, spruce, oaks, and sycamores. The campground and creek are named for William (Davy) Brown, who lived in a cabin here from 1879 to 1895. Davy Brown Creek, a tributary of Manzana Creek, flows year-round through the 13-site campground.

The Davy Brown Trail follows the creek through the deep, narrow confines of Fir Canyon. This hike utilizes the lower section of the Davy Brown Trail and forms a loop through Willow Spring Canyon. En route, the hike passes an old chrome mine and the remains of miner Harry Robert's cabin from the 1920s, which burned in the 1993 Marre Fire.

Driving directions: FROM SANTA BARBARA VIA HAPPY CANYON ROAD: From Highway 101 in Santa Barbara, take the State Street/Highway 154 exit. Turn northwest on Highway 154 (San Marcos Pass Road), and drive 22 miles to Armour Ranch Road. (The turn-off is located 4.6 miles past the entrance to Lake Cachuma.) Turn right and continue 1.3 miles to Happy Canyon Road. Turn right and drive 13.7 miles to the posted Cachuma Saddle and a road junction. Continue straight ahead on Sunset Valley Road, and gently wind 3.8 miles downhill to the Davy Brown Campground. Turn left into the campground and park.

FROM SANTA BARBARA VIA FIGUEROA MOUNTAIN ROAD: From

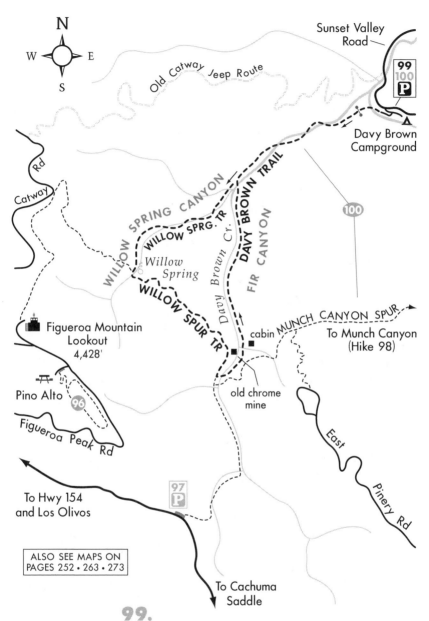

Davy Brown Trail: Lower Trailhead
Willow Spring Loop
FIGUEROA MOUNTAIN RECREATION AREA

Highway 101 in Santa Barbara, take the State Street/Highway 154 exit. Turn northwest on Highway 154 (San Marcos Pass Road), and drive 29.4 miles on Highway 154 to Figueroa Mountain Road at Los Olivos. Turn right and continue 20 miles to a T-junction with the Happy Canyon Road on Cachuma Saddle. Turn left on Sunset Valley Road, and gently wind 3.8 miles downhill to the Davy Brown Campground. Turn left into the campground and park.

FROM BUELLTON VIA FIGUEROA MOUNTAIN ROAD: From Highway 101 at Buellton, take the Highway 246 exit. Drive 8.4 miles east on Highway 246 (Mission Drive), passing through Solvang and Santa Ynez, to Highway 154. Turn left and continue 5.3 miles to Figueroa Mountain Road at Los Olivos. Turn right and continue 20 miles to a T-junction with the Happy Canyon Road on Cachuma Saddle. Turn left on Sunset Valley Road, and gently wind 3.8 miles downhill to the Davy Brown Campground. Turn left into the campground and park.

Hiking directions: From the restrooms and kiosk near the campground entrance, curve right on the paved road to the shady bank of Munch Creek. Cross the creek and pass through a metal gate to the mouth of Fir Canyon. Follow the east side of Davy Brown Creek through the broad oak-studded meadow. Rock-hop over the creek three consecutive times. Pass numerous pools, cascades, and small waterfalls. Traverse the west canyon slope to a posted junction at one mile, just before the fourth creek crossing.

Leave the Davy Brown Trail, and begin the loop to the right on the Willow Spring Trail. Cross a fork of Willow Spring, just above its confluence with Davy Brown Creek. Curve right and head up the north wall of Willow Spring Canyon among the oaks. Pass a moss-covered grotto with a waterfall on the left. Cross the stream a few times, and climb through small chaparral thickets. Curve around a distinct rocky peak to Willow Spring and a large horse trough in a small meadow. Just past the spring is a junction at two miles. The right trail connects to Catway Road and the Figueroa Mountain Lookout.

Instead, veer left on the Willow Spur Trail and traverse the hillside, overlooking the hills and ridges of the San Rafael Mountains. The view to the west includes the fire lookout atop Figueroa Mountain. Gain a little more elevation on the chaparral slope, covered with toyon, black sage, and scrub oak, before descending back into Fir Canyon. Follow the west canyon wall to Davy Brown Creek and a junction. Straight ahead 80 yards is a trail junction on the left (east) with the Munch Canyon Spur Trail. The Davy Brown Trail continues up-canyon to Figueroa Mountain Road (Hike 97).

For this hike, cross Davy Brown Creek and veer left, heading downstream. Follow the east side of the creek, watching for an old chrome mine tunnel in the hillside across the creek to the west. One hundred yards ahead, by a side drainage on the right, are the rock foundation ruins of miner Harry Robert's cabin. Continue downhill on the east canyon wall, passing cascades and small pools. Weave past huge moss-covered sandstone boulders and more small waterfalls. Rock-hop over Davy Brown Creek, and complete the loop at the Willow Spring Trail junction on the left. Retrace your steps one mile back to the campground. ■

100. Davy Brown Trail—Munch Canyon
Loop from Davy Brown Campground
FIGUEROA MOUNTAIN RECREATION AREA

Hiking distance: 5.4-mile loop
Hiking time: 3.5 hours
Elevation gain: 1,500 feet

map
page 273

Maps: U.S.G.S. Bald Mountain and Figueroa Mountain
 Backcountry Guide: San Rafael Wilderness

Summary of hike: Munch Canyon stretches between Figueroa Mountain and Sunset Valley near the Davy Brown Campground. The Munch Canyon Trail weaves across chaparral slopes and offers spectacular backcountry vistas of the San Rafael Wilderness.

The trail, originally a chrome ore mine road, follows Munch Creek, passing old excavation sites.

This loop hike begins at the Davy Brown Campground and climbs up the lower end of Fir Canyon along Davy Brown Creek. En route, the trail passes a series of pools, tumbling cascades, small waterfalls, and the remains of miner Harry Robert's cabin from the 1920s.

Driving directions: FROM SANTA BARBARA VIA HAPPY CANYON ROAD: From Highway 101 in Santa Barbara, take the State Street/ Highway 154 exit. Turn northwest on Highway 154 (San Marcos Pass Road), and drive 22 miles to Armour Ranch Road. (The turnoff is located 4.6 miles past the entrance to Lake Cachuma.) Turn right and continue 1.3 miles to Happy Canyon Road. Turn right and drive 13.7 miles to the posted Cachuma Saddle and a road junction. Continue straight ahead on Sunset Valley Road, and gently wind 3.8 miles downhill to the Davy Brown Campground. Turn left into the campground and park.

FROM SANTA BARBARA VIA FIGUEROA MOUNTAIN ROAD: From Highway 101 in Santa Barbara, take the State Street/Highway 154 exit. Turn northwest on Highway 154 (San Marcos Pass Road), and drive 29.4 miles on Highway 154 to Figueroa Mountain Road at Los Olivos. Turn right and continue 20 miles to a T-junction with the Happy Canyon Road on Cachuma Saddle. Turn left on Sunset Valley Road, and gently wind 3.8 miles downhill to the Davy Brown Campground. Turn left into the campground and park.

FROM BUELLTON VIA FIGUEROA MOUNTAIN ROAD: From Highway 101 at Buellton, take the Highway 246 exit. Drive 8.4 miles east on Highway 246 (Mission Drive), passing through Solvang and Santa Ynez, to Highway 154. Turn left and continue 5.3 miles to Figueroa Mountain Road at Los Olivos. Turn right and continue 20 miles to a T-junction with the Happy Canyon Road on Cachuma Saddle. Turn left on Sunset Valley Road, and gently wind 3.8 miles downhill to the Davy Brown Campground. Turn left into the campground and park.

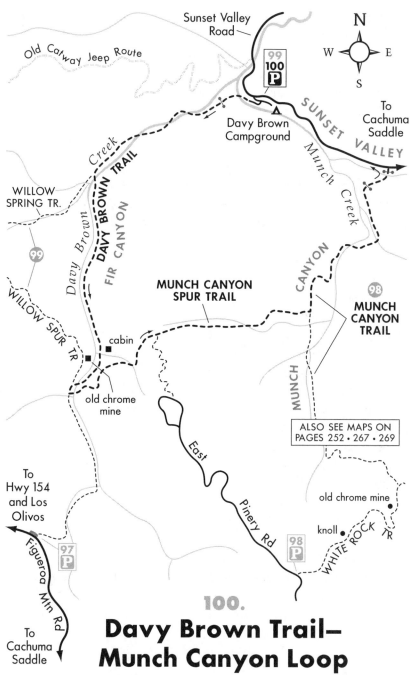

Sunset Valley Road

Old Catway Jeep Route

N
W E
S

99
100 P

To Cachuma Saddle

Davy Brown Campground

SUNSET VALLEY

Creek

DAVY BROWN TRAIL

WILLOW SPRING TR.

99

Davy Brown

FIR CANYON

Munch Creek

WILLOW SPUR TR.

cabin

old chrome mine

MUNCH CANYON SPUR TRAIL

CANYON

98
MUNCH CANYON TRAIL

MUNCH

ALSO SEE MAPS ON PAGES 252 · 267 · 269

To Hwy 154 and Los Olivos

East Pinery Rd

old chrome mine

knoll

WHITE ROCK TR

97 P

98 P

Figueroa Mtn Rd

To Cachuma Saddle

100.

Davy Brown Trail– Munch Canyon Loop

FIGUEROA MOUNTAIN RECREATION AREA

Hiking directions: From the restrooms and kiosk near the campground entrance, curve right on the paved road to the shady bank of Munch Creek. Cross the creek and pass through a metal gate to the mouth of Fir Canyon. Follow the east side of the creek through the oak-studded meadow. Rock-hop over the creek three consecutive times. Pass numerous pools, cascades, and small waterfalls. Traverse the west canyon slope to a posted junction with the Willow Spring Trail (Hike 99 loop) at one mile, just before the fourth creek crossing.

Stay on the Davy Brown Trail and cross the creek. Follow the east side of the creek. Pass the foundation ruins of miner Harry Robert's cabin on the left. One hundred yards ahead is an old chrome mine tunnel in the hillside across the creek to the west. Continue uphill and cross the creek to a junction with the Willow Spur Trail (Hike 99 loop). Veer left, following the creek upstream 80 yards to a junction and a rock-embedded bronze plaque. The plaque honors Edgar Davidson, a forest ranger who patrolled the Zaca Lake Forest Reserve and built the Davy Brown Trail in 1898—1899. The Davy Brown Trail continues straight ahead, climbing to Figueroa Mountain Road (Hike 97).

For this hike, cross Davy Brown Creek and veer right, heading up the hillside on the Munch Canyon Spur Trail. Traverse the slope above Fir Canyon, steadily gaining elevation to a saddle and a signed junction on the right. The right path zigzags 0.8 miles up the hill to the north end of East Pinery Road. Continue straight and follow the contours of the hill into Munch Canyon and a T-junction with the Munch Canyon Trail. The right fork leads into White Rock Canyon (Hike 98). Bear left and descend down the canyon to Munch Creek. Curve left and follow the west side of the creek. Cross the creek and a couple of tributary streams to the mouth of the canyon. Pass through two trail gates to Sunset Valley Road. Bear left on the narrow road, and wind 0.8 miles downhill. Complete the loop at the Davy Brown Campground. ■

101. Lower Manzana Creek Trail to Coldwater Camp

FIGUEROA MOUNTAIN RECREATION AREA

SAN RAFAEL WILDERNESS

Hiking distance: 5.6 miles round trip
Hiking time: 3 hours
Elevation gain: 250 feet
Maps: U.S.G.S. Bald Mountain
Backcountry Guide: San Rafael Wilderness

*map
page 280
and 282*

Summary of hike: Manzana Creek is a major tributary of the Sisquoc River, draining westward through the San Rafael Wilderness. The Lower Manzana Creek Trail follows the creek for 8.5 miles along the southwest corner of the wilderness, from Davy Brown Canyon to the Sisquoc River by the historic Manzana Schoolhouse. This remote hike follows the first 2.8 miles of the trail through cool riparian vegetation to Coldwater Camp on the banks of Manzana Creek. The primitive camp sits in a meadow shaded by digger pines and stately oaks. En route to Coldwater Camp, the trail passes Potrero Camp on a creekside flat among oaks and pines. The trail follows Manzana Creek on a gentle grade for the entire hike. There are overlooks of the lush, isolated canyon and numerous creek crossings.

For a longer hike, the trail continues along the creek to the old Manzana Schoolhouse at the confluence of Manzana Creek and the Sisquoc River. The one-room wooden structure was built by religious fundamentalists from Kansas in 1893, and was abandoned in 1902 after drought and hardships drove them away.

Driving directions: FROM SANTA BARBARA VIA HAPPY CANYON ROAD: From Highway 101 in Santa Barbara, take the State Street/Highway 154 exit. Turn northwest on Highway 154 (San Marcos Pass Road), and drive 22 miles to Armour Ranch Road. (The turn-off is located 4.6 miles past the entrance to Lake Cachuma.) Turn right and continue 1.3 miles to Happy Canyon Road. Turn right and drive 13.7 miles to the posted Cachuma Saddle and a road junction. Continue straight ahead on Sunset Valley Road, and gently wind 5.1 miles downhill to the posted trailhead on the left. It is located 1.3 miles past Davy Brown Campground, just before the second creek crossing. Cross the creek and park in the trailhead parking area on the left.

FROM SANTA BARBARA VIA FIGUEROA MOUNTAIN ROAD: From Highway 101 in Santa Barbara, take the State Street/Highway 154 exit. Turn northwest on Highway 154 (San Marcos Pass Road), and drive 29.4 miles on Highway 154 to Figueroa Mountain Road at Los Olivos. Turn right and continue 20 miles to a T-junction with Happy Canyon Road on Cachuma Saddle. Turn left on Sunset Valley Road, and gently wind 5.1 miles downhill to the posted trailhead on the left. It is located 1.3 miles past Davy Brown Campground, just before the second creek crossing. Cross the creek and park in the trailhead parking area on the left.

FROM BUELLTON VIA FIGUEROA MOUNTAIN ROAD: From Highway 101 at Buellton, take the Highway 246 exit. Drive 8.4 miles east on Highway 246 (Mission Drive), passing through Solvang and Santa Ynez, to Highway 154. Turn left and continue 5.3 miles to Figueroa Mountain Road at Los Olivos. Turn right and continue 20 miles to a T-junction with Happy Canyon Road on Cachuma Saddle. Turn left on Sunset Valley Road, and gently wind 5.1 miles downhill to the posted trailhead on the left. It is located 1.3 miles past Davy Brown Campground, just before the second creek crossing. Cross the creek to the trailhead parking area on the left.

Hiking directions: Rock-hop over Davy Brown Creek just above its confluence with Manzana Creek. Enter the San Rafael Wilderness, and head up the hillside on the south canyon slope. Traverse the hillside northwest, following the contours of the mountain on a shelf carved into the steep canyon wall. Zigzag down three switchbacks to Potrero Camp on the banks of Manzana Creek under oaks and pines at 1.3 miles. Wade or rock-hop to the north banks of Manzana Creek, and walk sixty yards to a signed junction. The Potrero Canyon Trail veers right; it climbs three miles to Hurricane Deck in the remote backcountry of the San Rafael Mountains.

Continue straight, staying on the Lower Manzana Trail among digger pines, sycamores, and oaks. Wade or rock-hop across the creek four more times, following the creek downstream. After the fourth crossing, pass through an open meadow dotted with oaks. Head up the northern slope and traverse the hillside. Drop back down into Coldwater Camp on the banks of the creek in a grassy meadow with majestic oaks at 2.8 miles. This is the turn-around spot.

To extend the hike, the trail parallels the creek downstream for an additional 3.5 miles to the Sulphur Spring Trail and 5.5 miles to the Sisquoc River and the Manzana Schoolhouse. ■

102. Upper Manzana Creek Trail to Fish Creek Camp

FIGUEROA MOUNTAIN RECREATION AREA

SAN RAFAEL WILDERNESS

Hiking distance: 5.2 miles round trip
Hiking time: 3 hours
Elevation gain: 250 feet
Maps: U.S.G.S. Bald Mountain
              Backcountry Guide: San Rafael Wilderness

map
page 280
and 282

Summary of hike: The Manzana Trail follows Manzana Creek for more than 18 miles through the San Rafael Wilderness, from its headwaters off of San Rafael Mountain to the Sisquoc River. The Upper Manzana Creek Trail begins from the NIRA Campground at the end of Sunset Valley Road and heads upstream. This relatively level trail is a popular route to Manzana Narrows, located seven miles from the trailhead where the walls of the canyon constrict. The Narrows has two campgrounds and fishing, wading, and swimming holes. The Upper Manzana Creek Trail is also one of the major access routes into the backcountry of the San Rafael Wilderness.

This hike follows the first 2.6 miles of the trail to Fish Creek Camp on a low, grassy flat at the confluence of Fish Creek and Manzana Creek. En route, the hike passes Lost Valley Camp near the mouth of Lost Valley Canyon. The primitive camp sits on the banks of Manzana Creek, shaded by oaks and digger pines.

Driving directions: FROM SANTA BARBARA VIA HAPPY CANYON ROAD: From Highway 101 in Santa Barbara, take the State Street/ Highway 154 exit. Turn northwest on Highway 154 (San Marcos Pass Road), and drive 22 miles to Armour Ranch Road. (The turn-off is located 4.6 miles past the entrance to Lake Cachuma.) Turn right and continue 1.3 miles to Happy Canyon Road. Turn right and drive 13.7 miles to the posted Cachuma Saddle and a road junction. Continue straight ahead on Sunset Valley Road, and gently wind 5.1 miles downhill to the posted trailhead on the left. It is located 1.3 miles past Davy Brown Campground, just before the second creek crossing. Cross the creek and park in the trailhead parking area on the left.

FROM SANTA BARBARA VIA FIGUEROA MOUNTAIN ROAD: From Highway 101 in Santa Barbara, take the State Street/Highway 154 exit. Turn northwest on Highway 154 (San Marcos Pass Road), and drive 29.4 miles on Highway 154 to Figueroa Mountain Road at Los Olivos. Turn right and continue 20 miles to a T-junction with Happy Canyon Road on Cachuma Saddle. Turn left on Sunset Valley Road, and gently wind 5.1 miles downhill to the posted trailhead on the left. It is located 1.3 miles past Davy Brown Campground, just before the second creek crossing. Cross the creek and park in the trailhead parking area on the left.

FROM BUELLTON VIA FIGUEROA MOUNTAIN ROAD: From Highway 101 at Buellton, take the Highway 246 exit. Drive 8.4 miles east on Highway 246 (Mission Drive), passing through Solvang and Santa Ynez, to Highway 154. Turn left and continue 5.3 miles to Figueroa Mountain Road at Los Olivos. Turn right and continue 20 miles to a T-junction with Happy Canyon Road on Cachuma Saddle. Turn left on Sunset Valley Road, and gently wind 5.1 miles downhill to the posted trailhead on the left. It is located 1.3 miles past Davy Brown Campground, just before the second creek crossing. Cross the creek to the trailhead parking area on the left.

Hiking directions: From the trailhead kiosk, walk down to Manzana Creek and rock-hop across. Enter the San Rafael Wilderness and head up-canyon to the east. Cross a seasonal drainage, and follow the north side of the creek on the dirt and sand path among digger pines and oaks. Cross a small tributary stream to a signed junction. The rugged Lost Valley Trail veers left; it climbs up to Hurricane Deck in the remote backcountry of the San Rafael Mountains. Stay to the right, following the creek 100 yards to Lost Valley Camp. The camp is tucked along the banks of Manzana Creek under oaks and pines.

The main trail continues through a grassy flat. Cross another drainage where the Lost Valley Trail can be spotted on the mountain slope above. Traverse the hillside above the creek, overlooking the forested canyon. Weave along the contours of the hill, and drop back down to the creek. Cross the creek into Fish Creek Camp, where Fish Creek joins Manzana Creek in a tree-dotted meadow. The primitive camp contains a sheltered toilet, a bench, and fire pits. This is the turn-around spot.

To extend the hike, the trail continues an additional 3.4 miles along the creek to Manzana Camp and 4.4 miles to Manzana Narrows. ∎

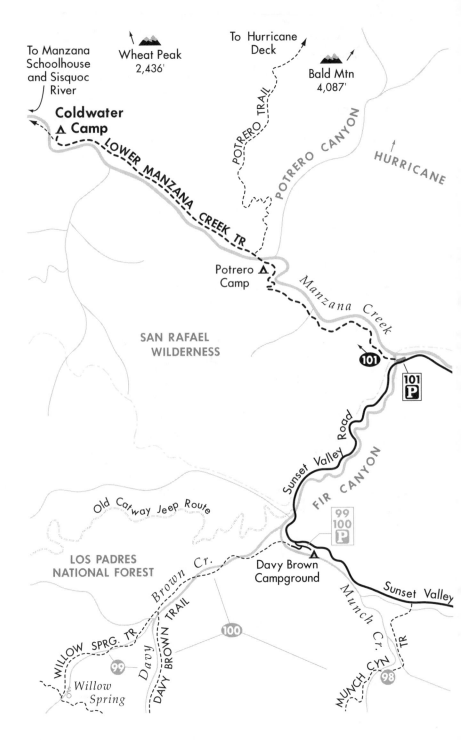

To Manzana
Schoolhouse
and Sisquoc
River

Wheat Peak
2,436'

To Hurricane
Deck

Bald Mtn
4,087'

Coldwater
△ **Camp**

HURRICANE

LOWER MANZANA CREEK TR

POTRERO TRAIL

POTRERO CANYON

Potrero △
Camp

Manzana Creek

101

101
P

**SAN RAFAEL
WILDERNESS**

Sunset Valley Road

FIR CANYON

Old Catway Jeep Route

99
100
P

**LOS PADRES
NATIONAL FOREST**

Brown Cr.

Davy Brown
Campground

△

Sunset Valley

WILLOW SPRG. TR

DAVY BROWN TRAIL

Davy

100

Munch Cr.

99

*Willow
Spring*

MUNCH CYN. TR

98

Manzana Creek Trail
FIGUEROA MOUNTAIN RECREATION AREA

HIKE 101: Lower Manzana Creek Trail
to Coldwater Camp

HIKE 102: Upper Manzana Creek Trail
to Fish Creek Camp

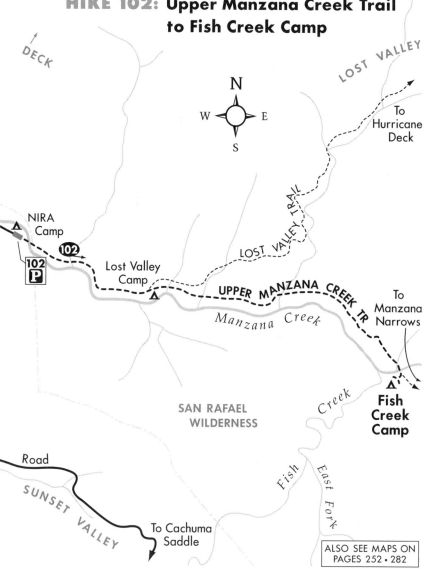

ALSO SEE MAPS ON
PAGES 252 • 282

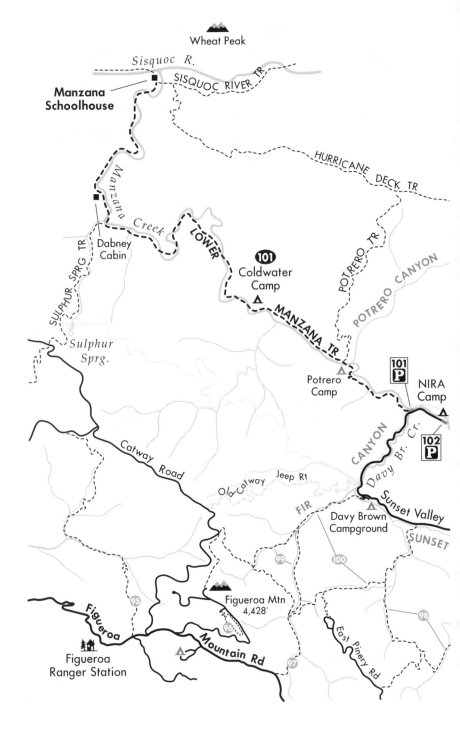

Wheat Peak

Sisquoc R.

SISQUOC RIVER TR

Manzana Schoolhouse

HURRICANE DECK TR

Manzana Creek

SULPHUR SPRG TR

Dabney Cabin

LOWER

101
Coldwater Camp

POTRERO TR

POTRERO CANYON

Sulphur Sprg.

MANZANA TR

Potrero Camp

101 P

NIRA Camp

CANYON

Davy Br. Cr.

102 P

Catway Road

Old Catway

Jeep Rt

FIR

Davy Brown Campground

Sunset Valley

SUNSET

99

100

East Pinery Rd

Figueroa Mtn 4,428'

95

98

Figueroa

96

Mountain Rd

97

Figueroa Ranger Station

(extended hikes)

Manzana Creek Trail:
Manzana Schoolhouse to Manzana Narrows

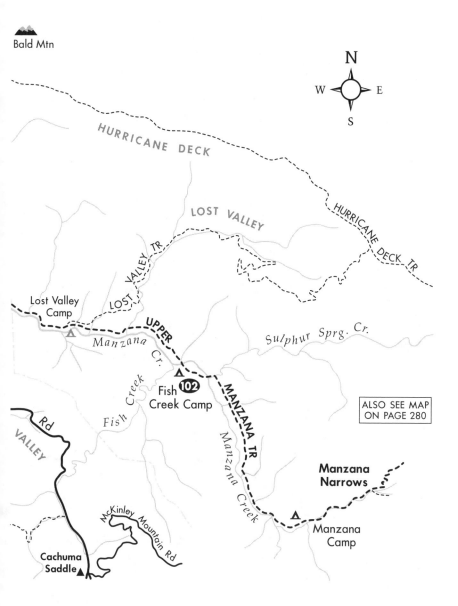

Bald Mtn

N
W E
S

HURRICANE DECK

LOST VALLEY

HURRICANE DECK TR

LOST VALLEY TR

Lost Valley
Camp

LOST

UPPER

Manzana Cr.

Sulphur Sprg. Cr.

Fish Creek

Fish **102**
Creek Camp

MANZANA TR

Fish

Manzana Creek

ALSO SEE MAP
ON PAGE 280

Manzana
Narrows

Rd

VALLEY

McKinley Mountain Rd

Manzana
Camp

Cachuma
Saddle

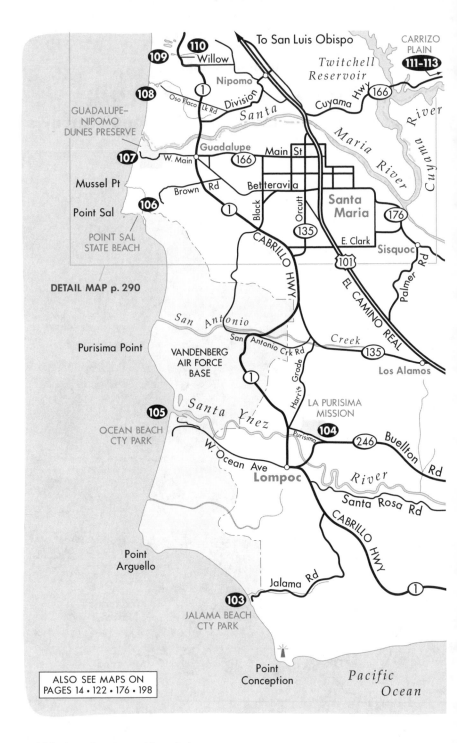

109
110
Willow

To San Luis Obispo

CARRIZO
PLAIN

Twitchell Reservoir

111-113

108

Nipomo

Oso Flaco Lk Rd

Division

Santa

Cuyama Hwy **166**

River

Cuyama

GUADALUPE–
NIPOMO
DUNES PRESERVE

107

Guadalupe

W. Main

166

Main St

Betteravia

Maria River

Mussel Pt

Brown Rd

106
Point Sal

POINT SAL
STATE BEACH

Black

1

Orcutt

135

**Santa
Maria**

E. Clark

176

Sisquoc

Palmer Rd

CABRILLO HWY

DETAIL MAP p. 290

San Antonio

San Antonio Crk Rd

Creek

135

Purisima Point

VANDENBERG
AIR FORCE
BASE

1

Harris Grade

101

EL CAMINO REAL

Los Alamos

105

OCEAN BEACH
CTY PARK

Santa Ynez

1

W. Ocean Ave

Lompoc

Purisima

LA PURISIMA
MISSION

104

246

Buellton

Rd

River

Santa Rosa Rd

Point
Arguello

Jalama Rd

CABRILLO HWY

1

103

JALAMA BEACH
CTY PARK

Point
Conception

*Pacific
Ocean*

ALSO SEE MAPS ON
PAGES 14 • 122 • 176 • 198

North Coast
Santa Barbara to Santa Maria

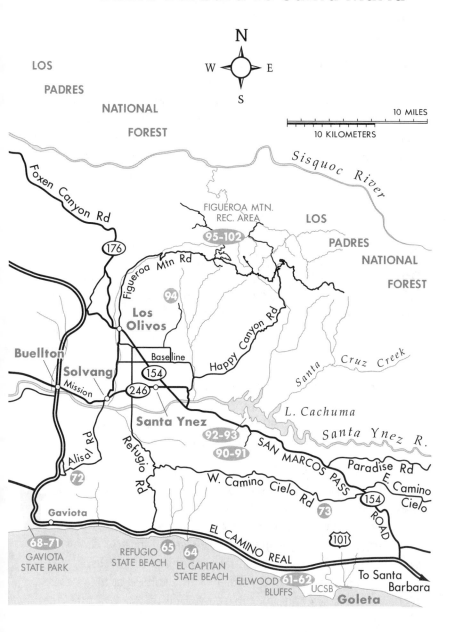

103. Jalama Beach County Park

Hiking distance: 2 miles round trip
Hiking time: 1 hour
Elevation gain: Level
Maps: U.S.G.S. Lompoc Hills, Tranquillon Mountain, and Point
Conception

Summary of hike: Jalama Beach County Park is a picturesque 28-acre park south of Lompoc in Santa Barbara County. The park surrounds the mouth of Jalama Creek between Point Arguello and Point Conception. The beautiful area includes a year-round campground with a half mile of shoreline, shallow dunes, a small wetland habitat, a picnic area, and a general store. This isolated stretch of coastline at the west end of the Santa Ynez Mountains is backed by cliffs and lush, rolling hills. For centuries it was a Chumash Indian settlement. (*Jalama* is the Chumash name for *blowing sand*.) It is now bordered by Vandenberg Air Force Base.

Driving directions: BUELLTON/HIGHWAY 101. From Highway 101 in Buellton, take the Highway 246/Lompoc exit. Drive 16.2 miles west to Highway 1 in Lompoc. Turn left and continue 4.2 miles to Jalama Road. Turn right and continue 14 miles, weaving up and over the Santa Ynez Mountains, to the campground and parking lot. A parking fee is required.

GAVIOTA/HIGHWAY 1 EXIT. From the Highway 1/Lompoc exit off Highway 101 by Gaviota State Park, turn left and drive 13.5 miles to Jalama Road. Turn left and continue 14 miles to the oceanfront campground and parking lot.

Hiking directions: Follow the shoreline north for a short distance to the park boundary near a small estuary along Jalama Creek. The 30-foot bluffs above the creek are fenced. At low tide you may beachcomb northwest for a mile beyond the creek to the Vandenberg Air Force Base boundary. Along the way, cross narrow, rocky beaches with sheer cliff walls.

Heading south, the sandy beach with cobbled stones begins to narrow and ends along the seawall cliffs. At low tide, the shoreline can be followed along the rock formations and tidepools for one mile to a view of the lighthouse at Point Conception. ■

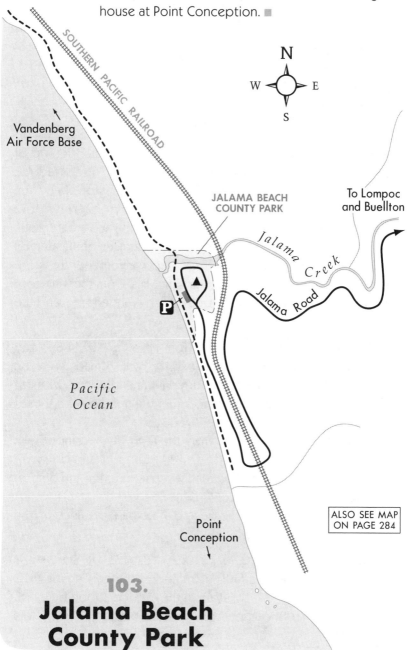

N
W ←◈→ E
S

SOUTHERN PACIFIC RAILROAD

Vandenberg
Air Force Base

JALAMA BEACH
COUNTY PARK

To Lompoc
and Buellton

Jalama Creek

Jalama Road

P

Pacific
Ocean

ALSO SEE MAP
ON PAGE 284

Point
Conception

103.
Jalama Beach
County Park

104. La Purisima Mission
STATE HISTORIC PARK
Open daily from 9 a.m.—5 p.m.

Hiking distance: 5-mile loop
Hiking time: 2.5 hours
Elevation gain: 300 feet
Maps: U.S.G.S. Lompoc
La Purisima Mission State Historic Park map

Summary of hike: The historic La Purisima Mission is one of California's 21 original Franciscan missions. Ten of the adobe buildings, dating back to the 1820s, are fully restored and furnished. The natural setting lies within the Lompoc Valley. More than 900 preserved acres surround the mission and create a buffer from development. The area has twelve miles of maintained trails that wind through the stream-fed canyon and cross the dunes and rolling terrain of the Purisima Hills. From the 480-foot summit are 360-degree vistas of Lompoc, Vandenberg, and the undulating landscape.

Driving directions: BUELLTON. From Highway 101 in Buellton, take the Highway 246/Lompoc exit. Drive 13.5 miles west on Highway 246 to Purisima Road. Turn right and continue 0.9 miles to the posted state park entrance. Turn right and park in the lot 0.1 mile ahead. An entrance fee is required.

GAVIOTA/HIGHWAY 1 EXIT. From the Highway 1/Lompoc exit off Highway 101 by Gaviota State Park, turn left and drive 17.7 miles to the Highway 246/Ocean Avenue junction in Lompoc. Turn right and go 2.5 miles to Purisima Road on the left. Turn left and continue 0.9 miles to the posted state park entrance on the right.

Hiking directions: EL CAMINO REAL—SEDERO DE SOLIS—LAS ZANJAS LOOP: From the far (north) end of the parking lot, pass the visitor center and bookstore in the historic adobe buildings. Continue straight ahead past the mission buildings on the left. Walk past the picnic area in an oak grove to a gravel road and junction.

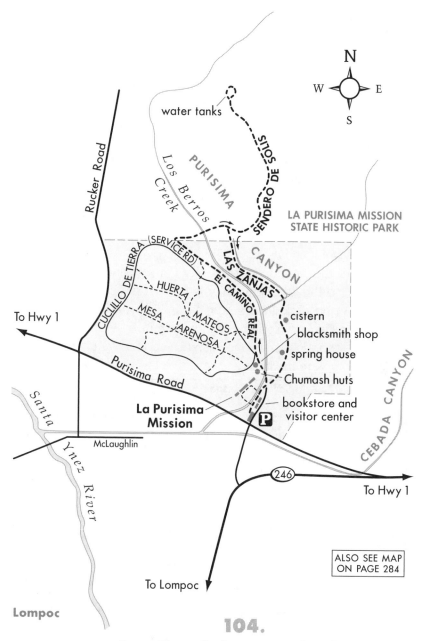

N
W E
S

water tanks

Rucker Road

Los Berros Creek

PURISIMA

SENDERO DE SOLIS

CANYON

LA PURISIMA MISSION
STATE HISTORIC PARK

(SERVICE RD)

LAS ZANJAS

CUCILLO DE TIERRA

HUERTA

EL CAMINO REAL

MESA

MATEOS

ARENOSA

To Hwy 1

cistern

blacksmith shop

spring house

Chumash huts

Purisima Road

CEBADA CANYON

Santa Ynez River

La Purisima Mission

P

bookstore and
visitor center

McLaughlin

246

To Hwy 1

ALSO SEE MAP
ON PAGE 284

To Lompoc

Lompoc

104.
La Purisima Mission
STATE HISTORIC PARK

Begin the loop to the left on El Camino Real, the original mission trail. Cross over Los Berros Creek towards the adobe blacksmith shop, passing Chumash Indian huts on the left. Stay on the main trail in Los Berros Canyon. Pass the Huerta Mateos Trail on the left, which climbs 100 feet up the dunes and through chaparral to a mesa and a network of trails. El Camino Real follows the west edge of the flat-bottomed canyon through open grasslands to the gated north boundary. Curve right along the boundary, crossing over Los Berros Creek, to a junction by ponderosa pines. The right fork, the Las Zanjas Trail, is the return route.

For now, continue straight on Sendero De Solis, an unpaved maintenance road. Climb one mile up the hill on an easy grade to the water tanks at the summit. A path circles the two fenced tanks to magnificent vistas.

Return to the junction in Los Berros Canyon, and take the Las Zanjas Trail to the left. Return along the east edge of the meadow. Follow the rock-lined water channel on the left, the mission's original aqueduct and irrigation system. Pass an old cistern and circular spring house, once used to collect water from the springs. Complete the loop and return to the visitor center. ■

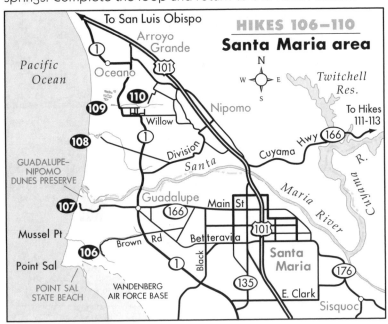

105. Ocean Beach County Park

Hiking distance: 7 miles round trip
Hiking time: 3 hours
Elevation gain: Level
Maps: U.S.G.S. Surf

map
page 292

Summary of hike: Ocean Beach is a 36-acre park between Purisima Point and Point Arguello west of Lompoc in Santa Barbara County. The park borders the Santa Ynez River by a 400-acre lagoon and marsh at the mouth of the river. The estuary is a resting and foraging habitat for migrating birds and waterfowl. This hike parallels the ocean along expansive sand dunes. Vandenberg Air Force Base, which surrounds the park, allows beach access for 1.5 miles north and 3.5 miles south.

Driving directions: BUELLTON. From Highway 101 in Buellton, take the Highway 246/Lompoc exit. Drive 25.7 miles west on Highway 246, passing through Lompoc, to Ocean Park Road. (In Lompoc, Highway 246 becomes West Ocean Avenue.) Turn right on Ocean Park Road, and go one mile to the parking lot at the end of the road by the Santa Ynez River.

GAVIOTA/HIGHWAY 1 EXIT. From the Highway 1/Lompoc exit off Highway 101 by Gaviota State Park, turn left and drive 17.7 miles to the Highway 246/Ocean Avenue junction in Lompoc. Turn left and continue 9.5 miles to Ocean Park Road. Turn right on Ocean Park Road, and go one mile to the parking lot at the end of the road.

Hiking directions: To the north, a path with interpretive nature panels borders the lagoon. After enjoying the estuary, take the quarter-mile paved path along the south bank of the Santa Ynez River. Cross under the railroad trestle to the wide, sandy beach. (Or take the footpath over the hill and cross the tracks.) Walk past the dunes to the shoreline, where the river empties into the Pacific. At times, a sandbar separates the ocean from the river, allowing access up the coast. This hike heads south along the coastline. At just over a half mile, the railroad tracks curve away from the water as the dunes grow higher, rising 120 feet. The wide beach narrows to a strip at one mile. Vandenberg Air Force Base sits atop the cliffs. At just over 3 miles, pass the mouth of Bear Valley, an extensive wetland. The beach soon ends as the cliffs meet the reef. Point Pedernales can be seen ahead, extending out to sea. Return along the same route. ▪

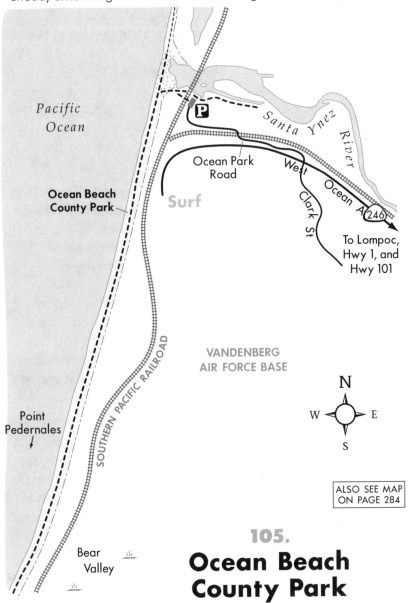

105.

Ocean Beach County Park

106. Point Sal Overlook
POINT SAL STATE BEACH

Hiking distance: 4 miles round trip to overlook
9 miles round trip to state beach
Hiking time: 2—5 hours
Elevation gain: 600—1,800 feet
Maps: U.S.G.S. Point Sal and Guadalupe

**map
page 294**

Summary of hike: Remote Point Sal, at the northwest end of Santa Barbara County, is backdropped by the 1,200-foot Casmalia Hills. The windswept point is located at the north end of Vandenberg Air Force Base and west of Santa Maria. This hike follows abandoned Point Sal Road to an overlook atop Point Sal Ridge. The road, which crosses the northern corner of the air force base, is open only to foot and bike traffic due to unstable soil, landslides, and washouts. The spectacular views include Point Sal Ridge as it emerges to Point Sal, the secluded Point Sal Beach at the base of the steep bluffs, and Lion Rock. The coastal views extend from Point Arguello in the south to Point Buchon at Montaña de Oro State Park in the north. Past the overlook, the old road descends 1,200 feet to the remote shoreline at Point Sal State Beach.

Driving directions: SANTA MARIA. From Highway 101 in Santa Maria, take the Betteravia exit, and head 7.7 miles west to Brown Road. Turn left on Brown Road, and continue 5.1 miles to the signed junction with Point Sal Road on the right. Turn right and park by the road gate.

Hiking directions: Walk past the locked gate, and follow the road uphill along the west edge of Corralitos Canyon. At 0.3 miles, the paved road turns to dirt, reaching a horseshoe bend at a half mile. Leave Corralitos Canyon and head south to the first ocean overlook at one mile. Continue gently uphill, crossing Point Sal Ridge to a cattle guard at a fenceline. The road enters Vandenberg Air Force Base and becomes paved again. A short distance ahead is an abandoned air force missile tracking station

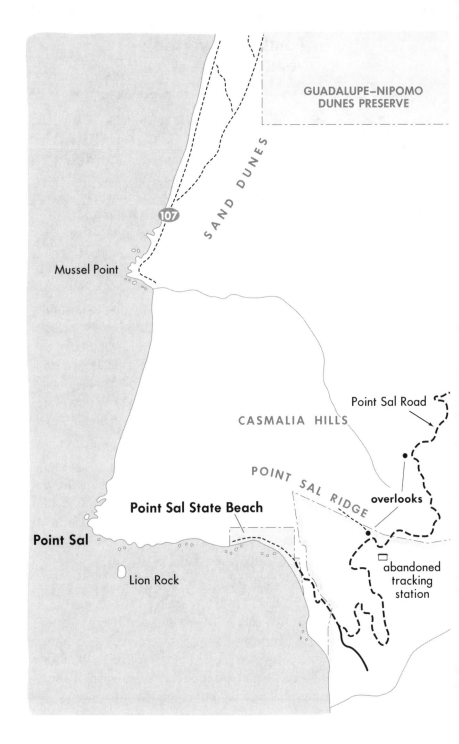

GUADALUPE–NIPOMO
DUNES PRESERVE

SAND DUNES

107

Mussel Point

CASMALIA HILLS

Point Sal Road

POINT SAL RIDGE

overlooks

Point Sal State Beach

Point Sal

Lion Rock

abandoned
tracking
station

on the left. The cinder block building has a wide stairway up to the concrete roof. From this overlook are commanding views up and down the scalloped coastline. Return to the road, and descend a few hundred yards to another overlook. The views extend along Point Sal Ridge to Point Sal. This is the turn-around spot for a 4-mile round-trip hike.

To hike farther, the road continues another 2.5 miles, descending 1,200 feet to the ocean. At the road fork, bear right. Near the shore, scramble down to the remote beach—with two miles of ocean frontage—at Point Sal State Beach. ■

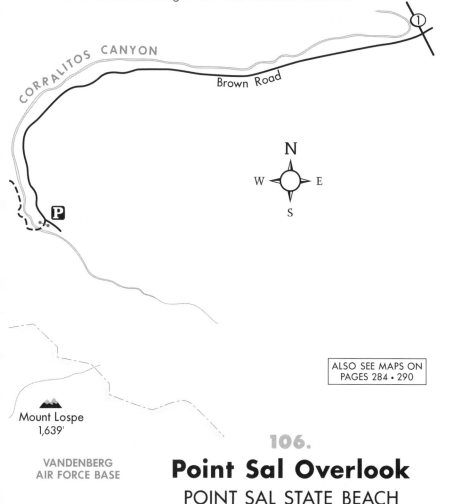

ALSO SEE MAPS ON
PAGES 284 • 290

106.
Point Sal Overlook
POINT SAL STATE BEACH

107. Guadalupe—Nipomo Dunes Preserve to Mussel Rock

Hiking distance: 6 miles round trip
Hiking time: 3 hours
Elevation gain: Level
Maps: U.S.G.S. Point Sal

Summary of hike: The Guadalupe-Nipomo-Oceano dunes complex composes the largest remaining coastal dune system in the nation. The windswept dunes stretch for 18 miles, from Pismo Beach to Vandenberg Air Force Base by Point Sal. The Guadalupe-Nipomo Dunes Preserve encompasses over 3,400 acres at the county's southern coast, west of Santa Maria. The preserve sits among towering, rolling sand mountains that were once inhabited by the Chumash Indians.

This hike follows the isolated shoreline along the sandy beach, parallel to the highest sand dunes on the west coast (which reach a height of 500 feet). The north end of the preserve is bordered by the Santa Maria River and the county line. At the mouth of the river is a wetland area, providing a habitat for migrating shorebirds and native waterfowl. The south end of the dune complex is bordered by Mussel Rock, a towering 450-foot promontory jutting out into the sea.

Driving directions: SANTA MARIA/HIGHWAY 101. From Highway 101 in Santa Maria, take the Main Street/Highway 166 exit, and head west towards Guadalupe. Drive 11.7 miles, passing Guadalupe, to the Guadalupe-Nipomo Dunes Preserve entrance. Continue 2 miles to the parking area on the oceanfront.

Hiking directions: Walk to the shoreline. First head north a half mile to the mouth of the Santa Maria River. The river widens out, forming a lagoon at the base of scrub-covered dunes. At low tide, a sandbar separates the river estuary from the ocean, allowing easy access from the north along the Nipomo Dunes.

Return to the south, meandering along the beach. Various side paths lead inland and up into the dunes. Follow the coastline towards the immense dunes at Mussel Rock. At 3 miles, reach the cliffs of Mussel Rock at the foot of the dunes. The enormous, jagged formation extends out into the ocean. For great coastal views to Point Sal (Hike 106), head a short distance up Mussel Rock to a sandy path that contours around to the south side of the formation. Return back along the beach to the parking area. ■

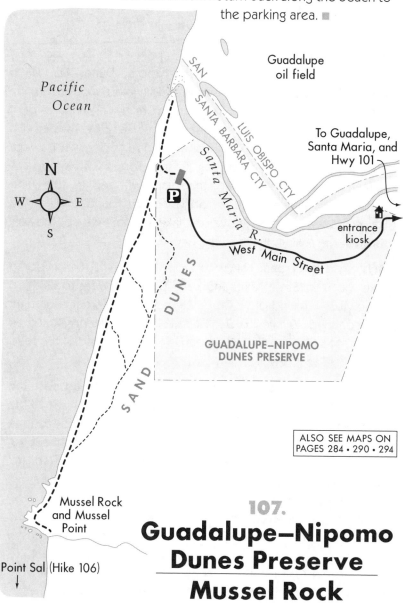

Pacific Ocean

Guadalupe oil field

SAN LUIS OBISPO CTY

SANTA BARBARA CTY

Santa Maria R.

To Guadalupe, Santa Maria, and Hwy 101

N
W — E
S

P

West Main Street

entrance kiosk

DUNES

SAND

GUADALUPE–NIPOMO DUNES PRESERVE

ALSO SEE MAPS ON
PAGES 284 • 290 • 294

Mussel Rock
and Mussel
Point

Point Sal (Hike 106)

107.
Guadalupe–Nipomo
Dunes Preserve
Mussel Rock

108. Oso Flaco Lake Natural Area

Hiking distance: 2.2 miles round trip
Hiking time: 1 hour
Elevation gain: Level
Maps: U.S.G.S. Oceano
Oso Flaco Lake Natural Area map

Summary of hike: The Oso Flaco Lake Natural Area is located east of Nipomo in the heart of the Nipomo Dunes. Oso Flaco Lake, Oso Flaco Creek, and the surrounding wetlands are among the central coast's largest refuges for migrating and resident birds, with more than 300 species. The 75-acre freshwater lake is surrounded by a variety of habitats, including dry, wind-swept dunes with low-growing shrubs; riparian forest with arroyo willow and wax myrtle trees; and marshland with sedges, tules, and cattails. It is a great place for observing birds and wildlife. The trail crosses a footbridge over the lake and follows a boardwalk through the rolling dunes to the ocean.

Driving directions: NIPOMO. From Highway 101 in Nipomo, take the Tefft Street exit, and head 0.8 miles west to Orchard Road. Turn left and drive 0.7 miles to Division Street. Turn right and continue 3.2 miles to Oso Flaco Lake Road. Bear right and go 5.3 miles to the Oso Flaco Lake parking lot at the end of the road. A parking fee is required.

Hiking directions: Head west on the paved road past the trailhead gate and through the shady cottonwood forest to the north shore of Oso Flaco Lake. Bear left on the long footbridge spanning the lake. From the west end of the lake, continue on a boardwalk that ambles across the fragile, vegetated coastal dunes. Most of the trail follows the boardwalk except for a short, well-marked sandy stretch. The boardwalk ends at the ocean on a long and wide stretch of beach at 1.1 miles. To the south, the trail crosses the mouth of Oso Flaco Creek to the Mobil Coastal Preserve and Coreopsis Hill, a prominent dune at 2.3 miles. To the north is Oceano Dunes Natural Preserve. Explore at your own pace along the coastline, returning on the boardwalk. ■

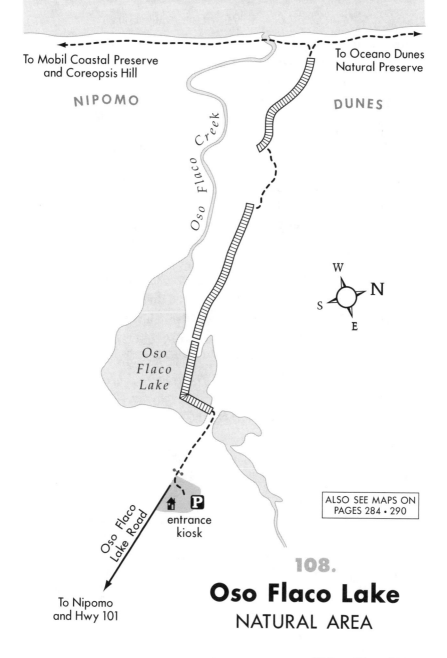

Pacific Ocean

To Mobil Coastal Preserve
and Coreopsis Hill

To Oceano Dunes
Natural Preserve

NIPOMO

DUNES

Oso Flaco Creek

W
N
S
E

Oso
Flaco
Lake

ALSO SEE MAPS ON
PAGES 284 • 290

Oso Flaco
Lake Road

entrance
kiosk

P

To Nipomo
and Hwy 101

108.

Oso Flaco Lake
NATURAL AREA

109. Black Lake

Free docent-led hike by
The Land Conservancy of San Luis Obispo County
Call (805) 544-9096 for scheduled hikes

Hiking distance: 2 miles round trip
Hiking time: 2 hours
Elevation gain: 100 feet
Maps: U.S.G.S. Oceano

Summary of hike: Black Lake is tucked into the Oceano Dunes at the west end of Nipomo Mesa, west of Highway 1. It is owned by the Land Conservancy of San Luis Obispo and is bordered by private property. The lake is one of a series of small lakes adjacent to the huge dunes. The lakes are hidden away in a natural depression and were formed from fresh water perched from the water table. Black Lake was named for the color of the water, darkened by peat deposits beneath the lake. It is among the last remaining coastal freshwater lakes in California and serves as a resting and foraging area for shorebirds and migrating waterfowl. The docent-led hike circles the lake through the wind-sculpted coastal dunes, weaving past eucalyptus groves and coastal scrub. The views extend across the dunes to the Pacific Ocean.

Driving directions: NIPOMO. From Highway 101 in Nipomo, take the Tefft Street exit, and head 0.6 miles west to Pomeroy Road. Turn right and drive 2.3 miles to Willow Road on the left. Turn left and go 2.5 miles, merging with Highway 1/Cabrillo Highway. Continue 2.4 miles to an unpaved road on the left, 0.5 miles north of Callender Road. Turn left and follow the directions above.

Hiking directions: Begin the hike under a stately eucalyptus grove. Head south along the two-track road. Cross over a small hill through coastal dune scrub and sagebrush. From atop the hill are the first views of Black Lake. Descend to a junction, beginning the loop. Take the left fork and cross the wetlands. The

wide path curves right and climbs a hill to a row of large eucalyptus trees bordering a meadow. Continue along the meadow
through another eucalyptus grove to the sand dunes at the west
end of the lake. Descend the ridge and loop around the lake to
a T-junction. Bear to the right and complete the loop. ■

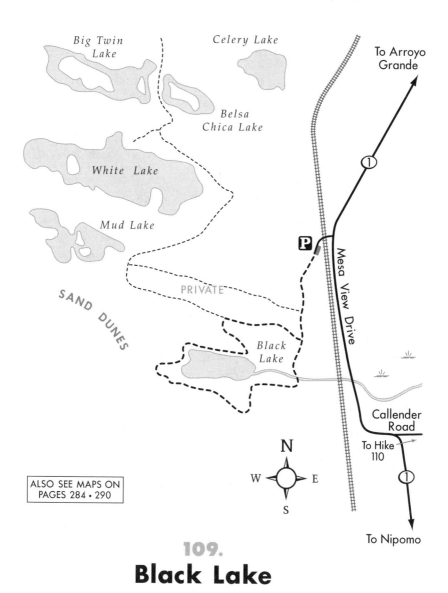

109.
Black Lake

110. Black Lake Canyon

Hiking distance: 1.5 miles round trip
Hiking time: 45 minutes
Elevation gain: 50 feet
Maps: U.S.G.S. Oceano

Summary of hike: Black Lake Canyon stretches inland through Nipomo, from Nipomo Mesa to the Oceano Dunes. The canyon encompasses 1,500 acres and is home to oak and eucalyptus woodlands, dune scrub, chaparral, marshes, ponds, and a year-round stream. This hike strolls through a small section of the canyon managed by the Land Conservancy of San Luis Obispo. The path meanders through the open space wetlands under a canopy of towering eucalyptus trees and oak woodlands.

Driving directions: NIPOMO. From Highway 101 in Nipomo, take the Tefft Street exit and head 0.6 miles west to Pomoroy Road. Turn right and drive 2.3 miles to Willow Road and turn left. Go 2.5 miles, merging with Highway 1/Cabrillo Highway. Continue 1.9 miles to Callender Road. Turn right and drive 1.3 miles to the end of the road.

Hiking directions: Walk past the wood barrier and "END" of road sign. Descend into a massive eucalyptus grove to a wide hillside perch. Traverse the grassy shelf along the south canyon wall. Descend to the canyon floor just above the wetlands. Continue east through the eucalyptus forest, overlooking a pond and the lush riparian vegetation. Ascend the hillside to a dirt road that connects Guadalupe Road and Zenon Way. At the junction is a plaque honoring Bill Denneen for his dedication in preserving Black Lake Canyon. From the forested junction, the right fork leads to the north end of Guadalupe Road. The left fork crosses the creek to the south end of Zenon Way. Return along the same route. ∎

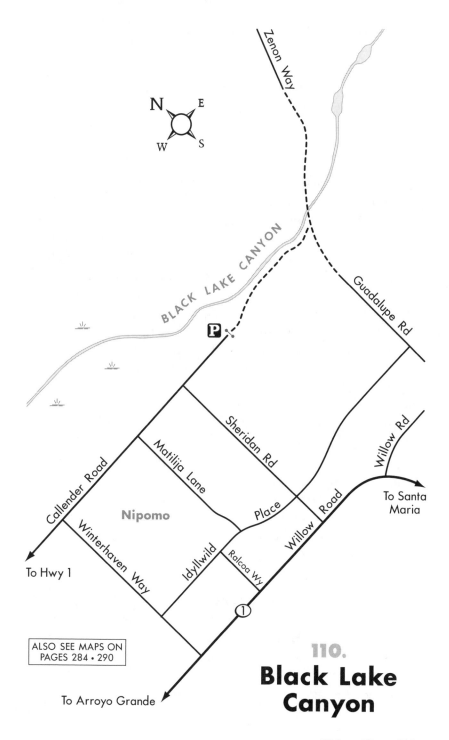

N E W S

Zenon Way

BLACK LAKE CANYON

Guadalupe Rd

P

Sheridan Rd

Matilija Lane

Callender Road

Nipomo

Place

Willow Road

Willow Rd

To Santa Maria

Winterhaven Way

Idyllwild

Ralcoa Wy

To Hwy 1

1

ALSO SEE MAPS ON
PAGES 284 • 290

To Arroyo Grande

110.
Black Lake Canyon

Carrizo Plain National Monument

HIKES 111—113

Goodwin Education Center

Thursday—Sunday · 9 a.m.—5 p.m. (December—May)

During wet weather, dirt roads may be impassable.
Call for road conditions: (805) 475-2131

The Carrizo Plain sits on the east edge of San Luis Obispo County at the Kern County boundary. The expansive plain is frequently referred to as "California's Serengeti" because of its resemblance to the rich grasslands in Africa. The beautiful and remote plain is 8 miles wide and 50 miles long, covering 253,000 acres. It is the largest contiguous remnant of the San Joaquin Valley ecosystem. The massive basin is tucked between the Temblor Range on the northeast and the Caliente Range on the southwest. Caliente Mountain, the highest peak in San Luis Obispo County, stands at 5,106 feet in the south-central side of the park. The San Andreas Fault runs through the center of the plain. The movement of the Earth's tectonic plates has cut a deep trench along the fault line and formed an exceedingly unique landscape.

The arid basin is rich with undeveloped rolling grasslands, drought tolerant shrublands, alkali desert scrub, juniper woodlands, and wetlands. The Carrizo Plain has the highest concentration of rare and endangered plant and animal species in California. Herds of pronghorn antelope and tule deer live on the plain.

Soda Lake Road crosses through the plain. This 45-mile-long road connects Highway 58 (east of Santa Margarita) in the north with Highway 166 (east of Santa Maria) in the south.

Driving directions to Carrizo Plain:

SANTA MARIA. From Highway 101 in Santa Maria, exit on Highway 166 (the Cuyama Highway). Drive 68 miles east, through the Los Padres National Forest and Cuyama Valley, to Soda Lake Road. Turn left and continue 30 miles north (entering the Carrizo Plain National Monument at 2.8 miles) to the posted Goodwin Education Center turnoff on the left. (Twenty-one miles of the road are unpaved.) Turn left on the dirt road, and go a half mile to the education center on the left.

Driving directions for Hikes 111–113 begin from the Goodwin Education Center. ■

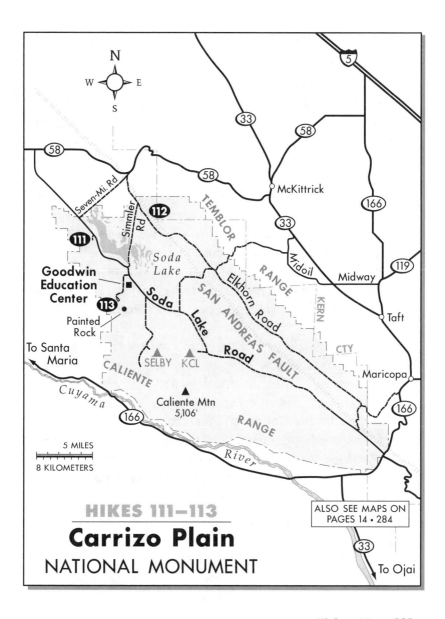

HIKES 111–113

Carrizo Plain

NATIONAL MONUMENT

ALSO SEE MAPS ON
PAGES 14 • 284

111. Soda Lake
CARRIZO PLAIN NATIONAL MONUMENT

Hiking distance: 1 mile round trip
Hiking time: 1 hour
Elevation gain: 50 feet
Maps: U.S.G.S. Chimineas Ranch
Carrizo Plain National Monument map

Summary of hike: Soda Lake is the dominant feature of the Carrizo Plain, encompassing 3,000 acres (12 square miles) with 102 miles of shoreline. It is one of the largest undisturbed alkali wetlands in California and provides a refuge for migrating shore birds and waterfowl. Sandhill cranes congregate in the thousands each winter at the lake.

Soda Lake is the internal drainage for the entire Carrizo Plain. Water gathers in the basin from the adjacent mountain slopes during the winter. The lake has no outlet, but evaporation exceeds the rainfall, leaving a massive expanse of dry, powdery, sodium sulfate and carbonate salts. In the 1880s, the lake was mined for saline deposits used for salt licks and preserving meat. In 1908 a chemical plant processed sodium sulfate, used for the production of paper, glass, and detergents. Production ended in the 1950s.

This hike is divided into two parts: One short trail leads to the Soda Lake Overlook. Atop the overlook are views across the huge expanse of the usually dry lake. From mid-December through February, it is a great spot for observing sandhill cranes roosting on the lake. The second trail crosses the plain a quarter mile to the lakeshore. An 816-foot boardwalk follows the shoreline, offering a close-up look at the fragile wetland. Interpretive panels describe the history, mining, geology, vegetation, and how wildlife adapted to this harsh environment.

Driving directions: SANTA MARIA. Drive to the Goodwin Education Center in Carrizo Plain National Monument—reference page 304. From the Goodwin Education Center turnoff, drive 5.3 miles north on Soda Lake Road to the posted Soda Lake

Overlook turnoff on the left. (The lakefront trailhead is at the large dirt parking area on the right.) Turn left and continue 0.2 miles around the backside of the hill to the overlook trailhead and parking area at the end of the road.

Hiking directions: From the Soda Lake Overlook trailhead, climb 100 yards to the saddle between the two rounded peaks. Go to the right and climb another 70 yards to the higher southern peak. At the summit is an interpretive map and views of the entire lake and the boardwalk along the Soda Lake Trail. Return on the same trail.

From the Soda Lake Trailhead across the road, cross the plain on a wide path through drought tolerant shrubland and alkali desert scrub. At 0.2 miles, the path reaches the usually dry lakeshore and a short pier. Go to the right and head south on the boardwalk. Follow the lakeshore, passing a series of interpretive panels. Return by retracing your steps. ■

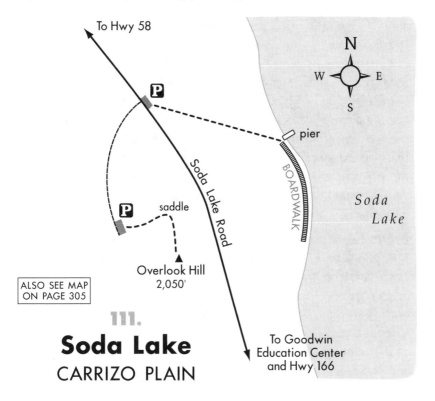

To Hwy 58

N

W ← → E

S

P

pier

Soda Lake Road

BOARDWALK

P   saddle

Soda Lake

Overlook Hill
2,050'

ALSO SEE MAP
ON PAGE 305

111.

Soda Lake
CARRIZO PLAIN

To Goodwin
Education Center
and Hwy 166

112. Wallace Creek Interpretive Trail
CARRIZO PLAIN NATIONAL MONUMENT

Hiking distance: 0.5—2 miles round trip
Hiking time: 20 minutes—1 hour
Elevation gain: 100 feet
Maps: U.S.G.S. McKittrick Summit
Carrizo Plain National Monument map

Summary of hike: The San Andreas Fault marks the division where the North American and Pacific continental shelves (tectonic plates) are joined. The Pacific plate is moving 1.5 inches north a year, an equivalent of 125 feet every 1,000 years. The lateral fault stretches 800 miles, from Cape Mendocino to the Salton Sea, and accounts for more than half of the sliding movement between the plates. It has cut a deep trench along the base of the Temblor Range and is visible for hundreds of miles. The fracture in the earth's crust is most visibly evident at Wallace Creek. It is among the world's best examples of a stream offset by a fault. Wallace Creek and numerous tributaries originally drained out of the Temblor Range and intersected the San Andreas Fault. Movement and earthquakes along the fault dammed up and displaced the streams as they crossed the fault line. Realigned Wallace Creek shifted 430 feet northwest and the movement formed a complex and corrugated topography. This hike explores the unique geography along the fault line and the jagged creek, with endless vistas across the plain. An interpretive pamphlet describing the geography is available at the education center.

Driving directions: SANTA MARIA. Drive to the Goodwin Education Center in Carrizo Plain National Monument—reference page 304. From the Goodwin Education Center turnoff, drive 0.8 miles north on Soda Lake Road to posted Simmler Road on the right. Turn right and continue 6 miles on the dirt (berm) road along the south end of Soda Lake to Elkhorn Road near the base of the Temblor Range. (Elkhorn Road parallels the Temblor Range and the San Andreas Fault.) Turn right and go 1.4 miles south, parallel to the mountains, to the signed trailhead and parking area on the left.

Hiking directions: Walk north, parallel to the fenceline, toward the Panorama Hills at the foot of the Temblor Mountains. The path reaches a T-junction at the San Andreas Fault and Wallace Creek at the base of the scarp by Post 1. This is where the creek exits from the Temblor Mountains and enters the Carrizo Plain. The trail follows the fault in both directions, with amazing views of the jagged fault line and wrinkled topography. The right fork climbs the slope and follows the grassy ridge above the deep fracture. Another path follows the valley along the fracture. Explore along your own route. ■

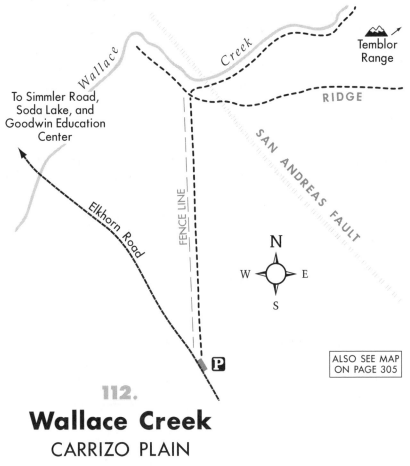

To Simmler Road, Soda Lake, and Goodwin Education Center

Elkhorn Road

FENCE LINE

Wallace Creek

Temblor Range

RIDGE

SAN ANDREAS FAULT

N
W · E
S

ALSO SEE MAP ON PAGE 305

112.

Wallace Creek
CARRIZO PLAIN

113. Painted Rock Trail
CARRIZO PLAIN NATIONAL MONUMENT

Hiking distance: 1.5 miles round trip
Hiking time: 1 hour
Elevation gain: 50 feet
Maps: U.S.G.S. Painted Rock
        Carrizo Plain National Monument map

Summary of hike: Painted Rock, a unique treasure in the Carrizo Plain, rises out of the grassy plain in the rolling foothills of the Caliente Range. The 55-foot, horseshoe-shaped sandstone formation is a sacred ceremonial site for the Yokut and Chumash Indians. The area was a hunting, gathering, and trading site for American Indians. The isolated uplifted boulder has a 20-foot-wide portal leading into an enclosed and protected amphitheater, inscribed with significant American Indian rock art. The pictograph site is rich with abstract and stylized paintings of bears and other animals dating from 200 to 2,000 years ago. Shamans likely created the paintings, expressing cultural and religious beliefs. Within the grotto are numerous encampment sites and bedrock mortars used to grind seeds and nuts. The amphitheater is home to cliff swallows and white-throated swifts that nest on the vertical rock walls. This hike follows a well-defined path along the easy, rolling terrain to the rock monument.

Driving directions: SANTA MARIA. Drive to the Goodwin Education Center in Carrizo Plain National Monument—reference page 304. From the Goodwin Education Center, turn left on the dirt road behind the education center, and drive 2.7 miles south to the picnic and trailhead parking area at the end of the road.

Hiking directions: From the trailhead are views across Carrizo Plain and Soda Lake. Take the posted trail south, and cross over a saddle to a surreal view of Painted Rock, sitting on the plain and backed by the rolling hills and the Caliente Range. Descend to the west edge of the plain at the base of the rounded hills. Follow the level path, passing lichen-covered sandstone outcroppings eroded into intricate shapes. With every step, more details are revealed in weatherworn Painted Rock. Two hundred yards before reaching the sculpted formation is a Y-fork. Begin the loop to the right and head to the northeast corner by a group of caves. Circle the sandstone formation, marveling at the finely etched erosion. On the north side, enter the horseshoe-shaped cavern. Explore the enclosed bowl, respectfully viewing the pictographs, caves, and nesting birds while sensing the timelessness. Complete the loop and return to the right. ■

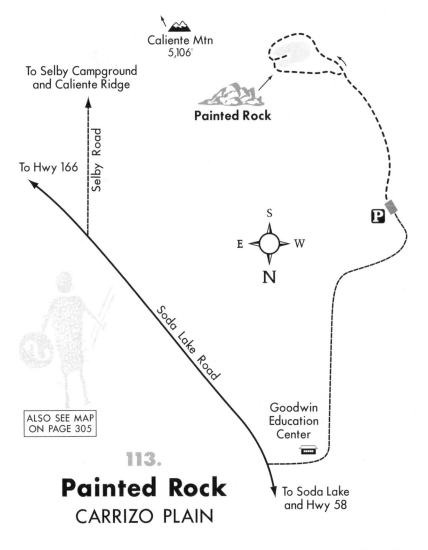

Caliente Mtn
5,106'

To Selby Campground
and Caliente Ridge

Painted Rock

Selby Road

To Hwy 166

Soda Lake Road

S

E W

N

ALSO SEE MAP
ON PAGE 305

Goodwin
Education
Center

113.

Painted Rock
CARRIZO PLAIN

To Soda Lake
and Hwy 58

DAY HIKE BOOKS

These books may be purchased at your local bookstore or outdoor shop. Or, order them direct from the distributor:

The Globe Pequot Press

246 Goose Lane • P.O. Box 480 • Guilford, CT 06437-0480
on the web: www.globe-pequot.com

800-243-0495 DIRECT   **800-820-2329** FAX

Day Hikes On the California Central Coast

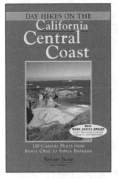

The California central coast has some of the most diverse and scenic geography in the state. This guide includes the most picturesque and rewarding day hikes in the coastal counties of Santa Cruz, Monterey, San Luis Obispo, and Santa Barbara. All of the hikes are adjacent to the scalloped Pacific coastline, with an emphasis on spectacular views and breathtaking overlooks.

320 pages • 120 hikes • 2nd Edition 2009

Day Hikes Around Ventura County

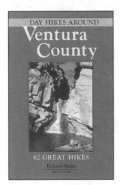

Ventura County's unique topography includes national forest land, wilderness areas, several mountain ranges, and over 50 miles of coastline. The many communities that lie throughout the county have been thoughtfully integrated within the green space and undeveloped land. This guide includes an excellent cross-section of hikes, from relaxing beach strolls to mountain-to-coast hikes with expansive views.

184 pages • 82 hikes • 2nd Edition 2003

Day Hikes Around San Luis Obispo

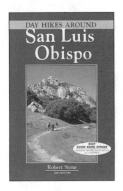

San Luis Obispo County is located where the white sand beaches of central California merge with the dramatic Big Sur coastline. Inland from the Pacific Ocean are oak-studded hills, verdant farmland, mountain lakes, and the Santa Lucia Range. These 128 day hikes explore the coastline, rocky promontories along a chain of volcanic morros, wetland sanctuaries, and cool interior valleys.

288 pages • 128 hikes • 2nd Edition 2006

Montecito Trails Foundation

P.O. Box 5481 • Santa Barbara, California 93150
(805) 568-0833 • www.montecitotrailsfoundation.org

The Montecito Trails Foundation has worked to preserve, maintain, and expand trails within Montecito, Summerland, and Carpinteria since 1964. The private, non-profit organization plays an active role in the acquisition of trails, raising funds, and working with land owners and local governments. Volunteers clear, build, and brush trails, keeping more than 300 miles of trails open to hikers, bikers, and equestrians. Members receive quarterly newsletters with trail updates, a detailed trail map of Santa Barbara County (not available anywhere else), monthly group hikes, and are invited to an annual BBQ each September. To find out more on how to become a volunteer or a docent, make a tax-deductible donation, or just enjoy one of their activities, call or visit their website. The Montecito Trails Foundation is connected with Hikes 25, 27, 28, 29, 3o, 34, 36, 37, 42 and 43.

The Land Trust for Santa Barbara County

P.O. Box 91830 • Santa Barbara, California 93190
(805) 966-4520 • www.sblandtrust.org

Since 1982, the Land Trust for Santa Barbara County—a membership-based, non-profit organization—has been working in the public interest to protect land from development. They work with land owners to preserve open space, wildlife habitat, scenic landscape, and agricultural land. Their dedicated work serves as a bridge between private landowners, government agencies, and the public, preserving open land through negotiated conservation transactions. Currently over 13,000 acres have been preserved through the land trust. To find out more on how to become a volunteer or a docent, make a tax-deductible donation, or just enjoy one of their activities, call or visit their website. The Land Trust for Santa Barbara County is connected with Hikes 21, 23, 61, 66, 67 and 94.

INDEX

LINDA STONE

About the Author

Since 1991, Robert Stone has been writer, photographer, and publisher of Day Hike Books. He is a Los Angeles Times Best Selling Author and an award-winning journalist of Rocky Mountain Outdoor Writers and Photographers, the Outdoor Writers Association of California, and the Northwest Outdoor Writers Association. He is also an active member of the Bay Area Travel Writers.

Robert has hiked every trail in the Day Hike Book series. With 23 hiking guides in the series, many in their third and fourth editions, he has hiked thousands of miles of trails throughout the western United States and Hawaii. When Robert is not hiking, he researches, writes, and maps the hikes before returning to the trails. He spends summers in the Rocky Mountains of Montana and winters on the California Central Coast.